D0701325

Ski
Mountaineering

Ski
Mountaineering

Peter Cliff

UNWIN HYMAN

London   Sydney

First published in Great Britain by Unwin Hyman,
an imprint of Unwin Hyman Limited, 1987

© Text: Peter Cliff
© Line drawings: Doug Godlington
All rights reserved. No part of this publication may be
reproduced, stored in a retrieval system, or transmitted in any
form or by any means, electronic, mechanical, photocopying,
recording or otherwise, without the prior permission of
Unwin Hyman Limited.

UNWIN HYMAN LIMITED
Denmark House, 37–39 Queen Elizabeth Street,
London   SE1 2QB
and
40 Museum Street, London   WC1A 1LU

Allen & Unwin Australia Pty Ltd
8 Napier Street, North Sydney, NSW 2060, Australia

Allen & Unwin New Zealand Ltd with the Port Nicholson Press
60 Cambridge Terrace, Wellington, New Zealand

British Library Cataloguing in Publication Data
Cliff, Peter
   Ski mountaineering
   1. Mountaineering   2. Skis and skiing
   I. Title
   796.5'22   GV200

ISBN: 0 04 440085 3

Designed by Julian Holland

Printed and bound in Great Britain by Scotprint Ltd, Musselburgh

Front cover photograph: Skiing down the Haut Arolla Glacier
in Switzerland, with l'Evêque in the
background.

Back cover photograph: A party climbing the Brenay Glacier
in Switzerland.

Contents

Acknowledgements

In writing this book I have relied heavily on the knowledge and writings of others, and some specific acknowledgements appear in the text. Also, the many different people with whom I have skied and climbed have indirectly contributed to this book. Of them all I owe the greatest debt to a fine master of off-piste skiing who at an early age pointed my skis in the right direction, namely my father.

Specific thanks are due to the following, and if I have inadvertently missed someone I apologise:

Bob Barton and Martin Burrows-Smith for checking the chapters on avalanches and glaciers respectively; Stewart Potter for photographic advice; Tania Alexander, John Cleare and Ken Wilson for literary advice; Maggie Barclay for typing; Marie Françoise Gaff for translating the chapter on Ski Extrème; Ivar Lund-Mathieson for research on the history of skiing; Camila Buxton of the S.C.G.B.; the Zermatt Tourist Office and Connie Austin Smith, my editor.

Equipment was supplied by Badger Sports, Berghaus, Lyon Equipment, Europa Sport, Marshalls of Aberdeen, and Sports International.

Individual chapters were contributed by: Anselme Baud (Ski Extrème), Jeremy Whitehead (Vanoise and Dauphine), John Cleare (Gran Paradiso and China), Hamish Brown (Morocco), Bruce Clark (New Zealand), Derek Fordham (Greenland), John Harding (Pyrenees), Lito Tejada-Flores and Rob Collister (U.S.A.).

I am grateful to the following for their photographs:
Anselme Baud (Colour pic 6)
Hamish Brown (Figs 111, 114)
Martin Burrows-Smith (Figs 9, colour pic 1)
Bruce Clark (Fig 117)
John Cleare (Figs 79, 109,110, 125 and 126 and for the map Fig 66)
Rob Collister (Figs 120, 123, 124)
Dave Ellis (Fig 116, colour pics 15, 16)
Derek Fordham (Figs 118, 119)
Phillip Lindsay (Colour pic 18)
Ivar Lund-Mathieson (Fig 60)
Raymond Renaud (Colour pics 2, 3)
Patrick Vallençant (Fig 90)
Jeremy Whitehead (Figs 102, 104)
Figs 2, 3 and 5 are reproduced from *The Guinness Book of Skiing* by Peter Lunn. Pub: Guinness Superlatives Ltd 1983.
Figs 6, 7 and 98 are reproduced from *The History of Skiing* by Sir Arnold Lunn. Pub: Oxford University Press 1927.
Fig. 4 is reproduced from *Oistoria Om De Nordiska Folken* by Olaus Magnus. Pub: Gidlunds Förlag 1982.

Finally, I am especially grateful to Doug Godlington for the illustrations, a magnificent job made all the more difficult for him by being handicapped, at the time, by a badly injured leg.

Foreword

In this book, Peter Cliff brings together a wide knowledge and experience of ski mountaineering techniques and locations, not only his own, but of other ski mountaineers; and sets it all in its historical perspective.

Peter is well qualified for this role, possessing both skills and knowledge, and a personal enthusiasm for mountains and skiing. I first met him on the British Alpine Ski Traverse in 1972, when we skied over the mountains from Kaprun in Austria to Gap in France, climbing major peaks on the way. Before and since then, he has spent a great deal of time in the Alps, usually doing several ski tours each year, as well as climbing rock or ice routes in the summer; and he has been to Scandinavia where we once did a Nordic ski journey through the Sarek Park together. Living in Scotland as he does, he is very active on Scottish hills, in summer and winter, and is leader of the Cairngorm Mountain Rescue Team, which has its own ski patrol. He has also written an important book on Mountain Navigation.

The first part of the book gives a comprehensive and sound coverage of modern Alpine ski mountaineering, from both the mountaineer's and the skier's point of view, and with helpful comments on the differences between the two. By drawing on his own extensive experience, Peter is able to give practical examples of many of the points under discussion. The chapter on extreme skiing by Anselme Baud adds perspective on the outer limits of the sport.

The second part is, however, equally valuable, with its extensive coverage of some of the best ski touring areas, and it should give the reader a good idea of where to go for several years at least. It also serves to demonstrate the varying nature of the sport, as for example in Lito Tejada-Flores' explanation of the importance of telemark skiing in North America.

Now is a particularly appropriate time for the book to appear, as more and more people are turning away from the crowded pistes to the stillness and silence of the unspoilt snow to be found, perhaps just round the corner from the resort on day tours, or on hut to hut tours away up in the mountains. Although some of the more popular tours, such as the Haute Route Chamonix–Zermatt, have now themselves become over-crowded, most of the other areas recommended in the second part of the book will not be so.

There is a great deal to be learned in order to travel safely and well in these different, more remote, conditions, with the attendant risks of avalanche, crevasse and weather, or of just losing the way. Although you are advised to go with an experienced skier from one of the ski mountaineering clubs, or with a guide, you will enjoy it so much the more if you also acquire a thorough understanding of the necessary skills.

Peter Cliff's book, with its wide and comprehensive coverage of these matters, and clarity of explanation, can be recommended with confidence for this purpose. And it will also, I am sure, be of interest to ski mountaineers, more generally as an exposition of the current state of the ski mountaineering art.

Alan Blackshaw
London 1987

Introduction

The first book devoted entirely to ski mountaineering, *Alpine Skiing At All Heights and Seasons* (Methuen 1921), was written by an Englishman, Sir Arnold Lunn. Of this book Marcel Kurz said:

> It is a curious fact that the British, who were the first to explore our Alps and the last to explore them on ski, possess, since 1921, the best work on this subject.

If he were alive today, Sir Arnold would not only agree that a new book was well overdue, he would have written it himself – my gain to have the chance to write this book and my loss not to have met such a great man. In *A History of Skiing* (Oxford University Press 1927) he muses about an unborn writer relying on his own published work, and wonders, '. . . if he may be sufficiently magnaminous to immortalize me in a footnote'. Sir Arnold is already immortalized as having made a contribution to skiing which is second to none, not only by his formidable exploits on skis but also by his prolific writings, on which I have relied in the preparation of this book, particularly the historical background.

He once said, 'Ski mountaineering is no mere variation of mountaineering. It is the result of the marriage of two great sports, mountaineering and skiing.'

For many this was no love at first sight. Limited time and funds usually meant that only those living in the mountains could indulge in both sports, while those living further away had to choose between one or the other. And of course the appeal of each sport was different and this invariably resulted in little contact between the enthusiasts. This was sometimes taken to extremes, witness this remark from one of the 'old guard' of the Alpine Club:

> When God made the hills He intended them to be climbed and not to be used as glorified toboggan runs.

But the marriage survived and went from strength to strength, and rightly so. By using a combination of mountaineering and skiing skills, the ski mountaineer is able to travel among mountains at a time when it would be, normally, difficult if not impossible, due to the great depth of unconsolidated snow. For the mountaineer there is the great satisfaction of solving mountaineering problems, be it assessing a change in weather pattern, navigating in bad weather, or choosing a route through a heavily crevassed section of glacier. For the skier there is the indescribable thrill of sweeping down deserted snowfields, using different turns and techniques as the conditions require.

The skills required are many and I have tried in this book to cover the most important ones. But there is no substitute for personal experience, and I hope that the chapters on tours will not only show what is available and possible, but will go some way in helping people to obtain that experience.

Fig. 1   'The indescribable thrill of sweeping down deserted snowfields . . .'

1 The History of Skiing

PRE-HISTORY

The oldest ski ever discovered is the Hoting ski which was found at Honne, Sweden, in 1921. It is estimated to be 4,500 years old. Unfortunately it is not complete, which is hardly surprising; but from what there is, it can be seen that it was short (111 cm/44 in long), made of pine, and rounded at the tip. There is a scoop for the foot and a hole which could have taken a retaining strap.

Dating back to the same time, about 2,500 BC, are two rock carvings found at Rödöy, a Norwegian island just north of the Arctic Circle. The better of the two carvings shows a figure on very long skis. He is wearing a head-dress with hare-like ears, in his hands he carries a pole with a right-angled hook at the bottom, which may have made it useful as a hunting weapon, and he is in a good skiing stance, with his knees forward over his toes.

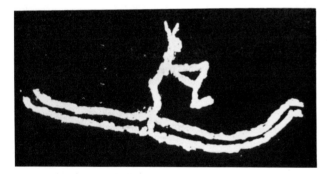

Fig. 2   Rödöy carving.

Another pair of skis and sticks were found at Kalvträsk, Sweden, in 1924. These have been dated back to 2000 BC. They are longer than the Hoting ski (204 cm/80 in) and are the same length as many skis used today. There are holes for a retaining cord for the feet; and the pole is 156 cm (61 in) long, with a scoop at the bottom, which could have been used for shovelling snow.

Some remarkable rock carvings have been found in north west Russia, around Lake Onega and the White Sea. One of them depicts three naked figures on skis. They are so obviously naked that they are usually known as the 'three phallic figures on skis'. These rock carvings cannot be dated accurately and estimates vary widely between 2,000 and 500 BC.

EARLY HISTORY

Early references show that the Chinese were using skis in the seventh century: 'riding on pieces of wood, they hunt deer over the ice' and, 'as their country is so soon covered with frost and snow, they used wooden boards ... with which to glide over the piled up ice'. The wooden boards measured 210 cm (83in) long and 15 cm (6 in) wide (Dr Joseph Needham, *Science and Civilisation in China*).

The official history of the Tang dynasty (AD 618–907) has a reference to skiers: 'The wooden-horse Turks are accustomed to skim over the ice on so-called wooden horses, that is, on sledges or runners which they bind to their feet to run over the ice. And they take poles as supports, and push themselves rapidly forward' (Carl Luther *1952 British Ski Year Book*).

MEDIEVAL HISTORY

In 1200 at the Battle of Oslo, King Swerre sent in a company on skis to reconnoitre the enemy's position. And in 1206 the infant King Häkon was rescued by two men on skis and taken in a blizzard across the Dovre Mountains to safety.

Fig. 3   Nineteenth-century painting depicting rescue of the infant King Häkon in 1206.

One of the earliest and most detailed references to skiing in Europe is contained in *Konungs Skuggsja* which was probably written about 1230. It takes the form of a dialogue between father and son and deals with a variety of topics including a chapter on 'strange and unbelievable things'.

People outside Norway will find it an even greater wonder if they are told about men who can use wood or planks in such a way that as soon as they fasten those planks, seven or nine feet long, to their feet, they are able to move faster than the bird in flight or the fastest racing hound, faster even than the reindeer. These men are, however, no faster on foot than other people, when they are wearing ordinary shoes.

Many people are so good at skiing that they can, in one ski run, kill nine or more reindeer with their spears. . . . when a man with the skis on his feet reaches his top speed, nothing on earth can escape him . . . However, where people are unaccustomed to the skis, even a fast-footed man would soon lose all his speed the moment the skis were tied to his feet.

Now we know the facts about these things, and when the snow comes in the winter, we can enjoy watching the people who master these skills.

(This is the first reference in any literature to skiing bringing enjoyment, and to being of interest to spectators.)

Competitions

Various sporting competitions formed a regular part of the pre-Christian mid-winter celebrations in Scandinavia, and regular meets continued long after the area was converted to Christianity in the tenth and eleventh centuries. Skis were used, those people from the forest regions using long skis and a stick, while others sported very much shorter ones.

The long skis were definitely the fastest, while the short type seemed to be much more versatile. Many of the short models were not made from wood, but from deer bones, and were sometimes only 30 cm (1 ft) long. To improve the facility for gliding they were filed smooth underneath and greased with pig's fat. The short version was known throughout northern Europe; it was often used on ice, very much like a modern ice-skate – particularly by children.

Vasa Ski Race

In 1521 Gustav Vasa fled from Sweden in the face of the invading Danes. He headed for Norway on a pair of snowshoes, but was chased by two Swedes on skis who, moving much faster, were able to catch up with him and managed to persuade him to return. He subsequently became King of Sweden. The annual Vasa Ski Race commemorates this event.

Olaus Magnus

In his *History of the Nordic People* (1555) Olaus Magnus describes in great detail, and with amazing accuracy, natural phenomena common in the northern regions, such as the structures of snow, avalanches, ice conditions, etc., and also how the northern people coped with everyday life in such a hostile environment. In each chapter the most important points are illustrated with neat little drawings.

He uses the name 'Scrickfinnia' when describing the northern part of the Scandinavian peninsula and Finland. He had taken the name from the works of ancient sixth and seventh century scholars, and its literal meaning is probably 'the land of the gliding Finns'. (For centuries it was common to refer to the Laplanders as 'Finns'.) He describes skiing as:

> The inhabitants use long, flat pieces of wood curved up at the front for their speedrunning. They tie these skis to their feet and with the aid of one stick held in their hands they can steer themselves and thus run easily up and down the snow-covered mountains at their will. A noticeable characteristic of these skis is that one ski is a foot longer than the other; and the shorter of the two skis should be as long as the skier. The underside of the ski is covered with soft reindeer skin.

Olaus explained that the reason for the skins was to enable the skier to move faster across snow, avoid dangerous crevasses or cliffs and to climb steep hills, as the hairs would rise up and create friction, thus stopping the ski from gliding backwards. This is the first reference in literature to skins.

> . . . these people managed to ascend mountains and rush down the steepest valleys which otherwise would have been completely inaccessible to man. There is not a single mountain too steep for them to ascend. They climb up from the valley by zig-zagging their way up the side of the mountain, negotiating difficult terrain and crevasses until they reach their goal: the top.

There is one rather strange aspect to all of this. In all his drawings, Olaus Magnus shows the skiers standing on the very back of the skis, with no running surface behind the

Fig. 4   Two of Olaus Magnus's drawings.

feet. Such skis can hardly have worked efficiently, and it may be that his memory misled him. He was born in 1490, went north when in his twenties, was exiled in 1523, and published the book in 1555. His skiing experiences were gained on his trip north, so he was recalling events which took place thirty-five to forty years earlier.

Maybe he recalled people skiing in deep snow, when the ski tips would be clear of the snow, and the backs of the skis buried, so giving the impression of the feet near the backs of the skis. It seems strange, however, because in general his drawings are remarkable for their attention to detail. In any case, these 'beaked shoes' as they were known, set a precedent: people copied them for the next four hundred years, despite the existence of other, more accurate, pictures.

SEVENTEENTH CENTURY

In the seventeenth century skiing was obviously commonplace and popular in Scandinavia. Long skis were used for travelling very quickly and efficiently through frost and on open, easy-angled, ground. According to a reference in *Lorna Doone* by R. D. Blackmore, published in 1869, skis were used in Devonshire, England, in the great frost of 1628. And Valvasor, an Austrian, published a book in 1689 called *Die Ehre des Herzogtumes Krain*, in which he describes the peasants of Krain (near the Adriatic) as expert skiers. They had short skis, about 1·5 m (5 ft) long, on which they could turn easily, and could therefore ski down steep slopes. This is the first time that such a method of skiing has been heard of, in contrast to the Scandinavian method of using long skis for fast and straight running. Two hundred years later it developed into a furious debate; short, easily turned skis against long fast ones.

But before examining that debate in more detail, men-

Fig. 5 This mail service was known as the Snowshoe Express, and thus John Thompson became known as Snowshoe Thompson. He delivered the mail in this way for the next twenty years, until he died in 1876 at the age of forty-nine.

tion must be made of one of the earliest and greatest ski mountaineers of all time.

Snowshoe Thompson (1827–76)

A young Norwegian, Jon Thorsteinson, emigrated with his parents to America in 1837, where his name was changed to John Thompson. In the winter of 1856, when he was twenty-nine years old, he started carrying the mail across the Sierra Nevada. Each one-way trip lasted two to three days. As there were no huts, he slept out in the open. His skis were home-made: 3 m (10 ft) long and weighed 11 kg (24 lb.) The loads he carried weighed up to 45 kg (100 lb). And we complain today with skis at 5·5 kg (12 lb) and loads seldom over 13·5 kg (30 lb)!

INTRODUCTION OF SKIS TO THE ALPS

Skis were introduced to the Alps in the late 1870s and 1880s. The main developments are listed chronologically on page 152. It is interesting to note that skis were first introduced to Meiringen, Switzerland (nowadays a thriving ski resort) in 1890 – the same year in which Nansen traversed Greenland on skis.

THE GREAT DEBATE

The skis which were introduced to the Alps were, of course, Norwegian ones. But experiments found that shorter skis had certain advantages on the steep Alpine slopes, particularly if used with a different technique.

The Traditional Norwegian Technique The Norwegians concentrated on skiing as a sport, as opposed to a means to getting up and down mountains. They emphasized jumping and straight running. The only time they turned was when they wanted to stop, and the turn used was either the telemark or the christiania. Much of their skiing was track running on hard snow, and they became very good at long-distance racing techniques, developing very steady balance in the running position.

Adapted Norwegian Techniques The traditional Norwegian techniques were far from suitable for the steep sides of Alpine mountains, where the essential skill was soon found to be the ability to turn sharply and safely. Wilhelm Paulke adapted the Norwegian technique: he used the telemark, the christiania and the stem, not only for stopping, but also for turning. He developed his technique for high Alpine touring and he became expert at turning on steep ground in deep, soft snow.

Zdarsky and the Lilienfeld Technique Mathias Zdarsky argued that short skis were essential for steep ground. They were certainly easier to turn, but were unsteady in straight running. So rather than straight running, Zdarsky preferred to do endless turns, using the stick a great deal to aid

Fig. 6 The adapted Norwegian technique was practised particularly by the Black Forest School which was founded in 1892 and of which Wilhelm Paulke was the leading light.

Fig. 7 Zdarsky was a strange man, almost a hermit, and he appears to have had absolutely no sense of humour at all. Even thirty years after the feud started he was still slinging mud at Paulke, accusing him of being a sadist because 'as a small boy he squeezed his snowballs into ice before hurling them at his little friends'! Nevertheless, he enabled thousands of people to take up and enjoy skiing; people who might otherwise have been put off from ever trying the sport.

balance. This, of course, was still in the days of the single stick. So Zdarsky's pupils could get down slopes slowly with great use of the stick, but they could never progress as they did not learn about balance.

Quite a war developed between the Black Forest School (Paulke) and the Lilienfeld School (Zdarsky).

TWENTIETH CENTURY

If I had to name one event, one trip, one person, and say that ski mountaineering as we know it today began then, I would nominate Paulke's traverse of the Bernese Oberland in 1897. The group started from Grimsel without guides and went via the Oberaarjoch Hut, Grünhornlücke, Konkordia Hut, and down the Gr. Aletsch Glacier to Belalp. It was an extraordinarily bold expedition, and really set the stage for Alpine exploration on skis. For a more detailed account of Paulke's trip, see page 95.

In 1898 Monte Rosa was climbed and skied down for the first time. In the first ten years of the 1900s the following mountains were climbed and descended on skis: Finsteraarhorn, Mönch, Mont Velan, the Gr. Fiescherhorn, Mont Blanc, the Allalinhorn, Gr. Combin and Gr. Glockner. In 1911, the year in which Amundsen reached

the South Pole on skis, the Classic Haute Route was first completed. These then are the Golden Years of ski mountaineering. (Most of the major events are listed chronologically on page 152.)

Thereafter Alpine peaks were progressively ticked off, and ski traverses became more ambitious, leading to the various Alpine ski traverses.

An increasing number of people turned to ski mountaineering – either downhill skiers bored with and frustrated by the queues and confines of marked pistes, or mountaineers recognizing the advantages of skis for getting around the mountains in winter. This increase in popularity has been reflected by the readiness of manufacturers to invest money in ski mountaineering.

Exponents at the top end of the field are expanding the limits all the time (see Chapter 9, 'Ski Extrème'), and Alpine huts are being enlarged to cope with the increasing numbers, often far greater than the summer trade.

2 General Skills

If you are a skier looking to ski mountaineering as a way of escaping from crowded ski runs, you will need to learn mountaineering skills. If you are a mountaineer who recognizes the efficiency of skis for travelling around snow-covered mountains, you will need to learn how to ski. And just how good a skier or mountaineer you have to be depends to some extent on the difficulty of the tour, and to some extent on whether or not you have a guide or other competent leader.

GUIDED PARTIES

The following standards are suggested as being the minimum necessary for someone to be a competent member of a party being guided in the Pennine Alps of Europe.

Skiing skills

You need to be able to keep up a steady touring speed, without falls, in any kind of snow. By 'steady touring speed' I mean a steady rate of descent, which will vary enormously according to the type of snow. It is relatively easy to ski on hard, frozen snow, on hard, windblown snow, in spring snow and in a light fall of fresh snow resting on a firm base. Conversely, it is invariably extremely difficult to ski on breakable crust, in totally saturated snow, over frozen avalanche debris, or in a deep fall of fresh heavy snow. On an average Alpine tour, most of the above conditions will be met. So, to have any chance of acquitting oneself properly, the following minimum pre-tour standard is suggested:

– good 'basic' parallels on piste without falls. In the 'basic' parallel the skis are kept apart;
– any linked downhill turn in reasonable off-piste conditions without falling. The linked turns include the parallel, the stem christie, the basic swing and the snow plough. By 'reasonable' off-piste conditions I include both moderate depths of fresh snow and moderate depths of snow softened by the sun which, in the Alps, is prevalent around midday;
– fast and fluent kickturns, linked by descending traverses, in difficult off-piste conditions, without falling. These conditions include all the horrific ones like breakable crust and deep saturated snow. And, of course, these kickturns may have to be done on fairly steep slopes.

The skiing standard required is often hopelessly underestimated by mountaineers taking up ski mountaineering. They view, quite rightly, ski mountaineering as a part of, or as an extension to, mountaineering; and they presume, quite wrongly, that their mountaineering skills will compensate for their lack of skiing expertise. Time and again I

have seen competent alpinists brought literally to their knees – totally exhausted and dispirited – because they cannot ski well enough. And the whole unhappy business is usually made much worse by a party of European ski mountaineers blistering past in perfect style.

One year, at the start of a tour in the Bernese Oberland (on which the minimum previous skiing experience was clearly stated as 'good basic parallel on piste'), I noticed that one of the group was skiing rather poorly. However, he did not stand out as being exceptionally bad, because none of the rest of the party were doing much better. This was understandable, as we were skiing down from the Jungfraujoch to the Konkordia Platz on a hot afternoon in slightly difficult snow conditions, with rucksacks; and it was the first day, so we were all feeling the altitude. I presumed not only that he would get better, along with the others; but possibly quicker since he had a lot of summer Alpine experience. I was wrong. While the others settled down and improved, he, if anything, got worse.

The crevassed glaciers of the Bernese Oberland were no place for him to practise. And so, in the afternoon of the third day, I left the others at the Konkordia Hut and set off with him to the Jungfraujoch.

The weather became progressively worse; the wind increased, it became cold, and it started to snow. Soon the tracks had blown in and the visibility became very poor. My companion was convinced that we were going to spend a night out on the glacier. I was not quite so sure: I thought we might both fall into a crevasse first. In time, though, we came to the entrance to the tunnel that leads into the railway station, and suddenly found ourselves back in the world of postcards and ice cream, surrounded by a trainful of camera-flashing tourists.

I later found out that his total previous skiing experience had been two days on an artificial ski slope in England and one day on snow in Switzerland. He had assumed that his summer Alpine experience and his fitness would see him through, but he learned the hard way that it does not. A salutory lesson for us both.

Mountaineering skills

Provided there is a guide or some other competent person in the party, the rest of the party need not be experienced mountaineers, as long as they are good skiers. Depending on the type of tour, one guide or experienced mountaineer can relatively easily safeguard between three and six good skiers on mountaineering sections. Many good skiers with almost no mountaineering experience have joined parties on serious tours and have performed very well. The reason for this is that a good skier has a lot of experience of being on steep snow – most of it on skis, but some of it will have been on foot – resulting in a confident ability to move on steep snow.

This point is well illustrated by a friend of mine who

came across the Haute Route with me. He had never seen an ice axe or crampons in his life, but was a very strong skier and fit. We did the Classic Route, had a fast crossing and he did very well. It must be said, though, that we had good snow conditions. It would certainly be foolish to go on exposed slopes of hard snow without first being able to use an ice axe and without some experience of wearing crampons.

Fitness

Overall physical fitness is essential. In good conditions a day tour will make few demands on someone who is reasonably fit and who has the necessary skiing and mountaineering skills. It is quite likely, however, that during a week's tour adverse snow and weather conditions will be met, sometimes at the same time. To be able to ski in deep saturated snow, at the end of a twelve-hour day, with a rucksack weighing 11Kg (25 lb), demands high technical and physical preparation – and also a sense of humour

GUIDELESS PARTIES

As soon as you go off without a guide, the minimum standards indicated above become essential; and in the case of mountaineering many more skills are needed. It may be that just one person has these skills; but it is more common in guideless parties to find that two or more members of the party bring different skills and expertise to the expedition, resulting in the sharing of responsibilities and decision-making. Whatever the make-up of the party, the following skills are needed on glacier tours:

Weather: competence to assess the current situation and likely developments from visible signs; ability to obtain local forecasts from the telephone, tourist office or met office, which may require knowledge of a foreign language:

Avalanches: to obtain, and instruct the party in the use of, avalanche bleepers; obtain official avalanche warnings from the telephone, tourist office or met office; assess local conditions for avalanche risk; choose the appropriate route to minimize avalanche risk; in situations of avalanche risk, lead the party in such a way as to minimize the risk; in the case of an avalanche accident, organize a search and rescue.

Crevasses: to choose safe routes through crevassed areas; check that the party is properly equipped with harnesses and ropes, etc.; brief the party on crevasse rescue procedures; maybe organize a practice session; and in the case of a crevasse incident, take control and rescue the casualty.

Route Choice and Leadership: take into account all the physical factors such as weather, snow conditions, etc., and match these with the overall ability of the party; to select a suitable route for the day and anticipate the situation a day or two ahead; having selected the right route, then to follow it at the correct speed so that the whole party can establish a comfortable rhythm and pace.

Navigation: to navigate in all weather conditions.

Accidents: to have the equipment and knowledge to deal with any problem from blisters and headaches to broken legs and frostbite.

Bivouacs: to decide when and how to bivouac, and to ensure that the party is adequately bivouacked.

Steep ground: to assess the ability of the members of the party to move on steep ground; decide when extra safeguards are necessary in terms of use of the rope; and to be able to employ the rope effectively as a safeguard, both in ascent and descent.

Bearing in mind that it may be necessary to evacuate a casualty to a hut on an improvised stretcher, or that it may be necessary to help a tired colleague by carrying his rucksack for a time, at least one member of a guideless party should be a very strong skier, and one should be an experienced alpinist.

This is a bare minimum, and ideally the whole party should have broad skiing and mountaineering ability.

SKIING ABILITY VERSUS MOUNTAINEERING ABILITY

A good skier will enjoy the downhill sections and will be much safer on them. Skiing on crevassed glaciers requires, from time to time, the ability to ski very steadily and to stop quickly. The good skier will also cope well with most of the uphill sections. Being used to skiing down steep slopes, the ascent of them will not be such a problem, despite using unfamiliar equipment like ice axe and crampons.

The skier, however, must realize that ski mountaineering is a part of mountaineering; and that, as such, it is physically demanding. He must also realize that you cannot, for example, buy a 'package holiday' to do the Haute Route and, thereby, be guaranteed success. Weather conditions or general conditions on the mountains may dictate otherwise.

Conversely, the good mountaineer who is a poor skier will have a much rougher time on the whole. On skis he will be lacking in technique, so he will be forced to rely on his strength and stamina. On the steep mountaineering sections he will come into his own. But, on balance, his mountaineering skills are outweighed a thousandfold by his lack of skill. Ask any guide: who would you rather take, a good skier or a good mountaineer? The answer will always be 'the skier'.

3 Techniques

UPHILL TECHNIQUES

Walking, carrying skis

If there is just a short distance to walk, skis can be carried across the shoulder in the normal manner, although a high rucksack does get in the way. Ski sticks can sometimes be locked together by putting the tip of one through the basket of the other, and then both sticks can be easily carried in one hand. Telescopic sticks are even easier.

Over longer distances it is more convenient to carry the skis on the rucksack, in one of two methods.

Fig. 8 The more secure is the 'A' frame. Put the rucksack face down on the snow, attach a ski to each side using the straps supplied and tie the tips together. If the ground is not too steep and it is likely that you will need your hands for climbing or for holding the ice axe, put the wrist loops over the ski sticks and tie the sticks in tight with the ice axe strap on the back of the rucksack.

Be careful of two problems: the heels of the skis tend to catch the ground, especially on steep traverses, and, as one bends forwards, the ski tips can hit someone or something in front.

A quicker method is to put the skis under the lid of the rucksack, using the top straps on either side to secure them. The advantage of this system is that the skis move with the shoulders, which gives better control on difficult ground, for example on a delicate traverse.

Uphill on skins

When going uphill on skins, the movement is a gliding one, not a lifting one. Each ski is pushed well forward, to such an extent that on flattish ground the boot comes level with the tip of the stationary ski. On steeper ground it is not possible to push the ski quite so far forward, but,

nevertheless, it should be pushed as far forward as possible so as to get as long a stride as possible. As you come to the end of the push forward, put your weight on that ski. On flattish ground the ski will now glide forward, and when the glide has finished the other ski, the unweighted one, can be pushed forward. The work is done with the legs, the sticks being used only for balance.

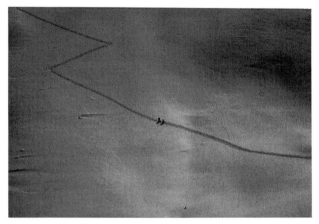

Fig. 9 It is much easier to follow someone else's track than to break a fresh one, which is why ski mountaineers tend to follow one behind the other when going uphill.

As the ground steepens, it will become necessary to zig-zag, each traverse being joined by one of the turns described below. On steep traverses it becomes difficult to hold the upper stick by the handle, so move the hand part of the way down the shaft. Normally when skiing on a traverse, the upper edges of the skis are used. When on skins this tendency must be resisted, because the priority is to get full skin contact with the snow.

Fig. 10 On a traverse this is usually obtained by rolling the knees and ankles downhill, which is contrary to the usual technique of edging. It will feel strange at first, but if correctly done it gives a much improved grip with the skins.

When going straight up a steep section, push each ski forward in turn, as far as possible. The skins get a better grip if the top surface of the snow is slightly soft, and conversely grip less well if it is very hard. If the ski is slapped down, this will help to get a good grip.

So, for maximum skin grip, on traverses roll the knees and ankles downhill; and on steep ground push the ski forward and slap it down.

(For the care of skins and how to put them on, see page 37.)

Walk-round turns

Fig. 11   If you want to change direction to the other traverse line, and if the slope is gentle, you can do this simply by walking round. Remember to keep the skins flat on the snow for maximum adhesion, and to slap them down if necessary.

Step-round turns

If the slope steepens too much for walk-round turns, try the step-round.

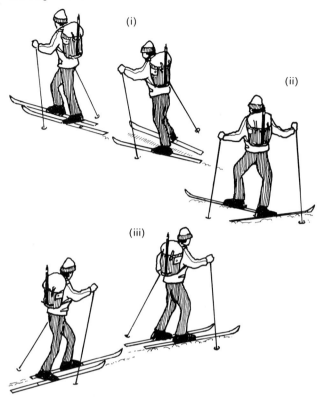

Fig. 12   (i) As you come up to do the turn, stamp down with the lower ski, and put your weight on its upper edge.
(ii) Turn the upper ski round to place it facing the new direction; and put your weight on its upper edge.
(iii) Bring the lower ski in parallel to become the new upper ski, and move off.

The common problem with the step-round turn is at stage (ii), in not getting the upper ski round far enough in the new direction. It must point along the traverse line; if necessary slap it down for good skin grip.

When performed fluently there is little break in rhythm, and because the turn is done facing uphill, there is little problem with the rope.

Uphill kickturns

As the ground steepens, it will become too difficult to do a step-round turn. The uphill kickturn is a similar turn except that the skis are placed carefully at a right-angle to the fall-line, both before and after the turn; whereas in the step-round turn the skis move from one traverse line to the next. The placing of the sticks is important.

There are two common problems with this turn. The first is a feeling of insecurity between stages (iv) and (v),

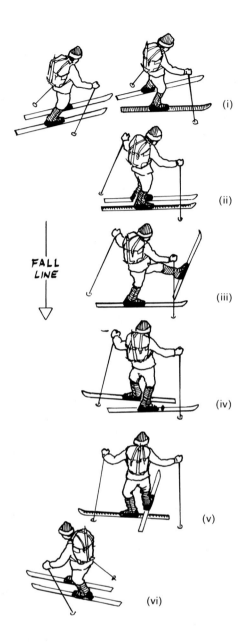

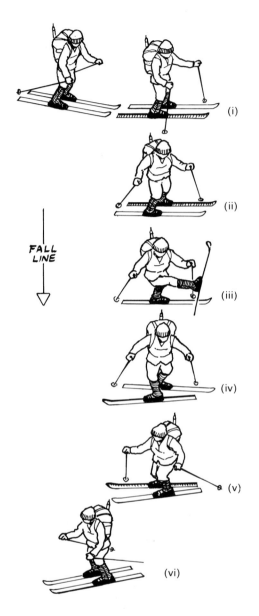

Fig. 13 The uphill kickturn.   (i) As you come into the turn from the traverse, place the lower ski at a right-angle to the fall-line. Stamp it down, making as good a platform as possible.

(ii) Bring the upper ski in parallel. Then put your weight on the upper edge of the lower ski.

(iii) Place the heel of the upper ski on the snow, as near to the tip of the lower ski as possible. The upper ski should be vertical.

(iv) Let the upper ski fall round to face the new direction, parallel to the lower ski.

(v) Put your weight on the upper edge of the upper ski. Bring the lower ski in parallel to become the new upper ski.

(vi) Move off.

Fig. 14 The downhill kickturn.   (i) As you come into the turn from the traverse, place the lower ski at a right-angle to the fall-line. Stamp it down, making as good a platform as possible.

(ii) Bring the upper ski in parallel, and stamp it down. Put your weight on the upper edge of the upper ski.

(iii) Place the heel of the lower ski on the snow, as near to the tip of the upper ski as possible. The lower ski should be vertical.

(iv) Let the lower ski fall round to face the new direction, parallel to the upper ski.

(v) Put your weight on the upper edge of the lower ski. Bring the upper ski in parallel to become the new lower ski.

(vi) Move off.

which is hardly surprising as one ski is facing one way and the other ski is facing another. It helps greatly to feel the upper edge of the upper ski firmly, and to get your weight on it.

The other common problem is at stage (v) when you bring the lower ski in parallel to become the new upper ski. Frequently the tip catches the snow, often to an extent that it will not come round. The steeper the slope, the more likely this is to happen. Try lifting the tip as much as possible, or clearing snow away with the ski stick, and if all that fails, do a downhill kickturn.

Again, since this turn is done facing uphill, there is little problem with the rope.

Downhill kickturns

This is an invaluable turn when descending in difficult conditions, and it can also be used in ascent. When used in ascent, it results in a slight loss of height (compared with the uphill kickturn) and rope management needs care and attention.

The common problem with this turn is sliding back in stages (ii) and (iv), usually because the skis were not placed at a right-angle to the fall-line, and also because the skis were not stamped down. There is also the sensation that one is going to ski away prematurely in stage (v). This can be avoided by making sure that the skis are placed correctly at a right-angle to the fall-line; and also by bringing the upper stick round at stage (v) at the same time as the upper ski, and placing the stick firmly near the tip of the ski.

Harscheisen

The advantages of harscheisen are that they give a grip on hard snow, they give confidence on steep snow, and they allow the traverse to be maintained. Without harscheisen on hard snow one cannot get enough skin contact with the snow to stop sliding backwards, and to make any progress uphill it is necessary either to go straight up on the skis, or take the skis off and go on foot.

The disadvantage of them is that they cause considerable drag, which is demanding on energy, and of course it is not possible to glide the skis at all.

When using them, try as far as possible to place the ski flat down on the snow, so as to get both sides of the harscheisen in contact – and to get the maximum skin contact as well, of course. The technique of rolling the ankles and knees downhill should be used.

Harscheisen are not very strong, particularly the side-fitting ones, and they will bend if subjected to such treatment as standing on rocks. They are excellent pieces of equipment, however, and can save a lot of time and energy on hard snow.

(For the different types of harscheisen and how to fit them, see page 36.)

Crampons

It is sometimes a difficult decision to make, whether to go on skis with the skins and harscheisen fitted, or whether to go on crampons and carry the skis. The advantage of crampons is that they give very good security on hard snow and ice. Really the only disadvantage is that the skis have to be carried and they are heavy.

On easy-angled ground the technique is to keep all the points on the bottom of the crampon, usually ten, in contact with the snow or ice. This can require considerable flexing at the ankle. When the ground steepens, try the front-pointing technique, where only the front two or four points on each crampon are used. It is tiring on the calves, but, on the other hand, it has the great advantage that one is facing into the slope, which not only gives a greater feeling of security, but also means that if the skis are being carried on the rucksack in the 'A' frame position, the heels of the skis will be well away from the snow.

If the snow is at an easy angle, a comfortable way of climbing is with the ski sticks in the hands. With steeper-angled snow the ice axe will be necessary: for security, by placing the shaft in the snow; for cutting steps, and for self-arrest in the event of a fall.

The most common cause of a fall with crampons is tripping over them, usually as a result of catching the front points of one through the straps of the other. I once witnessed a dramatic demonstration of this. A student caught his crampon straps at the top of a steep 213 m (700 ft) gully and fell head first down it. Because he had practised self-arrest with the ice axe, his reactions were quick and he stopped himself in about 30 m (100 ft). When using crampons, therefore, try to walk with the feet further apart than normal and make a deliberate effort to swing the moving foot wide of the stationary one.

Another point to watch with crampons is not to tighten the straps too much, as this can restrict circulation, which, in turn, can lead to cold feet and even frostbite.

Finally, be careful not to stand on the rope, as the sharp points can cause damage which may not be immediately obvious.

(For the different types of crampon, see page 38.)

Moving Roped-up

Reasons for roping-up: the main reasons for roping-up are: crevasses, ascending steep ground, descending steep ground, and bad visibility with consequent danger from crevasses and cornices, etc.

The decision whether or not to rope up on a glacier because of the risk of falling into a crevasse is often a difficult one. Safety is obviously increased by roping-up, but it takes time and the party will move more slowly on the rope. Few parties will rope-up in the following situation: clear visibility, cold conditions, early morning,

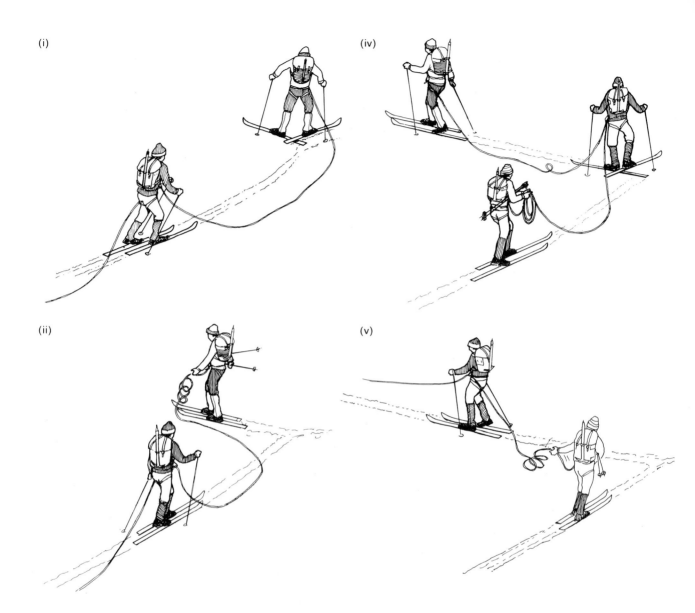

(i)

(iv)

(ii)

(v)

(iii)

Fig. 15 Roping-up method (1).   (i) As the leader does an uphill turn, the second keeps the same pace so that slack accumulates in the rope.
(ii) Having done the turn, the leader takes in the slack and drops the coils on the snow, while moving slowly on.
(iii) The second flips the rope over to the uphill side. The leader moves off.
(iv) As the second does the turn, slack rope is automatically taken up by the leader moving on. The third keeps the same pace and takes in coils.
(v) As the second moves off, the third flips the rope to the uphill side and drops the coils on that side. He then moves up and does his turn.

late in the season (when the bridges are strong), and on a glacier with few crevasses. Conversely, most parties will rope-up, if they have any sense, in this situation: poor visibility, warm temperature, midday or early afternoon, early in the season (when the bridges are weak), and on a heavily crevassed glacier.

There are many permutations between these two extremes. The rope gives extra safety, but what is safety? On the one hand a strong party might go unroped, while a less-experienced party correctly feels the need to rope-up. The strong party will move quicker, will therefore get better snow conditions, and will therefore use less energy. The usual reasons for forced bivouacs are injuries, sudden changes in weather, and parties being caught out because they went too slowly. Therefore speed is safety. On the other hand, one cannot afford to risk an unroped skier falling into a crevasse.

The best advice seems to be: when going uphill rope-up as soon as there is any danger. The extra safety will normally outweigh any loss of time.

Types of Rope: see page 39.

Types of Harness and Methods of Tying-in: see page 59.

Techniques on Crevassed Glaciers
Three people to a 45m (150 ft) rope are good, with four people as a maximum. When uncoiling the rope, do not throw it down on the snow, but hold it in one hand and take off one coil at a time with the other hand. This should avoid a tangle.

Two methods of handling the rope are shown.

(1) The first is suitable where the second person on the rope is inexperienced. (See Fig. 15.)

(2) This method is suitable where the second person on the rope is used to handling ropes. (See Fig. 16.)

This second method is easier for the leader and should be used where possible, as the leader has the additional problem of breaking the trail. The objective is to complete the turns with the minimum expenditure of energy and with the minimum loss of rhythm.

Fig. 16 Roping-up method (2). (i) As the leader does an uphill turn, the second keeps the same pace and takes in coils.
(ii) As the leader moves off, the second flips the rope onto the uphill side and drops the coils on that side.
(iii) The third comes up and does the same as he did in method (ii).

Ascending Steep Ground

Some Alpine cols are too steep at the top for skis, and are done on foot with the skis either carried over the shoulder or attached to the rucksack. If the rope is being used, its purpose will now be to stop anyone from falling a long way if he should happen to slip.

This is best done on a short rope of, say, 4–5 m (13–16 ft). The first thing is to shorten the rope.

Fig. 17   (i) Coils are taken under one arm and over the opposite shoulder.
(ii) The coils are tied off by passing a bight (loop) of rope round them and making two half-hitches.
(iii) To bring any pull onto the harness, make a figure of eight in the rope and clip it into the karabiner on the harness.

With such a short rope, a slip can be stopped from above before the person has gained any speed. It is not suitable for a leader fall, however, and if there is any risk of that happening a longer rope should be used and belays taken.

Holding a fall

1. On foot with a short rope: as just pointed out, a short rope can be very effective for steep snow, particularly when used by a competent leader to protect an inexperienced second. The leader will be able to contain the slip by holding the rope in both hands and absorbing the fall through his knees.

2. On foot with a long rope: in well-consolidated snow a leader can bring up and effectively protect a second using the *footbrake method*, providing he has practised it.

Fig. 18   (i) The shaft of the axe is driven into the snow, and the uphill boot forced against it. The rope is passed behind the axe and round the inside of the uphill boot.
(ii) The upper hand grips the head of the axe, the arm is kept straight and as much weight as possible is put on the head of the axe.
(iii) The lower hand holds the rope and applies friction by taking the rope round the inside of the upper ankle.

The footbrake can either be used as an emergency procedure – in which case it is doubtful of success even with practice – or it can be set up in advance and the rope taken round the footbrake as a precaution, which is a much safer method.

3. On skis: when going uphill on skis, the most likely fall is into a crevasse. The person next to the victim will be dragged towards the crevasse, maybe head-first and in an uncomfortable position. He must get his skis between himself and the crevasse, at a right-angle to the rope. Anyone else on the rope should get in the same position and help to arrest the fall.

The initial impact of the fall will be greatly reduced if the rope was being held fairly tight, without slack and without coils being carried in the hand. So, in crevassed areas do not carry coils in the hand. The rope will probably cut into the lip of the crevasse, and this will cause friction, thus helping to stop the fall.

Belays

Fig. 19 **Thread belay:** this is the most reliable belay, as it will take a pull from any direction. Either a sling can be threaded or the rope.

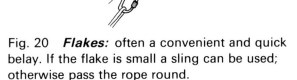

Fig. 20 **Flakes:** often a convenient and quick belay. If the flake is small a sling can be used; otherwise pass the rope round.

Fig. 21 **Rockpegs:** ski mountaineers are unlikely to carry these except on the most serious tours. But they might already be in place, and a decision will be needed as to their reliability. Ideally the crack should be at a right-angle to the direction of pull. The peg should be firm, i.e. no play. Do not trust rusty old ones.

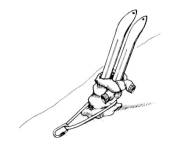

Fig. 22 **Skis:** of all the snow belays available, skis are the quickest, and in firm snow work well. They should be placed side by side at a 45-degree angle to the back slope, and forced into the snow as far as possible – certainly up to the bindings. The edges should be padded, and a sling or the rope passed round at snow level.

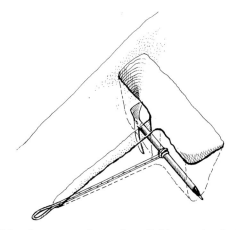

Fig. 23 **Ice axe:** the only reliable method of ice axe belay is the horizontally buried axe. Cut a slot in the snow at a right-angle to the direction of pull. Cut a groove for the rope. Tie the sling or rope to the shaft of the axe, at the point of balance, with a clove hitch. Place the axe in the slot and stamp it down.

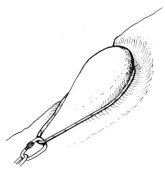

Fig. 24 **Ice bollards:** the size depends on the strength of the ice, from 35 cm (14 in) diameter in good ice. The channel should be deep enough to prevent the rope from jumping out, and it should be incut at the top of the bollard.

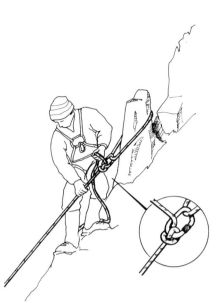

Fig. 25 *Ice screws:* it is common for ski mountaineers to carry one or two ice screws, as they can be useful in crevasse rescue (particularly where the casualty is injured and someone has to go into the crevasse to help), and they are also useful on windswept cols where the snow has been blown away to leave an icy surface. To get the screw started, chip a small hole in the ice with the ice axe. Then insert the ice screw at a right-angle to the ice. The head of the screw should point in the likely direction of fall. When used as a main belay, at least two screws and preferably three should be used.

Fig. 26 **Methods of belaying**
There are two methods:

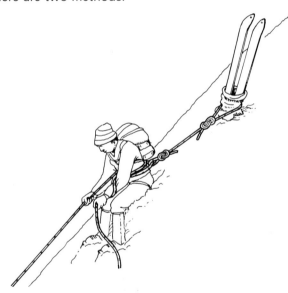

1. The dynamic or indirect method: the belayer is attached to the belay. In the example, the rope is attached to the belay by a figure of eight knot and to the belayer by another figure of eight knot into the back of his harness.

The rope is passed round the belayer's back, and he takes a twist in his 'dead' arm. The impact of the fall can largely be absorbed through the legs, so minimizing the shock-load to the belay point.

It is therefore suitable where the belay point is not so strong.

2. The static or direct method: the rope is belayed directly to the belay point.

In the example it is belayed using a friction hitch. The belayer stands by the belay and is not attached to it, unless he feels insecure.

The full impact of the fall goes directly onto the belay point, and, therefore, this method is only suitable where the belay point is very strong. This method has the advantage of being quick to set up.

Ice axe Techniques

Carrying positions: the best way of carrying the axe is so that it is instantly ready for self-arrest, i.e. with the uphill hand over the head of the axe, the thumb curled under the adze and the little finger towards the pick. The axe is then carried by one's side, with the spike down and the pick facing backwards. The spike can be put into the snow for security, and the axe is ready for self-arrest.

Self-arrest: this is one of the most useful techniques with the ice axe. A slip on steep snow can be stopped before it develops into a serious fall. It is essential, however, to apply the technique correctly and to practise it.

Here are techniques for three different types of fall.

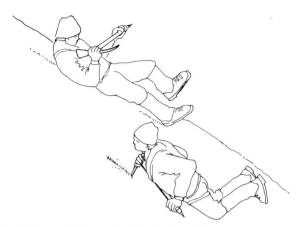

Fig. 27   *a. Fall on the back, feet first.*

(i) Bring the axe across the chest, one hand over the head of the axe and with the adze against the shoulder. The other hand holds the spike.

(ii) Turn over onto your front and press the pick into the snow with steady and increasing pressure. Since the shaft is across your chest, a lot of pressure can be brought to bear by pressing down with your chest.

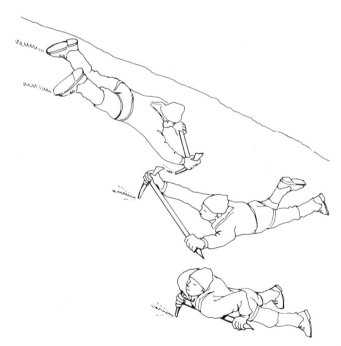

Fig. 28   *b. Fall on the front, head first.*

(i) Hold the axe in front of you with one hand over the head of the axe and the other over the spike.

(ii) Press the pick into the snow as far out to one side as possible.

(iii) This relatively small amount of friction will allow you to swing your legs over on the other side.

(iv) As the legs swing over, you will find yourself face-down with your feet below you, and you can brake in the normal way.

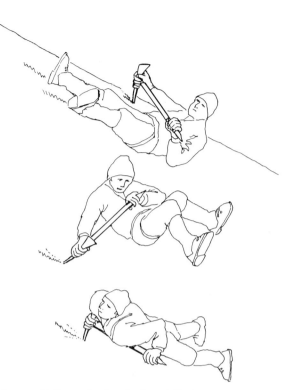

Fig. 29   *c. Fall on the back, head first.*

(i) Hold the axe across the abdomen, with the head in one hand and the spike in the other.

(ii) Press the pick into the snow at about hip level and keep steady pressure on it. This relatively small amount of friction will allow you to swing your legs over on the other side.

(iii) As the legs swing over, you will find yourself face-down with your feet below you, and you can brake in the normal way.

When braking hold the axe very firmly and make sure that the adze is kept in tight to the shoulder, to prevent the axe being ripped out of your hands.

Do not expect to come to an immediate halt. It may even feel as though you are never going to stop; but keep braking, as all the pressure you apply through the pick of the axe means that at least you are not accelerating, and you will probably manage to stop yourself.

If crampons are worn, keep the feet up, because otherwise you will somersault over them. If they are not being worn, the feet can be applied for extra braking.

DOWNHILL SKIING TECHNIQUES

There are many different skiing techniques, but all of them have four basic ingredients in common.

1. The legs must be turned and the feet pointed in the direction of the turn.

2. The edges of the skis must be used to enable the skis to go where you point them. So, to turn left, use the left edges.

3. Control of pressure between the skis and the snow. It is this pressure which pushes the skis round in a turn.

4. Balance. You need to stay roughly upright while you turn.

It is not the intention of this book to examine in detail the basic techniques of skiing. This is covered in many other books (see Bibliography). Not so readily available are hints on how to ski in the very variable and difficult conditions encountered while ski mountaineering.

General Skiing Hints

One of the first articles in German on ski technique gave this helpful advice: 'The skiers let the skis carry them where they will until the air acts as a natural brake and brings them to rest.' If only it were as easy as that!

Zdarsky, writing in the *Wiener Fremdenblatt*, gave details of a different technique:

> On the descent the skier leans back on his stick [this was in the days of the single stick], and shuts his eyes. Then he darts downward as straight as an arrow, and continues until he can no longer breathe. He then throws himself sideways on the snow, and waits until he regains his breath, and then once again hurls himself downwards until once more he loses his breath, and throws himself on the snow, and so forth until he reaches the valley.

Although possibly an accurate description of some skiing attempts, it hardly amounts to helpful advice. The following may be more useful.

In general, when skiing away from the prepared runs, adopt a defensive approach. Keep the skis slightly apart in the basic parallel position and continually flex the body and legs in order to absorb any changes in the snow. Sometimes these can be seen and the turning place chosen accordingly. If in doubt about the type of snow, test it by:

- making small jumps or bounces on the skis, either while stationary or on the move;
- poking the snow with one of the sticks;
- while on a traverse, dropping the lower ski into a plough and pushing away on it.

If in doubt about the chances of successfully turning, either stop and do a kickturn, or slow down and do a *survival snow plough*. On good firm snow a snow plough is done by pressing on the front of the boots which in turn press on the front of the skis, but in difficult, off-piste conditions it is safer to keep your weight on the back of the skis, to prevent the ski tips from burying themselves. The skis are turned by pressing the heels of the skis round, and this can be done very slowly and defensively. Hence the term survival snow plough.

Another reason for having your weight back is that it is safer to take a fall backwards than to go flying over the front of the skis.

While on the subject of falling, falls on crevassed glaciers must be avoided. When skiing smoothly forward, much of one's weight is transferred into kinetic energy forward, and very little weight is brought onto the crevasse bridges; whereas a hard fall shock-loads the bridge badly.

Most skiing falls happen when turning, and many of them are due to two mistakes:

1. The skier swings the upper body round, probably helped by an enormous swing of the outside arm. When this is done with a heavy rucksack on the back, the result is an overswing and a fall. So be careful to keep the upper body still and the outside arm back.

2. Another mistake is trying to stop the turn too quickly. As you turn, think of putting your weight onto the inside edge of the lower ski, and then do not try to stop the turn dead but look ahead to the new traverse line. There is a moment during the turn when one is skiing straight down the fall-line – this is the moment to look ahead to the new traverse line.

In going on now to consider four types of snow (deep dry snow, deep wet snow, breakable crust and hard icy snow), it must obviously be born in mind that snow comes in many degrees of depth, dryness, wetness, softness, hardness, crust, etc.

Deep dry snow (powder): this is probably the most exhilarating snow in which to ski, and it is deceptively easy because the snow is forgiving of errors. If you catch an edge on a well-prepared run, you might end up falling, but in powder there is nothing on which to catch the edge. And if you do not believe me, maybe it is because you have not discovered the four secrets to powder-snow skiing.

1. As you move off to go into a turn, bounce up and down on your skis. This is done for two reasons. Firstly, it may change you from a rigid, terrified coward into a relaxed, confident expert! Whenever we feel the skiing is getting difficult, we stiffen up which compounds the problem. So try deliberately to relax by bouncing up and down before the first turn. Secondly, it lets you feel the 'platform' for the turn. When skiing on the piste there is a firm platform from which to start a turn and on which to finish it. In deep snow the platform is still there, but not so definite. By bouncing up and down on both skis equally, before the turn, you will get a feel for the snow and will establish how far down the platform is. Also, you will know how far down into the snow you are likely to sink on completion of the turn; so helping you make the completion of the turn smooth and firm.

2. Keep the knees locked together. Once they wander apart, the skis will part and it is difficult to get them back

together again. So, as you go off into the first turn, bouncing away, consciously bring your knees together and from then on keep them locked together.

3. Imagine someone standing on your ski tips, facing you. As you unweight to start the turn, throw your outer arm forward and punch him on the nose! This helps lift the skis clear of the snow. Do not hold back: make it aggressive. This may sound as though it conflicts with the advice previously given, namely to keep the outer arm and upper body still. Well, to an extent it does, but it is a punch straight forward, and there should be no rotation of the shoulders in it. It is that rotation which is to be avoided at all costs.

4. As the depth of snow increases, the weight should be kept evenly on both skis. Do not weight the downhill ski on the completion of the turn (as on harder snow), but try to come down smoothly and equally on both skis. All skiing in deep snow should be done with smoothness and firmness.

Fig. 31 (i) When approaching the turn, the lower ski is stemmed down and most of the weight put on it. The shoulders are turned uphill. This is done in one fluid movement.
(ii) To turn, the weight is brought up onto the upper ski, and the shoulders are turned to face the new direction. With the added weight of the rucksack, this can be made into a forceful and aggressive turn.

Kickturns and traverses have to be resorted to in bad conditions.

Breakable crust: this may be a sun crust or a wind crust. With a sun crust the snow has probably been fairly well saturated and the lower evening temperatures have frozen the top surface. With a wind crust there is a soft layer (for whatever reason) with the top surface frozen hard by the wind. Sometimes the skis ride on the hard surface, and sometimes they break through into the soft snow below. It can be very unpredictable, and therefore difficult to ski on.

Jump turns are the most effective, if you are a good enough skier. The whole turn, while being strong and determined, must also be smooth. The landing must be on both skis equally, because if the skis break through the crust, it will then be like skiing in deep snow. Avoid doing jump turns, however smoothly, on crevasse bridges.

All the other turns may be used, but must be performed smoothly with the weight equally on both skis.

Fig. 30 Skiing in powder.

Deep wet snow: this can be very difficult to ski in. An aggressive approach and leg strength are required. Jump-turns can be used, but they are sometimes difficult to do because there is no base from which to jump. If snow ploughing, do it with the weight evenly on both skis and towards the back of the skis – a survival snowplough.

A very useful turn is the lower ski stem. The lower ski is stemmed down as this is less tiring than continually lifting the upper ski in this heavy snow. The stem can be combined with a counter-rotation of the upper body:

Careful route choice may make all the difference to the descent. For example, a slope which has not received so much sun will not have become so saturated, and therefore it may not have frozen on the surface (e.g. slopes with a more northerly aspect, slopes which receive shade from a mountain, deep-sided gullies and slopes shaded by trees). If the problem is breakable wind crust, either try a more exposed slope (e.g. the crest of a ridge) because the crust there might be so hard as not to break, or try the bottom of a gully, where the wind might not have penetrated – indeed it might have deposited some nice powder!

In extreme cases it might be better to sit down and wait for an hour or two for the crust to harden.

Hard icy snow: sharp edges and a reasonably stiff ski are needed to give confidence on really hard snow. Do your boots up tightly and press forward on the front of the boot, in order to get good edge control. The side-slip is really useful, and can be used very effectively in a diagonal side-slip, going forward and backward. To go forward, weight the front of the skis; and to go backwards, weight the backs of the skis.

Avoid kickturns, because it is impossible to stamp out a good platform and, without a good platform, a kickturn on hard icy snow can be a bit too exciting.

Skiing Downhill Roped

When to ski roped: skiing downhill roped to other people is, at the best of times, difficult. It can rapidly develop into a fiasco, causing more problems than it resolves.

If one can ski downhill with smooth turns, following the track of the person in front, the chances of falling into a crevasse are fairly remote. The problem, therefore, is for the person in front who is choosing the line, and the decision to rope-up will probably be made when that person begins to find route-finding difficult, for example when:

1. there is poor visibility and a danger of falling over a drop or a cornice;
2. there is poor visibility and the party is on a crevassed glacier;
3. there is good visibility, but the crevasse bridges are particularly dangerous. This might be because it is late in the day, or because it is unusually warm, or after a heavy snowfall.

While the rope is readily used when going uphill, it is used very much as a last resort when skiing down. Because of the difficulties of skiing roped, a normal procedure for a large party is for the first three people to ski roped, and the remainder of the party to follow exactly in their tracks, working on the principle that if three people have been safe, the others probably will be as well.

Methods

1. Two people to a rope of 25–30m (80–100 ft). This is the fastest method, but a fall might be difficult for just one person to hold.
2. Three people to 45–60m (150–200 ft) rope, with the end people tied onto the rope and the middle man floating. He does this by clipping the rope into a karabiner on his harness, without tying a knot. This enables him to ski more freely, and therefore to fall less, but it is more difficult to hold a fall.
3. Three people to a rope of 45–60 m (150–200 ft). Each person is tied on to the rope, and this is the normal method.

Techniques

Fig. 32   (i) The leader skis as near the fall-line as possible, making steady, predictable turns. He picks the safest and easiest line, and keeps a steady pace. (ii) The middleman follows exactly in the leader's track. (If he needs to catch up, he might have to turn slightly inside the track.) He holds both sticks together and he holds the rope.

The rope should be kept as tight as possible, with as few coils as possible.

During the turn, the middleman flips the rope over his skis, just before crossing the fall-line.

He keeps a steady pace, with predictable turns for the last man to follow.

(iii) The last man follows the track, sometimes turning inside in order to catch up. He keeps the rope as tight as possible on the middleman, with as few coils as possible. And he carries both sticks together.

Things to avoid: the emphasis is on steady, predictable skiing, so avoid skiing fast and sudden turns. On the whole, coils should not be carried, as they simply mean that the fall will be longer than necessary. Slight differences in skiing speed will result in slack rope which can be taken up temporarily in coils by the middle and last man; but they should be discarded as soon as possible, by slowing down.

Do not ski over the rope, as it cuts it. And the most important thing to avoid is falling – it causes chaos, particularly if it is the last man, as he inevitably takes the other two with him.

To hold a fall: if the leader falls into a crevasse, the middleman will take the brunt of the fall. He should fall over, if he has not done so already, get his skis between himself and the crevasse, and use his sticks for self-arrest. The rope will cut into the lip of the crevasse, so causing

friction and helping to arrest the fall. The last man will have no problem in holding the middleman.

Climbing Down

If it is too steep to ski, one of the following four methods of descent can be used.

1. Walk down with the skis in one shoulder, facing out, and the ice axe in the other hand for self-arrest. To avoid slipping at the heels, bend the upper body forward over boots and kick the heels into the snow. The legs and body should be flexible, and a slightly bouncing gait used. If wearing crampons, on hard snow keep the feet flat (French technique) and do not use a bouncing gait. If the snow is soft enough to allow the heels to be kicked in, use a bouncing gait. With crampons, beware of the snow balling up under the foot.

2. Climb down with the skis on the rucksack, facing in, and the ice axe in use. If there are steps in the snow, place your feet carefully in them. If there are no steps and the snow is hard, kick your toes in to make a step. On a long or awkward descent wear crampons and follow the same techniques of placing the feet in any steps or kicking the toes in. One hand should be over the head of the ice axe, which should be driven in, spike first, for support. In the event of a slip, if the shaft is well in, the axe will hold you; otherwise use it in the normal self-arrest technique.

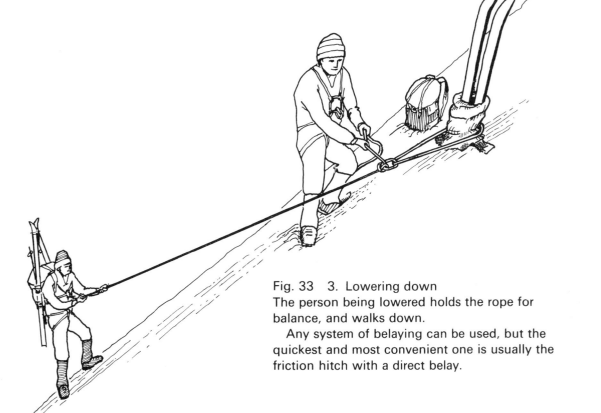

Fig. 33 3. Lowering down
The person being lowered holds the rope for balance, and walks down.

Any system of belaying can be used, but the quickest and most convenient one is usually the friction hitch with a direct belay.

Fig. 34   4. Abseiling or rappelling
The climber leans back on the rope, with the feet apart. The rate of progress is controlled by the climber feeding the rope through a friction device.

There are many methods of abseiling, using different friction devices. In ski mountaineering the most convenient one is the friction hitch. One hand is kept on the rope above the karabiner for balance. The other hand controls the rate of descent and should be kept down by the thigh, well away from the karabiner.

To save time on easy abseils, keep the skis on, side-slipping at a right-angle to the fall-line. Again, the friction hitch is suitable.

The last person down will have to pass the rope round the belay and abseil on a double rope. When he comes to

Fig. 35   Abseil off the Fenêtre du Chamois.

the end of the abseil, he pulls on one of the ends and recovers the rope.

Often two ropes are joined together to get a longer abseil. Be careful to place the knot on one side of the belay and to pull the rope on that side, to avoid the knot being pulled round behind the belay and jamming.

4 Clothing

As ski mountaineering is a combination of skiing and mountaineering, the question which usually arises is what to wear – skiing or mountaineering clothing? The requirements are stringent: wind and low temperatures may combine to give temperatures of − 40°C or lower, and at those temperatures exposed flesh freezes in less than a minute. It may be desperately hot, it may snow or it may rain. What you take in terms of clothing is, like everything else, severely limited by the weight of your rucksack. Different fabrics perform different jobs: some are bulky, some compact very tightly, some work well when wet, some do not, some have one function only, while some are multi-purpose.

Rain and Snow

Nylon is the most commonly used rainproof material. It is often proofed on the inside with either neoprene, which is hard wearing and very effective, or with polyurethene, which is not so hard wearing, but which is cheaper than neoprene. The very lightweight nylon garments are made from 56 gm (2 oz) material, while the heavier ones are made from 227 gm (8 oz) – these really are waterproof, especially if neoprene-proofed. However, there is very little ventilation with garments made from nylon, except through the following places: the neck, under the arms (if breathing holes are incorporated), up the arms and up the bottom of the jacket. This means that water given off by sweat cannot escape and one's inner clothing subsequently becomes damp.

There has, therefore, been a great search for a waterproof which breathes. Gore-Tex and Entrant are among the latest claimants. These may be snowproof, they may be rainproof for a time, they are usually light and comfortable to wear, they are usually expensive and they look good. Oiled cotton was once the traditional favourite, and there is no doubt it is effective. It has a certain rustic look to it, however, and you must not expect to be voted 'best dressed ski mountaineer of the year'! A friend of mine who lives on the Isle of Skye, off the west coast of Scotland, swears by it – and anyone who has been to Skye knows what the rain can be like there!

A material that has been around for a long time but which, for some reason or another has never really caught on, is Ventile. It is a very close-weave cotton and is sometimes known as 'the rich man's cotton'. It is no more expensive than many of the other materials around these days, and it is waterproof. One of the wettest weekends I ever had in the hills was in Dumfriesshire, when for two days it rained so hard that rivers broke their banks, roads were blocked and houses were flooded. On both days I was

out on the hills with a group of people, and between us we wore every type of waterproof available. I did a check on everyone later to see who had remained driest, and my double Ventile jacket was clearly the winner.

Wind

Nylon is a good windproof, but has the disadvantage already mentioned concerning condensation. Cotton has quite good windproof qualities and is cheap. If you waterproof it you will have a multi-purpose jacket. The best windproof is Ventile, the ultimate being double Ventile which is totally windproof, as well as snow- and rainproof. Gore-Tex and Entrant are fairly windproof and adequate for most purposes.

Cold

To keep warm you need layers which trap pockets of air which work as insulation. The traditional insulative material is wool. If worn in two or three thin layers, instead of one enormous great jersey, better insulation will be achieved as well as greater versatility. Wool still retains much of its insulating properties when wet. When pre-shrunk it makes very warm mitts, gloves and hats.

Nylon fibre-pile is a fabric which has good insulating properties, is light and comfortable to wear, and dries quickly when wet. It was originally designed to be worn as underlothing by fishermen, and, although it still performs this function very well, most designers now make it up as a kind of sweater.

Some designers are now making excellent underwear using blends of man-made fibres. Various trade names exist, but the normal collective name for this kind of underwear is 'thermawear'. Most thermawear works on the principle of combining very high insulation properties with very little absorption of moisture. Sweat, therefore, is able to evaporate away from the body, and the skin is left warm and dry. A word of warning with these fabrics: do not wash them in hot water, and never put them in a tumble dryer – they shrink!

Duck or goose down is the best insulation layer available, and in cheaper garments is mixed with feather. Its other important property is that it compresses down very small. Jackets and overtrousers made of down are normally called 'duvet' jackets and trousers. As long as they are kept dry, they will keep you very warm, but once wet, they lose most of their insulating properties.

Synthetic materials like polyester, hollofill and dacron are now used in many duvet-type jackets, waistcoats and overtrousers. Compared with down they are cheaper, bulkier and warmer when wet. Thinsulate is another synthetic material (a metallic/plastic fabric) which has great insulating properties and yet is not at all bulky. In fact, it is so effective, so light and so compact that many mountaineers have put all their woollen jerseys, nylon fibre-pile jackets, dacron waistcoats and duvet jackets into storage – replacing the lot with one Thinsulate garment.

Sweat

Taking the previous criteria into account, the answer would seem to be simple: a good insulating layer (say thermawear underwear with a nylon fibre-pile jacket), a Ventile jacket for windproofing, and a 227 gm (8 oz) neoprene-proofed nylon jacket for the rain and snow. And for the forced bivouac, pull a heavy gauge plastic bag over the lot. But this ignores sweat. Even at rest the body gives off water. Our average daily water intake is:

drink	1·4 litres	(2½ pt)
contained in food	·75 litre	(1⅓ pt)
from oxidization of food	·28 litre	(½ pt)
Total	2·5 litres	(4⅓ pt)

The average daily output is:

lost in urine	1·4 litres	(2½ pt)
lost from skin surface	·5 litre	(1 pt)
lost from lungs	·4 litre	(⅔ pt)
lost from faeces	·1 litre	($\frac{1}{6}$ pt)
Total	2·5 litres	(4⅓ pt)

So ·9 litre (1⅔ pt) is lost through the skin and the lungs, a process which is continuing even when asleep. This is why one's sleeping bag gets damp, why blankets in Alpine huts can be damp and cold (especially in the winter rooms where there is little chance of airing them), and why a bivouac spent in a big plastic bag results in one being wet in the morning.

It is very important to reduce sweating while ski mountaineering. One man with whom I toured treated his ski mountaineering the same way he would treat rugby training: he kept a lot of clothes on and went as fast as he could, so that he sweated as much as possible. He thought it was doing his fitness great benefit, and the more he sweated, the happier he was. Unfortunately, being his guide, I was responsible for his safety and I did not share his enthusiasm for his sweat. While he thought he was the strongest man in the party, the truth, of course, was that he was probably the weakest, since, in the event of a forced halt or deterioration in the weather, he would have cooled off very quickly and would have been a prime candidate for exposure.

There are four main ways in which to reduce sweating:
a) be fit;
b) regulate heat by taking clothes on and off, e.g. hats and gloves can be removed and put back on again continually;
c) use a regular pace, slowing for steep sections, so that breathing remains regular;
d) avoid nylon clothing.

Deciding what to wear

Let us return to the thorny problem of deciding whether to wear skiing or mountaineering clothing. When you visit your local sports shop, the choice of clothing is bewildering. The most important thing to clarify is what you require to be the primary function of a particular article of clothing. Is it to be rainproof, snowproof, windproof, an insulating layer against cold, or an item to combat sweating? Consider cost, design and comfort, and then it is a matter of avoiding a few bad mistakes, of which the following are the main ones:

Do not wear nylon next to the skin, whether as underwear or socks, as this really makes you sweat. The exception to this is nylon fibre-pile referred to above.

Make sure the clothing is long enough in the important places. For example, make sure that stockings overlap the bottom of breeches and do not leave a gap of flesh exposed to the elements – a prime place for frostbite or sunburn; make sure that shirts and jerseys are long enough so that no gap is left at the waist – general activity and carrying a rucksack will tend to make them ride up a little.

If you buy a new, coloured shirt, wash it first and test it for colour fastness. If you do not, you may end up doing what I did once, namely wearing it on a hot day and finding later in the hut that the green dye had left me looking like the 'Incredible Hulk'!

Useful tips

If you get cold hands, wear silk inner gloves or thermawear gloves with a pair of mittens over them. Climbing shops sell two very good types: pre-shrunk woollen mitts called Dachsteins, and nylon fibre-pile mitts marketed by Helly Hansen.

The best socks and stockings are loop-stitched wool, again obtainable from climbing shops.

Full-length zips in overtrousers allow them to be put on and taken off easily when wearing skis and boots.

Some garments, jackets in particular, combine two or more of the properties discussed above. For example: a Ventile inner (windproof) with a ripstop nylon outer (snow and rain-shower proof); Thinsulate inner (insulating) with a Gore-Tex or Entrant outer (snow- and rain-proof); or a fibre-pile inner (insulating) with a ripstop nylon outer (snow and rain-shower proof).

There is no clear answer as whether to wear your skiing or mountaineering clothing. Some salopettes are very comfortable, but many are too hot for the kind of weather to be expected in late March, April and May. Mountaineering breeches have the advantage of being more flexible, in that one can roll stockings down when it gets hot, and, on the whole, they are more comfortable than skiing salopettes. But many people go ski-mountaineering in skiing salopettes and this is quite acceptable providing they are comfortable.

5 Equipment

SKIS

When choosing skis for ski mountaineering, consider the following points:

Strength: they need to be strong because of the remoteness of the terrain in which they will be used where a breakage would, at the least, prove very awkward.

Lightness: the lighter the better from the point of view of saving energy.

Stiffness v. Softness: something in the middle of the range is the best compromise, because of the wide range of snow on which one will be skiing. For example, early in the morning it may be rock hard, almost ice, and this is where a stiff ski is best. Later in the day it will have softened up, and a soft ski will be best. For fresh powder snow a soft ski is best, whilst for spring snow a soft to medium ski is best. Avoid the temptation to buy a soft ski, because it will not grip on the steep ice slopes first thing in the morning.

Length: it is usual to have a ski about 10 cm (4 in) shorter than normal. Little is lost in terms of lateral stability and edge control, and the shorter ski will be lighter and easier to carry.

Colour: skis made specifically for ski mountaineering are usually brightly coloured. This means they are easier to find in a 'wipe-out' type of fall in deep snow, in avalanche search and in aerial search. They also happen to stand out well in photographs.

Specific Design Features: a hole in the tip is useful for making up an improvised stretcher and for crevasse rescue, as one can slot and tie ropes through the hole and also clip karabiners through it. Another common feature is a groove in the heel, which is useful for those types of skins which have a hook on the end for attaching over the heel of the skis. It is also useful if you lose a skin and have to make up an improvised one using, for example, a prusik loop – the hole in the tip and the groove in the heel are useful points for tying off the cord.

There are some points which, while important to normal downhill skiing, are not important to ski mountaineering. For example, a fast ski is unnecessary, since the emphasis is on controlled skiing without falls. Nor is directional or lateral stability very important, because one will seldom be going fast enough for that to be a problem. Far more useful is a ski which turns easily.

The classic test to see if a ski is soft or stiff is to put the heel of the ski on the floor, hold the tip in one hand and, with the other hand, press down fairly hard at about the mid-point, so inducing a bend. Let the ski bounce back into shape. However, unless one is doing this regularly, it is not possible to assess the difference between most skis and so, while one's performance in the ski shop might look knowledgeable and impressive, it will probably not reveal much about the relative properties of the ski.

It is best not to hot-wax ski mountaineering skis before using them, as the wax may stick to the glue of the skins. When putting the skis away for the summer, however, hot-waxing is a good idea as it provides moisture for the soles of the skis, and it can be scraped off easily.

BINDINGS

A ski mountaineering binding must keep the boot attached to the ski not only in the downhill position, but also the uphill one.

Downhill position: like any downhill binding, it must have sideways and forwards release – but this must be with a ski mountaineering boot, which has a thicker sole of the cleated vibram type. The problem is with the sideways release, because most bindings work on the basis of the sole of the boot sliding off the surface of the ski. This works well enough with the smooth sole of the normal skin boot, but the greater friction of the cleated sole of the ski mountaineering boot makes it very difficult to find the correct setting. One solution is to incorporate a sliding belt on the binding, which lets the boot slip out more easily. Mechanically more sound is to use a system where the boot is attached to a plate, the release being between the plate and the binding, i.e. the Marker and Silvretta.

Uphill position: the binding must allow the heel to lift, so that a comfortable gliding stride can be maintained. This is usually done through a front-hinging system, allowing the heel to be fully lifted to 90 degrees and more. Marker used to make a binding which allowed the heel to lift only to 45 degrees, the restriction being a wishbone plate attached from the binding to the heel of the boot. While there is no doubt that the length of the glide was restricted, there was, however, a great advantage with this binding: as the boot was attached at both the front and the heel, one had great lateral control of the ski – much more so than with the front hinging systems. This was particularly useful when doing kickturns in difficult situations, and when breaking trail in deep snow, especially where the snow had a crust on the surface. Some force is needed to push a ski tip out through crust, and where the boot is attached only at the front, there is a tendency for the ski to be knocked out of line. The ideal would be full heel lift with lateral control.

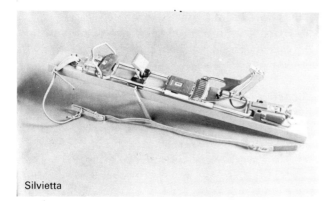
Silvietta

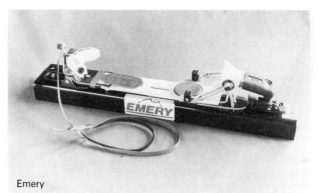
Emery

Marker M-Tour

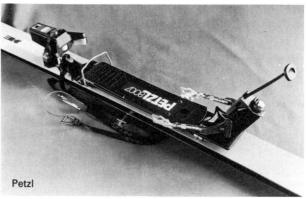
Petzl

Tyrolia

Fig. 36   A selection of bindings.

When in the uphill position, the binding must still have its full release properties. This could be important in the event of being avalanched; and also because from time to time one skis down short sections while still in the uphill mode.

Some bindings are difficult to change from the uphill to the downhill position, and vice versa. There is an advantage in having one that is quick and easy, and which does not require the boot to be taken out of the binding during the changeover.

Fig. 37   A useful aid for going up steeper slopes is the climbing step. Although it adds to the weight of the binding, it is an extra well worth having. Particularly good are those models which can be brought in and out of use by the ski pole, so avoiding having to bend down, which is tiring with a heavy rucksack.

Freezing up of mechanical parts can be a problem, to such an extent that some binding manufacturers supply (at a price) bottles of anti-freeze lubricant. This has to be applied regularly, making an extra item to be carried and an extra chore to cope with. There are many excellent bindings available which do not have this problem.

Snow can build up in recesses and grooves, perhaps to the extent that the binding will not operate in one, or either, of the positions. When you first get a binding, identify any problem areas, and use safety straps with stiff plastic tabs which can be used very effectively to clear out trapped snow.

If ski stoppers are used, they must be fixed between the boot and the plate. If they are fixed between the plate and the ski they will continually open in the uphill position. In a fall into a crevasse, safety straps are preferable as they minimize the risk of dropping a ski. On the other hand, in an avalanche ski stoppers are preferable as the priority is to get rid of the skis in order to avoid injury from them and to avoid their dragging you further under the snow. On all types of snow safety straps are more reliable: in deep snow ski stoppers are an actual menace as a ski can literally be buried beyond trace. Some safety straps have quick release systems and these are the ones to get.

Remember the situation in which you will be using the binding. Sometimes it will be windy and cold – can the binding be operated in these conditions with big gloves on?

Finally, the ideal binding is one which is light, strong and has all the properties mentioned above. To get a really light binding, strength and release properties will, to some extent, have to be sacrificed. Conversely, the binding which has a really good release system and which is strong will probably be heavy. Ultimately, it comes down to individual choice, depending on exactly what you want from the binding.

SKI STICKS

Consider for a moment what ski sticks are used for. In normal downhill skiing they are used for general stability and as a timing device when turning, in particular when doing linked turns. In ski mountaineering they are, in addition, used when going uphill for stability and for pushing; for testing snow conditions before turning; for testing crevasse bridges; and in improvised rescue for making up stretchers and splints.

Length: a ski stick is of 'normal' length if, when held upside with the hand just below the basket and the handle on the ground, the forearm is parallel with the ground. Long sticks are good for pushing uphill and for making emergency stretchers, while short ones are light and easier to carry on the rucksack.

Telescopic Sticks: the answer would seem to lie in telescopic sticks, which are very convenient to use. Really the only problem with them is the locking device, which can jam.

Baskets: big baskets were once fashionable, on the basis that you get a better push when going uphill in deep dry snow. This minor advantage is heavily outweighed by their general inconvenience in downhill skiing and their tendency to pick up a load of heavy wet snow on their upper surface. So it seems best to use a normal-size basket, some people favouring the ones which collapse when loaded on the upper surface.

Wrist Loops: wrist loops have specific advantages and disadvantages. Their good points are: they offer support when going uphill, they are useful in making up improvised stretchers, and they are convenient when tying the sticks and skis to the rucksack. They are positively dangerous if caught in an avalanche or if one slips on icy snow. In the latter situation use the sticks for self-arrest, but if the hands are in the wrist loops this will not be possible.

Handguards: handguards offer support on the uphill sections, and allow the stick to be thrown away if avalanched. But they are difficult to use in making up an improvised stretcher, and they are inconvenient when attaching sticks and skis to a rucksack.

The conclusion seems to be: keep about the same length as for normal skiing; have an average-size basket; strength is vital; wrist loops are good for everything except for downhill skiing – which, ironically, is the purpose for which they are intended.

BOOTS

Boots must give support to both the foot and the ankle for downhill skiing, which dictates a fairly high boot with some system of clips and/or zips for tightening up. At the same time the boot must be comfortable when skinning uphill and when walking along roads, paths and across fields. So a thick sole is needed for cushioning, and for climbing on rock and snow some form of cleated vibram sole is required. Finally, they must take crampons.

Lightness must be balanced against the need for warmth, yet sweating of the feet should be avoided, as wet feet cool quickly and may even freeze, for example in a forced bivouac. Warmth is currently obtained by wearing double boots; a light leather inner and a plastic outer shell. Leather is comfortable and lets the feet breathe, and the plastic outer provides insulation and is light.

The boots must be strong, as one cannot afford to have clips breaking and zips not working.

Few sports shops object to boots being taken home and

worn in the house for a day or two, on the understanding that they can be changed if unmarked. Wear them at home when your feet are cool and also when they are hot. Boots which are too tight will affect circulation which will mean cold feet and possibly frostbite. Whereas ones which are too big let the feet move around, with the inevitable result of blisters.

Normally one pair of thick socks is right, and there is a positive danger from wearing too many pairs – the socks ruck up against each other causing local pressure points, resulting in blisters and maybe cold feet as well.

HARSCHEISEN

These are crampons for the skis and are a great aid on hard snow. Without them it is very difficult to maintain a rising traverse line, to the extent that there may be only two options open: either go straight up, keeping the skis flat and getting maximum skin contact, or take the skis off and go on with crampons. But with harscheisen it is possible to keep a rising traverse on hard snow, so keeping to a good line and maintaining a normal pace and rhythm.

There are three types:
1. Those that fit on the side of the ski.
For each ski there are two knives with serrated edges. Each knife is attached to the ski by means of two lugs which are screwed permanently in place. In principle the ski is the right place for the harscheisen, but the big disadvantage of this system is that, with the full heel-lift binding, the harscheisen are dragged through the snow and this is

tiring. With a limited heel-lift binding, the harscheisen are lifted clear of the snow.

These harscheisen are rather weak and tend to come off. It can be a bad moment to be halfway round an exposed turn on a hard snow slope and to see a harscheisen go clattering off down the slope. To avoid this, join the two harscheisen together with a piece of wire, which lies across the top of the ski, below the boot.

Once the only type of harscheisen available, they are now fairly rare, being superseded by the next two types.
2. Those that fit between the ski and the plate.
For each ski there is a box-shaped harscheisen with serrated edges. Being fitted to the ski it is in principle in the right place. It is stronger than the side-fitting ones, but is heavier and bulkier.

Fig. 38 3. Those that fit between the plate and the boot. Again, a box-shaped harscheisen with serrated edges. Being between the boot and the plate, it cannot come off, and when the foot is lifted to glide the ski forward, the harscheisen comes clear of the snow. This makes it easy to move the ski as there is no drag from the harscheisen. This great advantage vastly outweighs one small disadvantage, namely, when in a precarious position it is not possible to move the ski and keep the harscheisen in contact with the snow at the same time – something one can do with harscheisen fitted to the ski.

With the climbing step in position, the harscheisen will not touch the snow, or at least only to a minimal extent; which means that you cannot get the benefit of both of these aids at the same time. On the other hand, the climbing step can be used to deliberately disengage the harscheisen thus enabling the ski to be pushed forward in a good glide without the restrictive friction of the harscheisen.

This third type is by far the most popular.

SKINS
Made originally from reindeer skins and then from seal, skins are now synthetic. They are attached to the sole of the ski and the grip of the fur allows the skier to climb uphill.

The original ones were attached to the ski by various straps and tensioning devices. It was difficult to get the tension right: too slack, and the skin came off; too tight, and the fittings on the skin pulled away. Another problem was that snow built up between the skin and the sole of the ski and this would eventually pull the skin off. Few days were ever completed without the cry of 'Skin off!'.

Modern skins are stick-on. A glue is applied to the sole of the skin by the manufacturer. This glue will stick the skin to the sole of the ski for the duration of the climb. The skin is then peeled off, leaving no traces of glue on the sole of the ski. The skin can be re-used many times.

The great advantages of these skins over the old strap-on type are: they are lighter, they are quicker to put on and off, and they stay on much better, mainly because it is not possible to get a build-up of snow between the skin and the sole of the ski.

Buying and sizing: there are two types of stick-on skin:

1. Those with a hook for the tip of the ski. These should be cut at the tail-end into a V-shape, allowing a 5 cm (2 in) gap between the apex of the 'V' and the heel of the ski. Cut in such a way, the skin seems to stay on much more securely than if the skin is left with a straight edge.
2. Those with a hook for the tip and a hook for the tail of the skin.
These should be bought according to the length of the skis.

Putting the skins on
The plastic protective strip can be thrown away, as it has no further use, not even for summer storage.

1. Stick-on skins with a hook for the tip of the skin.

– remove any snow from the sole of the ski and dry the sole with a glove, handkerchief, etc.;
– place the heel of the ski on the boot, to prevent snow getting on it;
– rip the skin apart, avoiding contact with the snow;
– place the hook over the tip and press the first 15 cm (6 in) of skin onto the ski sole;

Fig. 40   Grip this 15 cm (6 in) of skin with one hand and stretch the rest of the skin along the ski sole. The reason for gripping the first 15 cm (6 in) in this way is to avoid straining the hook as the rest of the skin is pulled apart.

– place the ski across the knee and rub the palm of a hand vigorously down the skin from tip to tail several times. This moves out any creases and generates heat which makes the glue stick better. The colder it is, the harder the rub.
2. Stick-on skins with a hook for the tip and a hook for the heel of the ski.
Proceed as above to the stage where you have put the hook over the tip of the ski. Then put the other hook over the heel of the ski, tension up on the front, and, finally, rub the skin down with the palm of the hand.

Fig. 39   Skins cut to shape at tail.

Taking the skins off

- rip the skin off, starting at the tail and avoiding any contact with the snow;
- fold the skin back on itself, sticky side to sticky side. If it is very windy, this can be tricky; so try ripping off only half of the skin at a time and folding each half back on itself;
- put the skins away in a plastic or nylon bag, and keep them as dry and warm as possible. In very cold weather it is worth putting them inside your jacket to keep them warm – the glue will stick better;
- at the end of the day put them out in the sun to dry, still folded up sticky side to sticky side. Avoid hanging them up by the hook, because the weight of the skin will slowly separate the two sides and the skin will be left hanging from the hook with the sticky side exposed to dust or dirt.

Care of skins

Stick-on skins must be looked after or they will not work well. Cut them to the V-shape already mentioned, unless you have the type which hooks on to the heel of the ski, and avoid at all times any contact between the sticky side of the skin and the snow.

Regluing: after about a week or ten days of use they will need to be reglued. Open up the skin and lay it down on a flat surface, sticky side up. Spread some glue down the skin, taking a third of the skin at a time, and spread it evenly with a piece of stiff cardboard or plastic. Leave it open on the flat surface for at least six hours, and then put the skin away as normal, with sticky side to sticky side.

The first part of the skin which is likely to start unsticking is the tail. The conditions in which this is likely to happen are when the weather is very cold, when it is very wet, or when snow or dirt have got onto the glue. If this happens, scrape any snow from the sole of the ski and from the sticky surface of the skin. If you have time, dry the ski and the skin in the sun for a few minutes. Then spread glue on the end 7–10 cm (3–4 in) of skin, stick the skin back on the ski, and add extra support by fastening some wide Elastoplast tape round the heel of the ski and skin. Skins with the hook over the heel are not nearly so susceptible to problems of unsticking.

Balling-up: another problem which can occur is that snow freezes onto the bottom of the skin, usually starting under the boot and then spreading, until one is walking on a platform of snow. You will notice it as soon as it starts because of the annoying drag it causes. Try tapping the side of the ski with the ski stick. If this does not move it, scrape the skin clear of snow with the ski stick – if it is really frozen on, use a knife – and then rub some silver wax or one of the proprietary liquids into the skin.

Dirty Skins: if dust and other dirt have got onto the glue, the skin will not stick properly. It is usually the tail of the skin which is particularly susceptible to this. Coat the affected glue with a proprietary glue dissolvant (usually obtainable from the same shop which sold you the skins) and then scrape it off, using a ski scraper. In theory one is supposed to be able to renew a whole skin this way, but I have never found it particularly successful and usually limit the operation to the tail.

End of Season: lay the skins down on a flat surface, still stuck sticky side to sticky side, in a dust-free room.

CRAMPONS

Crampons are invaluable when climbing steep hard snow or ice. The ones with front points are the best for climbing, and the ones without are best for walking.

Correct fit is essential. There should be about 15 mm ($\frac{1}{2}$ in) of front point in front of the boot. And the fit should be good enough so that, when the crampon is on the boot without the straps done up, it is possible to shake the boot gently without the crampon falling off.

There are many different types of strap on the market, as good as any are the neoprene ones with a ring at the front, sometimes called 'French' straps.

Fig. 41   Easiest of all are the quick-fit or snap-on type.

Rubber protectors should be put on the crampons when not in use to protect others from injury.

ICE AXE

A winter climber probably looks after his ice axe more carefully than any other item of equipment, as his life can literally depend on it. Whether everyone in a ski mountaineering party needs to have one depends on the type of tour, but serious tours certainly need axes.

Uses of the Axe: the axe can be used for many things, and some of these are described in Chapter 3, for example, self-arrest, as a climbing aid, for support and balance when traversing, for cutting steps, for cutting through cornices, for cutting stances and belays, as an aid to walking and as a belay.

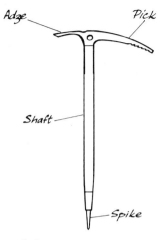

Fig. 42   Parts of the axe.

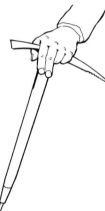

Fig. 43   ***Holding the axe:*** a good way to hold
the axe is in the uphill hand with the thumb under
the adze, the hand over the top of the head of the
axe, and the little finger towards the pick. Held like
this it is ready for self-arrest.

Length: a fairly short one, about 50–55 cm (20–22 in) is
good for self-arrest, for climbing and for general conven-
ience. A longer one is better for support, as an aid to
walking and as a belay point.

Shape: a slightly curved pick is recommended, as it gives
good holding power when climbing hard snow and also
gives good braking power when doing self-arrest. Avoid
straight picks which do not brake well, and heavily
dropped picks which grab badly when braking.

KARABINERS

If you look in a climbing shop, there will be a bewildering number of different types of karabiner. For ski mountaineering it is usual to use screwgate karabiners for the harness
and abseil points, and snaplinks for everything else. It is a
question of striking the right balance, again, between
lightness and strength. 2,500 kg (5,500 lb) is about the
breaking strength required for the screwgates, and

1,800 kg (3,970 lb) for the snaplinks.

The UIAA (*Union Internationale des Associations d'Alpinisme*) test karabiners and it is recommended to buy only
those which have on them the UIAA stamp or motif.

Also, those with a large gate will be easier to use when
working with gloved hands and frozen ropes.

ROPES

Modern climbing ropes have an inner core (kern) and an
outer sheath (mantel) and are called 'kernmantel'. They are
easier to handle than the old hawser-laid ropes, and
modern friction devices used for belaying and abseiling
work well on them.

Size: the full-weight climbing rope has a diameter of
11 mm ($\frac{1}{2}$ in), but one will seldom, if ever, get the kind of
forces associated with a climbing fall, since most of the falls
will be slips on snow, and probably the most severe will be
falls into crevasses, where the impact is reduced by the
friction of the rope biting into the lip of the crevasse. From
the strength point of view, a 9 mm ($\frac{1}{3}$ in) diameter rope is
therefore adequate in ski mountaineering, and it is a much
lighter rope to carry than an 11 mm. But from the
crevasse-rescue point of view an 11 mm rope is better, as
friction knots work much better on the thicker rope. If
using 9 mm in a heavily crevassed area, it is therefore a
good idea to carry some mechanical prusikers.

Stretch or Non-stretch: most climbing ropes stretch
which is an advantage as it reduces the impact on the
climber and on the belay. With an average leader fall the
rope may stretch 10 per cent, and it will stretch up to 60
per cent before breaking. In ski mountaineering one will
seldom, if ever, be holding this kind of fall, as the most
common use of the rope is for abseiling and crevasse
rescue.

In these situations the stretch of a rope is a positive
disadvantage, and there is therefore a lot to be said for
using pre-stretched ropes. These do not have quite the
same strength as normal ropes, so, in order to get the
equivalent strength, it may be necessary to go for a slightly
heavier rope. The other disadvantage of them is that they
are not so easy to handle, being stiffer.

Length: ropes can be bought in any length at all. In ski
mountaineering a useful gap to have between two people
is about 25 m (82 ft), which means that three people can
rope-up on a 50 m (164 ft) rope, and an acceptable maximum would be four people to a 50 m rope. A large party,
say nine people using three ropes, will have sufficient spare
rope if someone falls into a crevasse. But if a party of three
or four are all on one rope, they may find they do not have
enough for the crevasse rescue, and in that case there is a
good argument for the last man to carry spare rope.

50 m (164 ft) of 9 mm ($\frac{1}{3}$ in) rope is quite a heavy load for one person. One way round this is for everyone in the party to carry their own 25 m (82 ft) length of rope. This makes roping-up quick, no one has a very heavy rope to carry and there will be spare rope in case of a crevasse rescue, because three people will use only two ropes. It is a bit awkward when abseiling or lowering people down – you have to join the ropes together and pass the knots through.

The various methods of using the rope are discussed in Chapter 3.

RUCKSACKS

For anything more than a day tour, a fairly large-capacity rucksack is needed, something between 55 and 75 litres (12–16$\frac{1}{2}$ gal).

A lid which has at least two zipped compartments is useful for such odds and ends as maps, compass, sun cream, gloves, hat, skins and harscheisen – the things which are continually needed throughout the day. Ski-carrying straps on the side of the rucksack are essential, and so are straps for securing the ice axe. Straps for securing crampons are optional, as they can be kept inside the rucksack.

A wide waist-belt will not only give good support for load-carrying, but will also hold the rucksack steady when skiing. It is therefore an essential item and it should have an easily adjustable buckle. Some rucksacks have a small section of Karrimat down the front of the rucksack, giving some frame to the ruck-sack and making it more comfortable on the back. This Karrimat can also be removed in the case of a bivouac. You pull the rucksack up over the legs and sit on the Karrimat. If the rucksack has an extendable bivouac sheet, so much the better.

6 Avalanches

The first recorded incident of a fatal avalanche to a ski mountaineer happened on the Susten Pass in 1899, killing Dr Ehlert and R. Mönnichs, members of Paulke's successful traverse of the Bernese Oberland two years earlier.

And without doubt the biggest and most tragic avalanche in history happened on Huascaran (6,768 m/ 22,000 ft), the highest mountain in Peru. On 10 January 1962 a vast piece of the summit ice-cap broke away. The resulting avalanche covered a distance of 15 km (9 miles) with a vertical height drop of 4,250 m (13,900 ft). The avalanche obliterated six villages, partly destroyed three others, and killed more than 6,000 people.

To decide whether or not a slope might avalanche is a most difficult problem, full of scientific complexities. To get to grips at all with the problem it is essential to look first at the basic ingredient – the snow crystal.

HOW DOES SNOW FORM?

Two prerequisites for the formation of snow are near 100 per cent humidity and then cooling. This may occur by air being forced to rise up a mountainside and then cooling by expansion. The next part is not yet fully understood, except that it is known that a very cold (supercooled) droplet of water is formed by initial condensation on to a dust particle.

This supercooled droplet will not necessarily freeze, even if the temperature is below freezing. Another type of impurity is needed, namely a freezing nucleus. These are much rarer than the condensation nuclei. But if the droplet does find such a nucleus, it freezes and becomes ice.

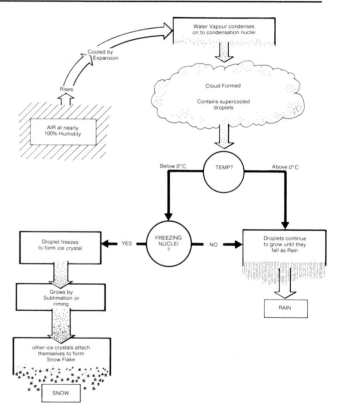

Fig. 44 How snow forms.

This ice crystal grows at the expense of other water droplets by one of two processes: (1) either the water vapour deposits directly onto the crystal by *sublimation*. (Sublimation is the process whereby vapour turns directly to solid without going through the intermediate liquid stage, and vica versa.); or (2) when a water droplet touches the ice crystal, the droplet freezes to it. This is called *riming*. Heavy rime can hide the shape of the crystal completely.

The ice crystal takes a hexagonal shape. There are many kinds of crystal: plates, stellar crystals, dendrites, needles, prisms, and columns, to name but a few of the basic ones. In his research, W. A. Bentley identified 6,000 different ones and reckoned he had only just scratched the surface (ref: *Snow Crystals* by W. A. Bentley and W. J. Humphreys, 1931). The one thing they all have in common is the basic hexagonal shape.

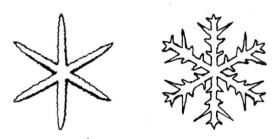

Fig. 45   Stellar and dendritic crystals.

When snow falls

Given fairly windless conditions, a uniform fall of stellar crystals or dendrites falls without drifting. The branches of the crystals interlock to give initial adhesion between themselves, which is why it is relatively safe to ski during the first day of a heavy snowfall.

The snow is then subject to three types of metamorphosis (from the Greek, meaning 'changing shape').

Equitemperature Metamorphosis: this stage is also known as destructive metamorphosis. Vapour is transferred from the points of the crystals to the valleys of the crystals by sublimation. The speed at which this happens depends on the temperature. At just below freezing it happens fast, and it stops altogether at $-40°C$.

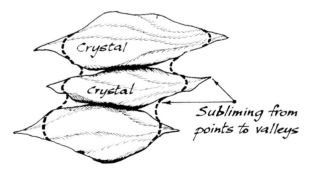

Fig. 46   Equitemperature metamorphosis.

This results in a loss of that initial adhesion, and there is a danger of a powder-snow avalanche at this stage. Depending on the temperature, this is within hours of the start of the fall. If it does not avalanche, the process of shrinkage continues with the crystals changing from branched forms to rounded crystals.

As each flake is getting smaller, the whole layer tends to

settle. An initial fall of 30 cm (1 ft) will settle down to about 20 cm (8 in) in the first two days.

At the same time, sublimation is causing bonding between individual crystals. This bonding is very strong and so the new fall of snow now forms a distinctive layer. Gravity tends to pull the layer down, so *creeping* of the snow layer down the slope occurs. This is frequently very obvious on the roofs of houses.

This equitemperature or destructive metamorphosis takes about two to three days in the Alps, depending on the temperatures. Once it has taken place, the snow pack is relatively safe, and this is the scientific reasoning behind the usual advice: wait for two to three days after a heavy snowfall. Note also that 90 per cent of Alpine avalanches occur on north- and east-facing slopes, presumably because they do not get much sun and therefore they take a long time to stabilize through equitemperature metamorphosis.

The end result of this process is well-consolidated snow, usually referred to as *firn snow*.

Temperature Gradient Metamorphosis: this stage is also known as constructive metamorphosis. The temperature at ground level under the snow is normally about 0°C., whereas at surface level it may be well below freezing. If this is the case, vapour sublimes off crystals low down in the snow pack, then rises and resublimes higher in the pack. The crystal created is stepped in shape, and, if the process continues, cup crystals (also known as depth hoar) are formed.

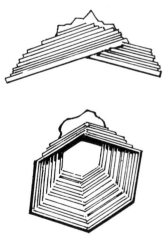

Fig. 47   Temperature gradient metamorphosis: stepped and cup crystals.

It takes one to two weeks for a formation of stepped crystals to develop and probably another two weeks for cup crystals. A stable steep temperature gradient must be present all the time, with a gradient of about 0.2°C. per centimetre. In other words, this will only happen in long, continuous cold spells.

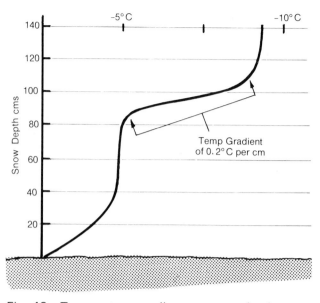

Fig. 48 Temperature gradient metamorphosis: optimum temperature gradient.

The process is helped if air is able to circulate at ground level, for example if the snow is lying on heather or small bushes. These cup crystals may be ·6–1·25 cm ($\frac{1}{4}$–$\frac{1}{2}$ in) across in size, they are very fragile and they do not bond to each other. The greater the temperature gradient, the greater the crystals. A layer of these crystals is a fragile and unstable layer, providing a sliding surface for the layers above. The most insidious thing about them is that, by a drop in temperature, they can form on what was previously a safe slope.

Melt/Freeze Metamorphosis: in a spell of good clear weather, daytime temperatures will melt the top surface of the snow and bring the temperature of the snow pack up to 0°C. – each crystal melts and gets coated with a layer of water and the original shape of the crystal is lost. At night the temperature will drop, resulting in the surface freezing and in a very strong bond being formed between each crystal. On the other hand, during the melt part of the cycle, the layer is very weak. Sublimation is not involved in this process, and the end result is glacier ice.

That is the usual process, but other events may take place, the most common being:

Rimed Crystals: the heavier the riming, the more resistant it is to equitemperature metamorphosis. The end-result of riming is *graupeln*. Because of its resistance to equitemperature metamorphosis it does not change shape easily and is therefore a big hazard. The only thing which will change it is melt/freeze metamorphosis. These rimed crystals or graupeln fall typically with a cold front.

Wind-transported Snow: when wind transports snow it physically damages the crystals so that they may be deposited as a slab of snow on lee slopes. The anomaly is that local physical features can cause eddies, resulting in the slab being deposited on what is basically a windward slope.

AVALANCHE CLASSIFICATION

If there was just one type of avalanche, the job of predicting it would be relatively easy. Unfortunately snow avalanches in many different ways, starting either as a loose-snow avalanche or as a slab avalanche.

1. Loose Snow
   dry – falls of 23 cm (9 in) or more with cold temperatures giving powder-snow avalanches, either airborne or surface.
   wet – occurring at any time of thaw and particularly in springtime.
2. Slab
   dry – windslab avalanches, either soft or hard slab. Maybe sliding on depth hoar, surface hoar or graupeln.
   wet – occurring at any time of thaw and particularly in springtime.

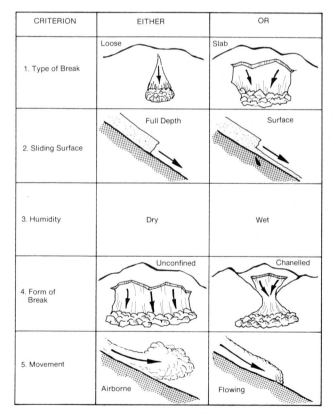

Fig. 49 Avalanche classification.

This classification unfortunately excludes one of the avalanches to which the ski mountaineer is particularly exposed – the ice avalanche.

Before going on to look at ways of predicting avalanches, it is important to look first in depth at the main kinds of avalanche, so that a full understanding of each one is acquired.

Powder-snow Avalanche

A fall of 23 cm (9 in) or more of snow on a steep slope in cold temperatures may result in the snow breaking away from a single point (loose-snow avalanche in the classification). While the snow is actually falling, there is reasonable stability due to the interlocking of the branches of individual crystals. But equitemperature metamorphosis rounds off the branches and creates an unstable period. The avalanche will normally take only the layer which has just fallen, but it may take the underlying layer and layers as well.

Fig. 50   Small powder avalanches are surface ones, flowing along the ground. Most of the small ones come down harmlessly. One situation, however, where they can be very dangerous is where they fall down the path of a recognized climb – for example a gully or couloir giving a good snow and ice climb. Even a very small powder avalanche, hardly warranting the title avalanche, but more of a snow slip, can be enough to knock a climber from a precarious position.

Some of the bigger ones, however, have a disturbing habit of becoming airborne. The reason they do this is not fully understood, but it is known that they generate enormous wind speeds, often in excess of 400 kph (200 mph). The snow may stop, say in a river bed down in the valley, but the windblast may well continue as a 400 kph (200 mph) maelstrom destroying everything in its path. Ski lifts, buildings, whole villages and forests are regularly destroyed by this, the most deadly, avalanche. The following account illustrates how destructive these avalanches can be.

In 1970 I worked for the Saas Fee Pistendienst (ski patrol) and lived with ten others in the Plattjen/Längfluh calbecar station. One night the door of my bedroom burst open and my bedclothes went flying out of the window, all accompanied by the sound of several express trains going through the room. Without too much thought I dived under my bed, and landed next to Bernhard, one of my colleagues, who had made the same decision fractionally ahead of me.

And then there was total silence. It was not until this silence fell that I realized just how noisy it had been. I had no idea what had happened, but it seemed a good idea to shut the door which, with the help of the moonlight, I could see was open. I stood up without a stitch of clothing on and plastered from head to toe with snow. As I reached the door, I met Frau Francesca, a very thin elderly Swiss lady who cooked for us. She was equally plastered with snow, but had more or less managed to retain her nightie. The Swiss are a well-mannered people, so I said, 'Guten Morgen, Frau Francesca'!

Perplexed people started to appear in the gloom, plastered with snow and in various degrees of undress. The lights were not working, so we found some torches. I went to dress, only to discover that all my clothes (including the chair on which they had been hung) had disappeared out of the window. In fact, the whole window frame had gone. The room next door was our dining room. Here the floor was three feet higher than usual. Every inch of every room had been penetrated by snow; curtains and bedclothes had been sucked out of the windows; the boss's office looked as though it had been ransacked.

We realized that we had been hit by an airborne powder avalanche, but it was not until daylight that we saw the full extent of the damage, and also how lucky Saas Fee had been to avoid a major catastrophe. The avalanche had come down at 0400 a.m. from the upper slopes of the Dom. It had flattened the woods leading down to the village, the snow had stopped in a stream and the windblast had continued, running parallel with, and missing by 100 m, the row of hotels leading up to the Längfluh and Plattjen lifts.

The first thing which the windblast had hit was the nursery ski lift: steel girders had been ripped out of their concrete bases and left twisted and buckled. It had then hit the ice rink, smashing the changing hut into small pieces and depositing it all over the mountainside. The only building to be hit which contained people was the cablecar station.

Running from this building was a steel gantry. The cablecars were run out on this in the summer for painting and other maintenance work. This gantry had been destroyed by the windblast. Behind the building, fully grown pine trees had been uprooted or snapped off.

If the avalanche had come down during the day, it would have smothered everyone on the nursery slopes. If it had been 100 m to the north, it would have hit the row of houses and hotels. Saas Fee was indeed lucky that night.

Wet Loose-Snow Avalanche

The powder-snow avalanche just described is a dry loose-snow avalanche. Also very dangerous is the wet loose-snow avalanche. By definition it starts from a single point (being 'loose' as opposed to 'slab'), it may be part- or full-depth, but in any case it is likely to gather a vast quantity of wet snow on its way down. Often slow moving, the enormous weight of this dense wet snow has great destructive power. During its descent, energy is released, and then, when it stops, it re-freezes into a solid mass.

The trigger for this avalanche is a rise in temperature, so it is most common in spring and summer.

Slab Avalanche

Of all the objective dangers facing the ski mountaineer, the slab avalanche is the greatest. This is because it is both common and difficult to predict.

Wind blowing over a mountain accelerates on the windward side of ridges and decelerates on the leeward. If it is snowing at the time, the snow will be blown along the windward slopes. As this happens, it can be readily appreciated that the stellar crystals get knocked about and lose their branches. When the wind decelerates on the lee slope, the snow is deposited. What happens next is not clearly understood, but the best theory would seem to be that each crystal now resembles a sphere (due to the mechanical damage) and that there is a small change in vapour pressure between these spheres, resulting in an immediate bonding between the spheres. The hardness or softness of the slab seems to depend on wind strength, temperature and humidity.

Fig. 51   Debris of wet loose-snow avalanche in Lötschental, Switzerland.

The end result is that a slab of snow, anything from an inch or two in depth to several feet in depth, is deposited on top of the previous snow pack. It may have little adhesion to the layer below.

Slab forms, therefore, on lee slopes when it is windy and snowing. Unfortunately, it also forms in many other situations. For example, rocky outcrops and gullies can cause eddies which in turn deposit slab on what are basically windward slopes. Also it need not necessarily be snowing at the time.

Fig. 52 In fact it might be a beautiful sunny day with just a light breeze blowing, but enough to pick up snow and deposit it somewhere else as slab.

One might not even be aware that this is happening, since 90 per cent of wind-transported snow travels in the area between the surface and one's knees.

It may be that a slope is crossed daily for months in complete safety, but then a cold spell sets up temperature gradient metamorphosis, resulting in a layer of cup crystals somewhere down in the snow pack, and the next person who comes along triggers a slab avalanche.

A dry slab avalanche will be of either hard or soft slab. As we have seen, the hardness or softness of the slab depends on the wind strength, temperature and humidity at the time it was formed. Soft slab can be penetrated by a boot or fist, and very soft slab makes excellent snow for skiing. Hard slab is so hard that one can walk on it. An unsuspecting mountaineer may flounder up some deep snow and then, to his relief, find that he has reached some hard snow which he can walk on. This hard snow could well be hard slab, and the mountaineer becomes the trigger for an avalanche.

The debris of a soft slab avalanche looks very much like that of a loose snow avalanche, whereas that of hard slab normally consists of well-defined angular blocks of snow.

A wet slab avalanche is in many ways similar to the wet loose-snow avalanche: a slow-moving, enormous weight of dense wet snow with great destructive power, and which freezes to a solid mass when it stops. A friend of mine released a very small avalanche of this type: it was a gentle slope, the slab was only a few inches deep and it travelled a very short distance – about 10 m (11 yd). He was on skis and he kept his balance. When he came to a halt, the snow was just up to his knees, no higher. But it had set solid and it took him half an hour to extract himself.

A rise in temperature might trigger a wet slab, or it might only break adhesion to a limited extent, the final trigger being a skier.

Where the slab avalanche differs from the loose-snow one is in the manner of break-off. Whereas the loose snow starts from a single point and fans out as it descends, the slab starts with a well-defined fracture line. This fracture line forms an irregular and often arc-shaped line across the top of the avalanche path with the face of fracture perpendicular to the slope.

Fig. 53 A small windslab avalanche.

For a windslab to start the following must be present:

- a sufficiently steep slope;
- a slope of the right aspect;
- a weak layer somewhere;
- a fracture along the top;
- some form of trigger.

We will look at these in turn:

Steepness of slope: most slab avalanches are on slopes angled between 30–45 degrees. Above that the snow tends to slough off, and below that, although one might easily get the vertical collapse of a slab, the slope is not steep enough for it to avalanche. Although this is the general rule, it must be stressed that there are many cases of 60-degree slopes going, and some of as little as 15 degrees.

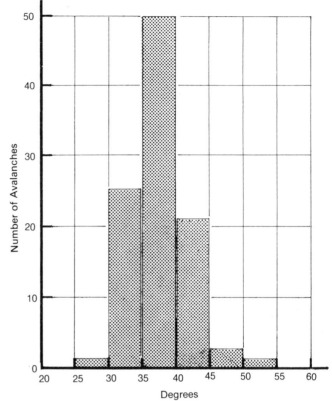

Fig. 55   Slope angles of 100 slabs observed in USA, Switzerland and Japan.

(iv) a cold spell may create a layer of cup crystals through temperature gradient metamorphosis, and these cup crystals are weak and fragile;
(v) a warm spell might cause melt-water to percolate down a slab of rock, breaking the adhesion of the snow-pack with the rock;
(vi) if a farmer was late in cutting his hay, an early snowfall would lay the grass down the slope, and any subsequent melting would lubricate the grass, creating an ideal sliding surface.

Fracture along the top: a skier traversing a slab may get quite a fright suddenly to see a small line appear across the snow, more or less under his skis. This may be enough to set the avalanche off, in which case it is the trigger of the avalanche. But often it does not actually go, in which case this line is what is known as a tension fracture. 'Creeping' of the slab may also cause these fractures, as can protracted cooling of the slab, which results in an increase in tensile stress. These tension fractures are dangerous, as they bring on the main fracture, namely the one at the bed surface. The most likely place for them to occur is in the area of greatest tension on a convex slope.

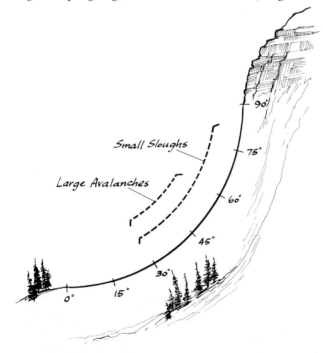

Fig. 54   Slope angle.

Aspect of slope: slab builds up on lee slopes, and so, subject to the vagaries of local eddies, it will normally be found on predominantly lee slopes.

Weak layer: somewhere in the snow pack there must be a weak layer, and this could mean one of many things, for example:

(i) sun crust which forms a good hard layer. Any slab subsequently forming on it will have little adhesion to it;
(ii) a layer of graupeln, acting like a layer of ball bearings for any subsequent build-up of slab;
(iii) both a light snowfall and a layer of surface hoar, when covered by slab, may melt and form a lubricating layer between the slab and the rest of the snowpack;

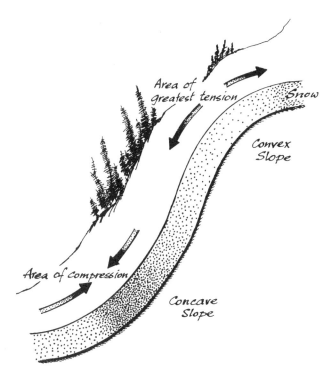

Fig. 56 Area of greatest tension on a convex slope.

Trigger: given the above-mentioned criteria (a slope of sufficient steepness with a build-up of slab, a weak layer and a tension fracture), the avalanche is ready to go. The final trigger may be one of many things:

1. a skier traversing the slope. If he traverses well below the tension crack, the slab may break off above him, putting him in a particularly bad position. If the slab breaks off under his skis, he may be able to put his ice axe in above him and hold himself there while the avalanche goes off below him;

2. other common triggers are cornices collapsing and falling onto slabs; small loose-snow avalanches doing the same, and even rockfalls;

3. ice breaking off from a hanging glacier may trigger a slab avalanche on the main glacier below;

4. temperature changes may be the cause of internal stresses and tensions. For example: warm temperatures resulting in melting may be enough to weaken the bed surface sufficiently to trigger it; conversely, cold temperatures may cause thermal contraction to increase the tension, as at sunset, or may create cup crystals to such an extent that the slab collapses and the avalanche is triggered.

Ice Avalanches

Ice may break off from the seracs in an ice fall or from a hanging glacier in such quantity as to warrant the term avalanche.

Fig. 57 An ice avalanche on Fee glacier, Saas Fee. Ice avalanches from hanging glaciers are quite common in spring and summer: the trigger being either a rise in temperature or the natural downward movement of the hanging glacier. The ice breaks off and falls with quite a noise, often throwing up a plume of snow which looks dramatic but which is not so dangerous as the ice. There is also a possibility that a secondary avalanche may be triggered. For example, a fairly small ice avalance may fall onto, and trigger, a much bigger slab avalanche below.

AVALANCHE PREDICTION

To be able to classify an avalanche correctly after it has happened may well be of academic interest only. The vital skill is being able to identify avalanche danger before the event.

Slopes do not just avalanche. There are good reasons why they do so. Unfortunately, the subject is full of scientific complexities and much of it is still to be discovered, which is the reason why so many experienced mountaineers, many of them experts in avalanche prediction, are regularly caught in avalanches. There is only one sure way of not being avalanched: do not go up snow-covered mountains.

However, much is known and it is possible to apply this knowledge and logic in many situations in order to assess avalanche danger, and thereby minimize the risk.

Weather

Find out from local people what the weather has been doing. Maybe there was a big snowfall shortly before your arrival, and due to continual low temperatures much of the fresh snow has not yet consolidated. Maybe strong winds indicate slab accumulation on certain slopes.

Weather forecasts can normally be obtained from the tourist office or guides bureau. In Chamonix, for example, weather bulletins are posted and regularly updated at the tourist office, and if you want more information, you can go to the weather office (the Météo) in the square and discuss it in English with one of the staff.

Snow Pits

Lightweight shovels should be carried by all ski mountaineering parties for digging out an avalanche victim. They can also be used for digging down into the snowpack in order to examine the layers of the snow. Theoretically, this pit should go down to the earth's surface. Practically, the time and effort involved usually limit one to going down about 1·2–1·5 m (4–5 ft), but this will be enough to examine the top layers.

There is no doubt that where there is physical similarity of adjacent layers, then a high degree of adhesion is likely to exist, and the avalanche risk is reduced. The converse applies. By digging a pit one can identify the layers, and then test each one for the following: hardness, wetness, crystal size and crystal shape.

Hardness – penetration by objects

1. Gloved fist ....soft (weak)
2. Extended gloved fingers (all)
3. Extended gloved finger (single)
4. Ice axe pick or ski-stick point
5. Too hard for all of the above ....hard (strong)

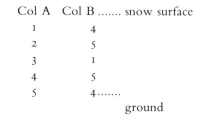

Col A	Col B	.... snow surface
1	4	
2	5	
3	1	
4	5	
5	4	....
		ground

Hardness Scale. Column A shows a steady change with no great differences between adjoining layers, and therefore relatively safe; while Column B shows big differences between some adjoining layers, with consequent avalanche risk.

Wetness – snowball squeezing

1. Snow will not make a ball ....dry
2. Forms dry snowball
3. When squeezed, drops of water appear
4. When squeezed, running water appears
5. Free water observed...wet

Crystal Size – measured in mm on compass base

1. Less than 1 mm...small
2. Less than 2 mm
3. Less than 3 mm
4. Less than 4 mm
5. More than 4 mm ....large

Crystal Shape – subjective estimate

Because there are so many different types of crystal, it is not possible to make any objective test. But it is possible to note any large differences in crystal shape and this indicates avalanche danger.

Specific Avalanches

Sometimes it is useful to consider the main types of avalanche, and to ask oneself questions relative to each one. For example:

Dry Loose Snow

Has there been a recent fall of snow of 23 cm (9 in) or more?

If so, have the temperatures been normal enough to allow equitemperature metamorphosis to take place, to the extent that the snow has consolidated?

If not, and if there is still a lot of fresh unconsolidated snow around, where is it?

Are the slopes we are going on likely to avalanche?

Or is there danger of avalanche from slopes above?

Remember: two to three days of normal temperatures (i.e. warm at midday and cold at night) is usually enough to consolidate fresh falls.

Skiing powder on the Pas de Chèvres, with the Petit Dru behind.

Anselme Baud on the Gervasutti Couloir, Mont Blanc du Tacul.

Anselme Baud on the Gervasutti Couloir, Mont Blanc du Tacul.

Climbing the steep section of the Brenay Glacier,
Haute Route, Day 6.

Climbing to the Plateau
du Couloir, Haute Route,
Day 5.

Climbing ice in the Talèfre Basin.

The start of a tour.

Planning the route.

Looking after the feet.

View from the Hollandia Hut down the Löschental, with Mont Blanc in the distance.

Group crossing the Konkordia Platz with
the Faulberg and Konkordia Hut behind.

Wet Loose Snow

As these are triggered by a rise in temperature, what is the temperature now?

Does the route take us across south- and west-facing slopes?

If so, when will that be and what will the temperature be?

Remember: 10 per cent of Alpine avalanche accidents are caused by people crossing south- and west-facing slopes too late in the day.

Slab – Dry

When was the last snowfall, and was it windy at the time?

Has wind been blowing loose snow around?

On which slopes might slab be?

Are there any rocky outcrops, etc., which might cause eddies?

Have I noticed any raised footsteps or *sastrugi*, indicating blown, loose snow and the direction in which it might have been blown?

What is the colour of the snow – old consolidated snow or firn or *névé* looks darker, whereas slab looks chalky.

What does a snow pit show?

If I kick the snow with the side of my boot, does it break away in slabs, so indicating slab?

Equally, does it fall away in small slabs from below the skis on a traverse?

Has there been a long cold spell, indicating cup crystals?

Remember: it does not have to be snowing for windslab to build up, and 90 per cent of wind-transported snow is blown around below your knees, so you might not be aware of it.

Slab – Wet

A rise in temperature is needed to saturate the snow, so what is the temperature?

Is the underlying surface likely to be smooth rock slabs?

Are there any signs of tension cracks?

Sometimes you can become completely baffled trying to decide whether a slope is dangerous or not, while all the time there might be a simple and logical answer.

This happened to me some years ago, skiing down from the Guslar Spitze to the Hochjoch Hospiz hut in the Ötztal Alps of Austria. It was late in the day, very hot, and the month was April. The slope down to the hut is south-facing for a vertical descent of 500 m (1,600 ft). The snow was deep and saturated. Not a nice place to be. I traversed out across the slope to see what it was like, and several tension cracks appeared as I went across. When I came to the end of the traverse, I sank up to my thighs in saturated snow, an enormous tension crack appeared beside me and the whole snowpack moved about two feet down the slope.

I looked down to the hut below me, and wished I was there. This was obviously a potential wet slab avalanche of large proportions. Using the map I worked out that the slope was at an angle of about 25 degrees. From being there in summer I knew that the surface under the snow was fairly rough, with no rock slabs.

Now, slopes which have been weakened, for example by saturation or by a layer of cup crystals, can settle. Even horizontal snowfields can settle, usually with a distinctive cracking noise which can be startling. So I decided that this slope was just settling, and that the fairly gentle angle of 25 degrees, combined with the rough bed surface, would hold it back.

I skied on down with the rest of the party, and have seldom skied in such dreadful snow. It took ages and all the time I was worried, because I was not entirely convinced of my diagnosis – and I do not think my companions were either! When we got to the hut I asked the guardian if the slope had ever avalanched, and he said that it had not. Although I had worked out correctly that it was safe to descend, I had missed the simple and logical answer, namely, these conditions were entirely normal for the time of year, and they would not have built a hut there if there was any danger at all of it being avalanched.

PRECAUTIONS IN POTENTIAL AVALANCHE DANGER

Bleepers: these are small transceivers and it cannot be recommended too strongly that everyone in the party wears one. There are several different types on the market, certain makes being more common in some countries than in others. The important point is that everyone in the party wears one, certainly on the same frequency and preferably of the same make. Practice sessions in their use must be run before the tour, and they must always be switched on before leaving the hut. For details on their use, see pages 51–53.

Fig. 58   Avalanche transceiver

Fig. 59   A bleeper practice session.

Avalanche Cords: these have effectively been superseded by bleepers.

Skis: release the safety straps.

Ski Sticks: take the hands out of the safety straps, so that the sticks can easily be discarded. Some sticks have quick-release straps; and many experienced tourers never put their hands through the straps, so the problem never arises.

Clothing: put on a jacket, gloves and hat. A balaclava or scarf should be used to protect the mouth.

Rucksack: undo the waistbelt, so that the rucksack can be discarded.

Escape Routes and Safe Points: before starting onto the suspect slope, identify possible escape routes and safe points. The best rule is to move one at a time, from safe point to safe point. If possible, avoid traversing the slope, particularly across the convex part of a slab. If it is necessary to traverse, this is better done across the top of the slope, working on the theory that, if it does go, it is better to have an exciting ride on the top of the avalanche than to be smothered from above.

It is much safer, however, to go straight up or down the slope, keeping to one side. If it looks particularly dangerous, it might be better to take off the skis and walk straight up or down until safety is reached.

Deliberate Release: if the avalanche risk has been clearly identified, the decision may be made to release it deliberately, by one member of the party skiing onto the slope and deliberately trying to get the avalanche to go. I hardly need say that this should only be done in an extreme situation and by someone who knows exactly what he is doing. If successful, it means that the danger has gone and everyone can proceed safely.

When working with the Ski Patrol in Saas Fee, we used to test ski runs, trying to release any avalanches – usually with a rucksack full of explosives, which was a great incentive not to fall!

In 1972 I was descending a very steep pass called the Pas de la Cavale, at the end of the British Alpine Ski Traverse (Austria to France). We had to cross three shallow gullies and they looked to be full of windslab. Alan Blackshaw skied steeply down to the first one and cut a profile with his ice axe, which clearly identified about 15 cm (6 in) of windslab on a hard base.

He skied gently to the middle of the gully, placed his axe in the snow above, and made one big slow, deliberate jump. The slab broke off at his skis and avalanched down the gully, while his axe held him steady. I did the next one, and Alan did the third – in each case there was an impressive little avalanche and the gully was made safe.

As a precaution, wear a rope, and check your insurance policy!

Route Choice: if the danger is from avalanches coming down from above, as opposed to the slope one is on avalanching, then careful consideration will have to be given to the choice of route. The middle of the glacier or valley might be the safest place, or it might be wise to cross to the other side in order to avoid threatening slopes above.

In ascent, it will normally be safer to take the slower but safer route, but, in descent, it may be better to take the faster and more dangerous route, working on the principle that time saved is worth the risk. It is a question of how long one will be exposed to risk, and what the alternatives are. In any case the party should be well spread out, minimizing the chance of more than one member of the party being hit.

ACTION IF CAUGHT IN AN AVALANCHE

As one of the precautions just mentioned, let us hope you will have identified a possible means of escape. A steep traverse is the best line. If there is no chance of skiing out, discard your skis by a sharp sideways twist of the feet, throw away your sticks and try to throw off your rucksack.

The main objective is to try to reach the side of the avalanche, and this can best be done by rolling sideways. The sharp sideways twist which has discarded the skis will initiate this rolling. Use your arms and legs to gain speed. Even if you go under the snow, keep rolling, because it will stop you sinking and keep you near the surface. You are literally fighting for your life here, so give it everything.

As the avalanche slows up, you must really fight to stay on or near the surface. Some people recommend going onto your back and using a very energetic backstroke. Others recommend that you keep rolling. At the same time, you have got to try first to keep your mouth and face clear of snow and, second, to try and push an arm out of the snow. Both pieces of advice are based on statistics: most avalanche fatalities die of asphyxia – having snow forced into the mouth and nose, thus cutting off the oxygen supply – and yet the average burial depth is only 1.3 m ($4\frac{1}{2}$ ft), which is not very deep at all.

It would require great presence of mind to think of all this at the right time, and few people will wish to gain the necessary practice which would result in automatic reaction.

Now that you are buried and the avalanche has stopped, the greatest self-control is required. If the snow is light,

you may be able to dig yourself out, provided you can work out which is the right way to go. Some victims have been so disorientated that they have dug in the wrong direction. Try spitting – gravity will take it down. If you are in a wet-snow avalanche, the snow will probably have set like concrete, and you will not be able to move even a little finger. If you hear someone above you, try shouting, but do not be dismayed if they do not hear you as snow transmits sound in quite easily, but out very poorly.

ACTION BY SURVIVORS OF AVALANCHE

Whether or not victims are found alive will depend very much on three things:

– whether part of them is showing;
– whether they are wearing bleepers;
– whether one of the survivors takes control and organizes the search efficiently.

Fig. 60 Digging out an avalanche victim.

Bleeper Search

If the party is wearing bleepers, the procedure is:

1. Someone takes control, and the others keep quiet.
2. If anyone saw a body disappear into the avalanche, he keeps his eyes on that point and another person is directed

to it. The watcher should not go, as he will probably become disorientated.

3. Check how many are missing.

4. Switch bleepers to 'receive' or 'off'. It is vitally important that everyone does this.

5. The most experienced person starts searching from the 'last seen' point. If no bleep is audible, he goes down the avalanche track, until he picks one up – at which point he goes into the 'close search' routine.

6. The organizer spreads other members of the party across the avalanche – the distance between each depending on the range of the transceiver. They then move down the avalanche, searching. Depending on the number of people available and on the width of the avalanche, he may have to use one of the systems shown in the illustrations:

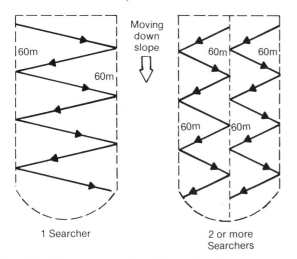

Fig. 61   Bleeper search, wide avalanche.

7. Once a signal has been picked up, one searcher only goes into the 'close search' routine. Others can get shovels, airways, spare clothes, etc.

8. 'Close Search' routine: See Fig. 62.

(i) Aerial alignment: soon after picking up the signal, stop and align your set so that you get the best signal from the victim. This does not mean that your set is now pointing towards the victim – just that the aerials of both sets are aligned in the same plane. Maintain this alignment throughout the search.

(ii) As you come down the slope, the signal gets stronger, so reduce the volume control (the human ear can detect differences between the quiet sounds much better than it can between loud ones).

(iii) X the signal decreases, and at A it is lost. Run back in your to X – the loudest point. Go at a right-angle, towards B. The signal will decrease, so run back in your steps to X.

(iv) As you go to C the signal increases, so decrease the volume. If you lose the signal, run back in your steps to

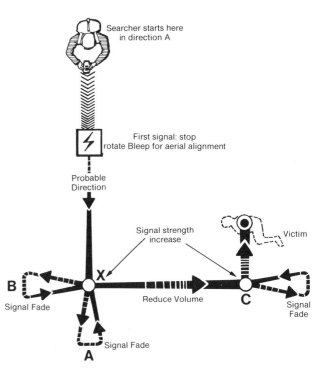

Fig. 62

the last loudest point, and go off from it at a right-angle.

(v) The final search can be done by sweeping the snow with the instrument and listening for a double signal.

Search by Parties without Bleepers

1. The first two steps of 'bleeper search' are done, i.e. someone takes charge, and people are directed to the last points where bodies were seen.

2. The points where the bodies were last seen are marked, and in each case a quick search is made of the debris below, looking for any signs of them.

3. A systematic search is then started. This is usually from the bottom of the avalanche, working back up, for two reasons:

(i) you get a better sight under blocks of snow;

(ii) it is less tiring for the rescuers.

It must be carried out with total discipline, one person standing at the end of the line and organizing.

Searchers are spread out with their hands on their hips, elbows touching. Using an inverted ski stick, each searcher probes to the full length of the stick, directly between his feet. Everyone advances 60 cm (2 ft), and in this way a grid of approximately 75 × 60 cm (2 ft 6 in × 2 ft) is built up.

Sending for Help

A party equipped with bleepers should be able to resolve the search without the need for external help, although they might need help with the evacuation of casualties. A

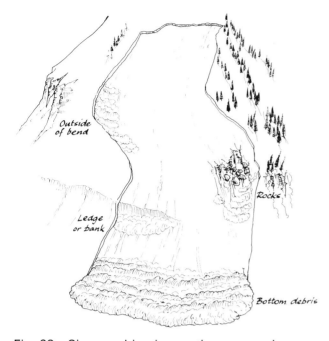

Fig. 63 Since probing is very time consuming, preference should be given to some of the more likely spots, e.g. by rocks, trees or any other projection; on ledges and banks; on the outside of bends, and at the bottom

As a general rule concentrate on the areas of greatest debris.

party which does not have bleepers may well find that their searches are in vain, and the question then arises: should they send for help, and, if so, when?

There is no clear answer and each situation must be taken on its own.

Conclusion

Ski mountaineering parties must be self-sufficient as regards avalanche rescue. Outside help will usually arrive too late to be of any use except in the recovery of bodies. The statistics show this conclusively.

This means that parties must carry bleepers and be totally practised in their use. Lightweight shovels should also be carried, preferably at the ratio of one shovel per person.

Bleepers are at a relatively early stage of development. The problem of different makes being on different frequencies must be resolved in the interests of safety of life. However, at the moment they offer by far the best method of avalanche search, and they can be bought or hired in many countries.

Bearing in mind everything that has gone before, it will be realized that the flow diagram overleaf is a huge over-simplification of the subject. However, for some it may help to see the problem more clearly, and for that reason it is included.

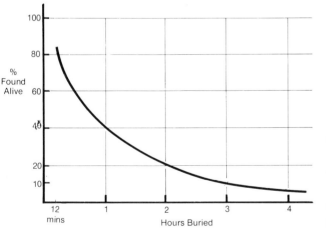

Fig. 64 Bear in mind that, according to statistics, if someone is buried and is found within twelve minutes, he has an 80 per cent chance of survival; within one hour, 40 per cent; within two hours, 20 per cent; within three hours, 10 per cent; and within four hours, 5 per cent.

If help is a long way off, it might be better to stay and concentrate your energies in your own search.

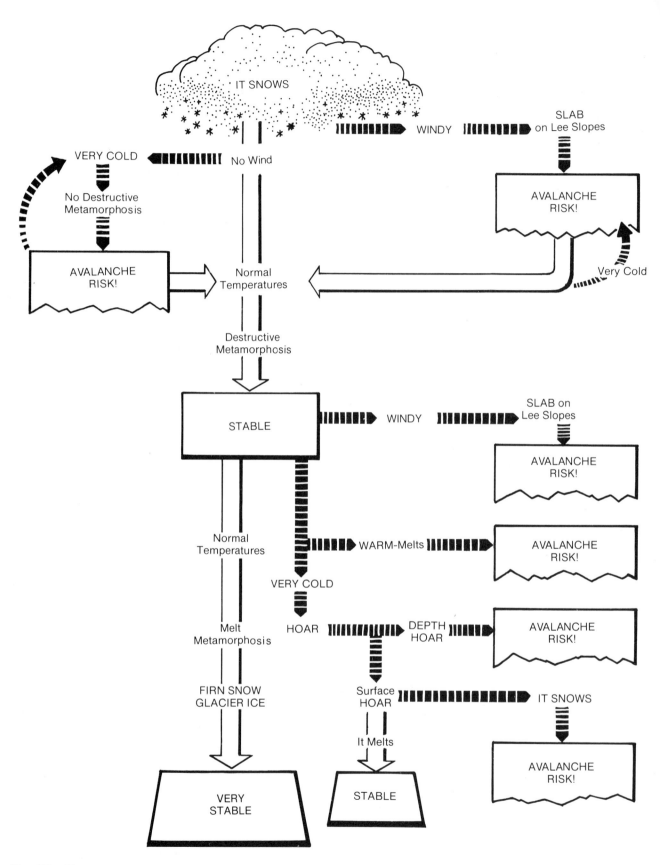

Fig. 65   'It snows..

7 Glaciers and Crevasse Rescue

Ski mountaineers spend a lot of time on glaciers. Any tour in the central Alps will involve glacier skiing, sometimes to an advanced level. For example, a traverse of the Classic Haute Route takes you on twenty-three different glaciers, and a tour in the Bernese Oberland will inevitably take you on the Gross Aletsch Glacier, which is 25 km (15½ miles) long and, at the Konkordia Platz, a staggering 800 m (2,600 ft) deep.

In the ski mountaineering season the glaciers are particularly prone to avalanches, and the crevasses are usually in a dangerous state. The ability both to route-find and to move safely on glaciers are two essential skills of the ski mountaineer, skills which must be developed to a higher level than for summer mountaineering.

The earliest record of a crevasse accident happening to Alpine ski mountaineers was a dramatic one. This account is taken from *A History of Skiing* by Arnold Lunn (Oxford University Press, 1927).

On February 24th 1902 a party of five amateurs – Paul Koenig, Egon von Steiger (afterwards killed on the Balmhorn), Dethleffsen, Walter Flender and Fehr – accompanied by four Zermatt guides, left the Bétémps Hut [Monte Rosa Hut] intending to climb the Zumsteinspitze of Monte Rosa. The party was ascending the Grenz Glacier, unroped and on ski, when suddenly a muffled crack was heard and Koenig, Flender and the guide Perren were seen to sink simultaneously into a concealed crevasse. Perren was rescued almost uninjured. Flender and Koenig were killed. Flender was a very fine skier and an enterprising mountaineer.

A remarkable feature of the accident was the thickness of the snow bridge which gave way. It was almost 65 feet in length and over 14 feet thick. In winter, snow bridges are composed of light powdery snow or snow covered by a wind crust. Whereas a bridge two or three inches thick composed of summer or spring crust will often hold, bridges composed of the powder snow of winter, of course, form a terribly insecure snow bridge compared to the snow which, in spring or summer has been melted and refrozen again and again.

This clearly illustrates how dangerous bridges can be early in the winter before they have had time to consolidate. Another point which emerges is that the three who fell in must have been very close together, so the moral of the story is, keep well spread out on crevassed glaciers. The fact that they were unroped was normal practice at that time, as it was thought to be too complicated to move roped on skis, even uphill. You see a lot of people doing the same today, but there can be no doubt at all as to the correct advice: if in any doubt at all, rope-up on crevassed glaciers when going uphill.

GLACIER FORMATION

Glaciers are formed by the accumulation of snow in the high altitude snowfields. These are permanent snowfields and are normally referred to as 'névé'. As the snow becomes more dense, through compaction caused by the weight of additional snowfalls, it turns gradually to ice. While the body of the glacier is being fed from the permanent snowfields, down at the foot, or 'snout', of the glacier the opposite process is taking place. The higher temperatures down there are melting the ice.

Glaciers are referred to as 'advancing' or 'retreating'. They are advancing when the snout is moving down the valley, because the temperatures there are relatively lower than previously; they are retreating when the snout is moving back up the valley, because the temperatures are now relatively higher than before.

Often glaciers are likened to rivers of ice, although it is more correct to think of their flow being like that of a metal close to melting point. In any case, the most important points to understand are that the centre flows quicker than the sides, and that the surface flows quicker than the bottom.

CREVASSES

The previously mentioned factors, namely that the centre flows quicker than the sides and that the surface flows quicker than the bottom, are the reason that crevasses occur. A crevasse is a cleavage in the ice, occurring at right-angles to tension. There are two main types.

The first is the *transverse* crevasse which runs across the main flow of the glacier. The main place for these is where the glacier gets steeper. This is, of course, a likely stopping place for ski mountaineers, either on the way up, to have a rest after doing the steep bit, or on the way down, to look at the ice-fall and identify a route through. The second main type of crevasse is the *longitudinal* crevasse which runs down the flow. The main places for these are where the glacier widens, and where any part of it is raised in a longitudinal ridge.

The other types of crevasse are the *bergschrund*, or *rimaye*: this is the big crevasse between the glacier and the permanent snowfield. Sometimes confused with the bergschrund, but strictly speaking a different crevasse, is the *randkluft*, which is the big crevasse between the glacier and the rock walls.

Two useful tips for route-finding are that crevasses are less frequent, first, below an *ice-fall*, where the ice is consolidating again and, second, where the glacier is

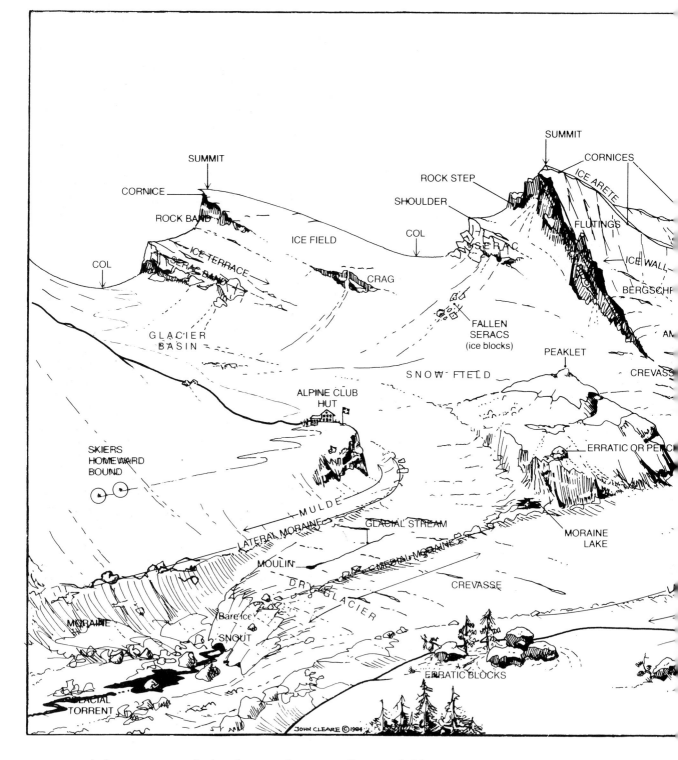

SUMMIT

CORNICE

ROCK BAND

ICE FIELD

ICE TERRACE

SERAC BAND

COL

GLACIER
BASIN

SUMMIT

ROCK STEP

SHOULDER

COL

CORNICES

ICE ARETE

FLUTINGS

SERAC

ICE WALL

BERGSCHR

CRAG

FALLEN
SERACS
(ice blocks)

PEAKLET

CREVASS

SNOW FIELD

ALPINE CLUB
HUT

SKIIERS
HOMEWARD
BOUND

ERRATIC OR PERC

MULDE

LATERAL MORAINE

GLACIAL STREAM

MORAINE
LAKE

MOULIN

MEDIAL MORAINE

CREVASSE

DRY GLACIER

MORAINE

Bare Ice

SNOUT

ERRATIC BLOCKS

GLACIAL
TORRENT

JOHN CLEARE © 1984

concave and the crevasses tend, therefore, to close up. Since an ice-fall is caused by a change in the gradient of the glacier, the point where the glacier is concave will often be the point below the ice fall. Sometimes big unstable towers of ice are thrown up. These are called *seracs*, and occur where tranverse and longitudinal crevasses occur in the same place, for example in a complicated ice-fall.

Crevasse bridges

In the heavy winter snow falls, the crevasses get filled in or bridged over. Then, in the early spring, with the hot weather, some of this snow falls into the crevasses. But not all of it falls in, and so we are left with crevasses which are open in places and which are bridged over in other places. At this stage, i.e. early spring, these bridges are very

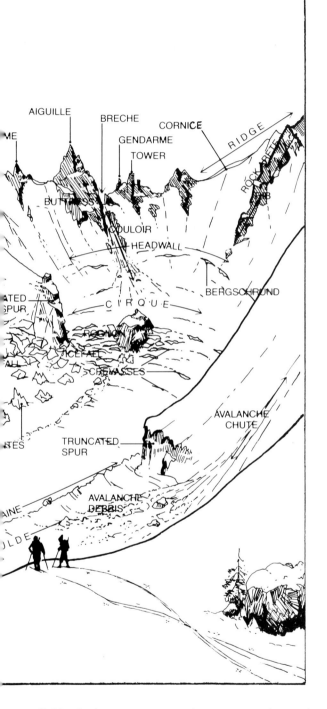

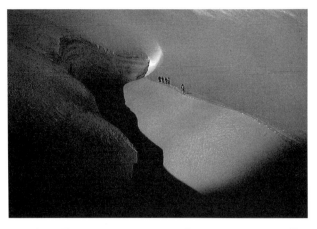

Fig. 67   Party moving beside large crevasse on Fee Glacier, Saas Fee.

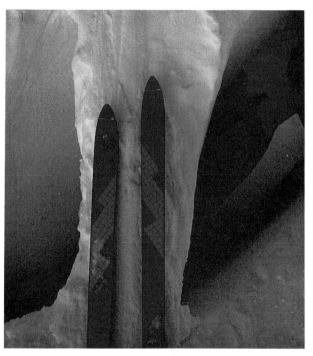

Fig. 68   Crossing crevasse bridge.

Undercutting

Another nasty factor at this time of year is that the crevasses often have undercut lips on them. These undercut lips can be very unstable and can collapse when weighted. The area of snow which falls in is surprisingly large, as is the case with collapsing cornices. I once saw this happen with a crevasse which was not particularly badly undercut.

It was in April 1970 on the Weissnollen, Bernese Oberland, with a winter touring leaders' course of the Swiss Alpine Club. What started as a practice crevasse-rescue session suddenly turned into the real thing when the side of one of the crevasses collapsed over a length of 15 m (50 ft) and 3·5 m (12 ft) back from the edge. Three people were standing in that area: an unroped student

unreliable. As the year progresses into summer, the continuous processes of thaw and freeze result in bridges which are well defined and strong. In summer, if you cross these bridges early in the morning or at any other time when the temperature is low, you will usually cross safely. But in the early spring – the time of the ski mountaineer – this is not necessarily the case.

who landed safely on a ledge; a roped student who was safely held, and one of the guides (Bruno Koller) who was unroped and who fell about 13·5 m (45 ft) into the crevasse where he jammed head-down with all the snow on top of him.

There was immediate confusion and a lot of shouting. I was roped to a man knicknamed 'the Weasel', whose profession was erecting high voltage electricity pylons and so was used to drama. Without a word he grabbed a shovel, glanced at me and jumped into the crevasse. I lowered him down to where he found the tip of one of Bruno's skis, and after a few moments of frantic shovelling he managed to free him. Bruno had been unable to breathe all this time, partly due to the constriction of his chest and partly due to the mass of snow around him. He was tied to a rope and pulled out by direct haul. With the exception of bruised ribs, he was none the worse for wear.

What struck me forcibly at the time was that the immediate reaction, even among experienced people, was panic, confusion and shouting. While this was going on, the Weasel quickly and calmly worked out what had to be done and did it, thereby saving Bruno's life. The story also shows how dreadfully unstable the sides of crevasses can be. It is not unusual for the uphill lip to be undercut and obviously dangerous, but this was the downhill one and it was not particularly undercut. Since then I have been very wary of the sides of crevasses!

A sad postscript is that Bruno Koller, who was a young guide from Meiringen, was killed soon after while on a false-alarm rescue on the North Face of the Eiger – the helicopter he was in crashed while the people for whom the alarm had been raised were safe and sound down in the valley.

Dry glaciers

When the snow melts, with the advance of summer, the top surface of the glacier reveals bare ice, and this is termed a 'dry glacier'. It is often running with water, so 'dry glacier' is something of a misnomer. In such conditions crevasses are easy to see; and such bridges that remain are well defined and stable.

Moraines

Moraines consist of long piles of stones, boulders and debris pushed out from the glacier as part of its continuous erosion process on the underlying ground. There are three types of moraine. The *terminal* moraine is the debris left at the foot or the snout of the glacier. A retreating glacier will have terminal moraine that can be hundreds of yards below the snout. *Lateral* moraines are the long ridges of rubble that run along the edges of glaciers. *Medial* moraines are the rubble ridges in the middle of glaciers, usually formed from the lateral moraines of two glaciers which have joined.

When loosened by the sun, stones and boulders crash down through moraines and present an obvious danger. Sometimes the crest of a lateral moraine gives good walking with a path in summer, and a safe (avalanche-free) route in snow conditions.

Muldes

Muldes are deep hollows lying between the lateral moraine on the one side and the valley on the other. Any avalanche coming down from the hillside above will end up in this hollow, being held back by the lateral moraine. So, at any time of avalanche risk, muldes should definitely be avoided.

Hanging glaciers

These glaciers are found on very steep faces, usually falling over a rock face. They literally hang there. They look very dramatic, these hanging glaciers, and they also present considerable danger. Lumps of ice may break off and fall down onto the main glacier below. These are a type of ice avalanche. They make a lot of noise and tend to throw up a plume of snow, particularly if they come down soon after a snow fall. The danger is from the falling ice, rather than from the snow. The normal trigger for such an avalanche is a rise in temperature, but this is not always the case and they have a disturbing habit of coming down at unexpected times. Although the danger is normally limited to the falling ice, on occasion a secondary snow avalanche may be triggered off and can develop into such proportions as to present by far the more serious danger.

AVALANCHES ON GLACIERS

The subject of avalanches is covered in depth in Chapter 6, so here it is enough just to summarize a few points on glacier avalanches.

They are basically of two kinds: those falling onto the glacier, and those occurring on the glacier.

1. Avalanches falling onto the glacier: these may be wet or dry avalanches from above, coming down onto the sides of the glacier. As discussed above, they may be ice avalanches coming down from a hanging glacier or from seracs of a neighbouring glacier. These ice avalanches may take snow with them and may occur at any time. Finally, they may be rock falls. The risk of rock fall increases proportionately with the rise in temperature. A slope exposed to rock fall generally shows traces of it, in the form of stones left on the surface of the snow and in grooves cut in springtime, and yet the signs of stones and grooves may be obliterated by a recent snowfall. Moraines, and particularly big lateral moraines, are a potential source of this danger.

2. *Avalanches occurring on the glacier:* these may be ice avalanches, for example bits of serac and other bits of falling ice. They are dangerous at any time, but particularly so as the temperature rises during the day. As seen above, they may trigger a secondary snow avalanche. And any of the snow avalanches may occur on a glacier, in particular the windslab and the fresh snow avalanche. The main places to watch are the steepest slopes below the final rock wall of the glacier, and the lee side of passes.

ROPES, HARNESSES AND KNOTS

Ropes
The type of rope to use for ski mountaineering is dealt with on page 39, and the way in which to use it is dealt with on page 19.

Harnesses
Whether custom-built or improvised, a harness must be of the full-body type. A fall into a crevasse may well result in the person hanging free 6 m (20 ft) or so below the lip of the crevasse. This is a very serious situation in which a harness of the sit-only or chest-only type is totally inadequate. A full harness supporting both the seat and the chest is essential. A lot of research, some of it of the involuntary and unexpected kind, proves how important this is.

1. Custom-built harnesses:

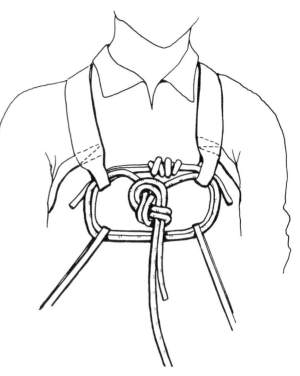

Fig. 70 Sometimes a different chest and sit harness can be combined to make a very satisfactory full harness.

A piece of 9 mm ($\frac{1}{3}$ in) or 10 mm rope about 1·5 m (5 ft) in length can be used to tie the chest to the sit part using a double fisherman's knot, and then the climbing rope can be tied in separately, as illustrated.

Fig. 69 The Petzl ski mountaining harness. The harnesses made for rock-climbing will do the job very well, but are really too heavy for our purposes. Some manufacturers make special lightweight glacier harnesses for the ski mountaineer, and these are excellent. Their advantages over improvised harnesses are that their strength is proved and known, particularly if they carry the motif of the UIAA (*Union International des Associations d'Alpinisme*), indicating that they have reached the rigorous standards of that association. A second advantage of these harnesses is that they are normally much more comfortable than an improvised one.

2. Improvised harnesses: The advantages of improvised harnesses over custom-built ones are that they are lighter, cheaper and much more versatile in that the slings can be used for other purposes, like making belays and emergency stretchers. The main disadvantage of them is that they are not so comfortable to wear.

There are several methods, of which the following are recommended, having been tested and found to work.

(a) Sit sling (Dülfer) with Parisian baudrier
For this you need two full weight tape slings, one 3 m (10 ft) long for the sit sling and the other 3·3 m (11 ft) long for the chest. Those lengths are for a man of average build.

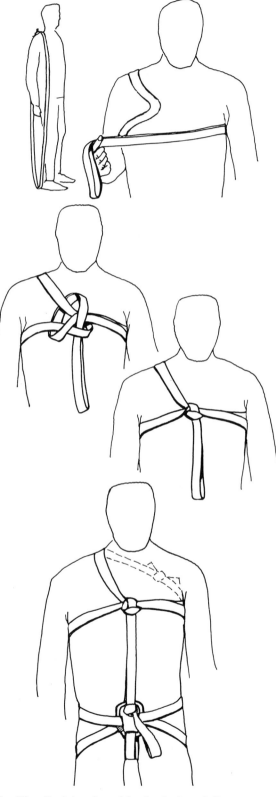

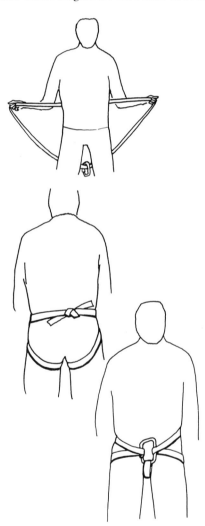

Fig. 71 Place the knot of the sit sling in the small of the back with a screwgate karabiner hanging down from it. Bring bights (loops) of rope from both sides and through the legs; and join all three with the karabiner.

If the sling is on the long side, a snugger fit can easily be obtained by tying an overhand knot on the side.

Fig. 72 The Parisian baudrier is tied as follows: place the sling over one arm, take it round the back and under the other arm, and tie off with a sheet bend.

There are two recommended methods of tying in to the rope.

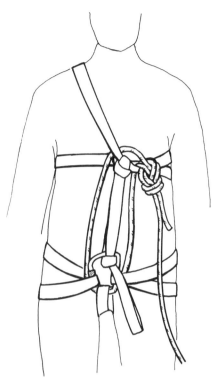

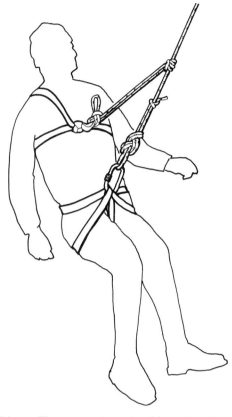

Fig. 73 The first is to tie an overhand knot in the chest sling and to clip this, either above or below the knot, into the karabiner. Then pass the rope through the three parts of the sit sling and the top two parts of the chest sling, and tie off with a bowline or figure of eight.

Fig. 74   The second method is to tie the climbing rope into the sit sling karabiner with a figure of eight knot, and to then attach the chest sling to the climbing rope by means of a short prusik loop tied off to the chest sling with a sheet bend. This method has the advantage of being able to adjust the hanging position easily by the prusik loop, but it runs the risk of a three-way pull on the karabiner.

The first method is probably the safest.

(b) Sit sling and Reepschnur

The sit sling is tied in the Dülfer method shown above. The Reepschnur is a 2·5 m (8 ft) length of 10 mm or 11 mm (½ in) rope.

(c) Single long sling

This method is probably the most one can achieve in terms of combining lightness with full body support.

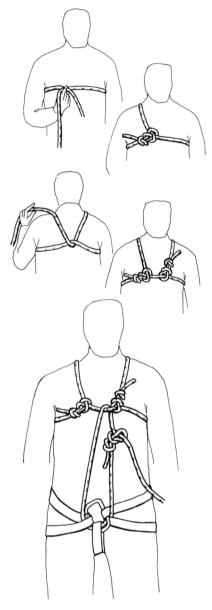

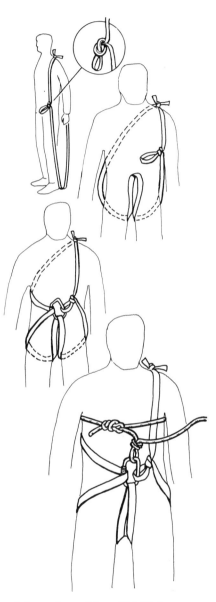

Fig. 75   One end is passed round the chest fairly loosely and tied off with a bowline. The long end is taken over the shoulder, threaded through the rope at the back, and passed back over the other shoulder. It is then tied off with a bowline and thumb knot. This gives a more secure chest harness than the Parisian baudrier, and is a method favoured in Austria and Germany.

The climbing rope is tied in by passing it through the three bights of the sit sling and through the chest harness, as shown. It is tied off with a bowline and thumb knot.

Fig. 76   A long tape (4 m (14 ft) for a man of average build) is tied with an overhand knot to make a sling. A second overhand knot forms a small loop. The sling is fitted as shown, the loops being joined by a screwgate karabiner. The sling can be adjusted for size by means of the first overhand knot at the shoulder.

The climbing rope is passed round the chest and is tied off with a bowline and thumb knot. A small loop is formed in the rope by an overhand knot, and this loop is clipped down into the karabiner.

3. Hybrid harnesses: we have looked at custom-built harnesses and at improvised ones. A hybrid one can be achieved by either taking a custom-built chest harness and combining it with an improvised sit one, or vice versa. The advantages are that you have the comfort and security of the custom-built part, and yet you have the versatility of a sling (for use in belaying, emergency stretchers etc.).

With all the improvised sit harnesses, there is an annoying tendency for the sling to drop down round the back of the thighs. This can to some extent be resolved by hitching the sling into the shoulder strap of your rucksack, using a very lightweight non-screwgate karabiner. Either one side or both can be hitched up. It is not necessary to use a separate karabiner for this, because, as will be seen under 'Crevasse Rescue' on page 64, a karibiner will be carried in this position anyway.

4. Harnesses made from the rope only: if someone comes without a harness or leaves it behind in the hut, an effective improvisation can be made from the rope only. A bowline on the bight, or a figure of eight on the bight, can make two loops either for thigh loops or for the chest, and a triple bowline can be made to give two small loops for the thighs and a third larger one for the upper body. When putting these on, you have to take off your skis, whereas the following system, devised by Martin Burrows-Smith, can be put on without taking them off.

(a) Sit harness

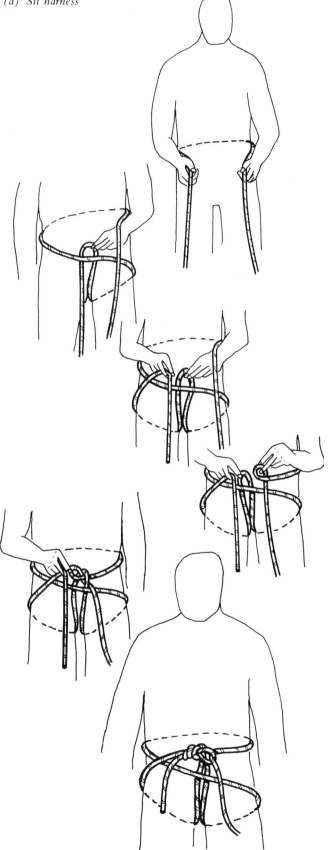

Fig. 77 (i) Pass the rope behind your back, with about 2 m (7 ft) spare held in your right hand.
(ii) Pass the spare across the front of the left thigh, round the back of that leg and up the front to pass as a loop under the cross-over part. Hold this with the left hand.
(iii) Pass the spare end round behind the right leg.
(iv) Tie off with a bowline by (a) making a loop with the rope in your left hand, standing part underneath; (b) passing this loop through the centre loop and (c) completing the bowline with the spare end, as shown.

(b) Full harness

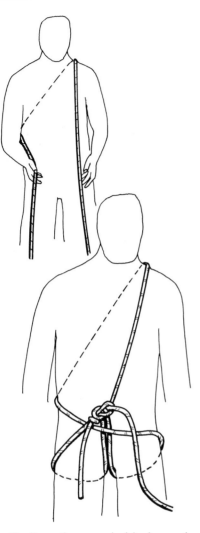

Fig. 78   (i) Pass the rope behind your back, with about 2 m (7 ft) spare held in your right hand.
(ii) Hook the rope over your left shoulder, as shown.
(iii) Complete stages (ii) to (iv) in Fig. 77.

Again, the thigh loops can be hitched up into karabiners attached to the shoulder straps of the rucksack in order to stop them rubbing against the backs of the thighs.

CREVASSE RESCUE

If someone does break through a crevasse, the fall may, with luck, be a short one with the person only going just below the lip of the crevasse. A good strong haul on the rope may be all that is necessary. Far more serious though is the longer fall, which may well result in the person hanging free a long way under the lip of the crevasse. This is a very serious situation, often grossly underrated by ski mountaineers. The person who has fallen in will be in a very uncomfortable position, will be very frightened, and

may well be incapable of assisting with the rescue except in a token way. For this reason, the person who has fallen will from now on be referred to as 'the casualty'.

The success or otherwise of the rescue will depend on whether or not a system of rescue has been agreed on beforehand, on whether it has been practised, and on how well the people on the surface operate in this emergency situation.

Holding the fall

If, as is usual, it is the leader who falls in, the second man should fall over (if he has not done so already), get his skis between himself and the crevasse, and use his sticks for self-arrest. While not wishing to underestimate the problem, it is easier to stop these falls than is perhaps imagined, helped by the friction of the rope cutting into the side of the crevasse. The third man will have no problem in holding the second.

One thing which will make it much more difficult is any slack rope in the system (e.g. people too close together, or holding coils in their hands). In this event, the fall will not only be longer than necessary, but the shock load on everyone will be that much greater. So the moral is clear: keep a fairly tight rope with a minimum of slack in crevassed areas.

Immediate priorities (preliminery steps)

Before a method of rescue can even be thought about, the casualty and those on the surface (the rescuers) must take the following action, and this must almost be automatic, as few people will be capable of clear thought in the first moments of this frightening situation.

Casualty   He must make himself as comfortable as possible by (i) taking off his skis and clipping them and the sticks into the karabiner which is on the shoulder strap of his rucksack; (ii) tying a long prusik loop to the rope, with a prusik knot or klemheist. The free end is passed down inside the chest harness, behind one leg and onto one foot. (A 3.3 m (11 ft) length of 6 mm ($\frac{1}{4}$ in) rope, when tied with a double fisherman's knot, gives about the right length of loop.) The loop can be secured to the foot by a lark's foot knot.

Rescuers Whatever they do, they must not themselves fall in, particularly if unroped. The strain must be taken off the person holding the casualty, and the rope belayed. The way in which this is done varies in each situation, depending on the weight of the fall, the strength of the person holding the fall, the type of snow and the number of people available. The illustrations overleaf show some examples.

Fig. 79   Practising crevasse rescue.

Fig. 80   (i) Third man (3) supporting the middle
man (2), while a fourth man (4) moves in to set up
the belay.

(ii) The fourth man has set up his skis as a belay,
and has taken the strain off the middle man (2) by
means of a prusik loop attached between the
middle man (2) and the casualty.

(iii) The rope is tied to the ski belay.

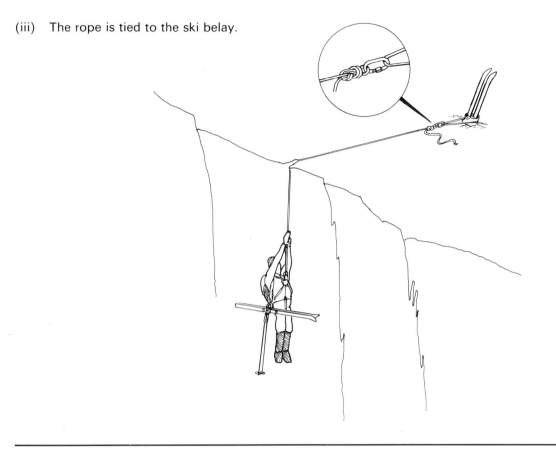

(iv) Rescuers safely position a man (2) to make verbal and, if possible, visual contact with the casualty.

(v) Rescuer (2) pads the lip of the crevasse with a
rucksack or skis, and secures this padding to an ice
axe. This padding is to stop the ropes cutting into
the lip of the crevasse.

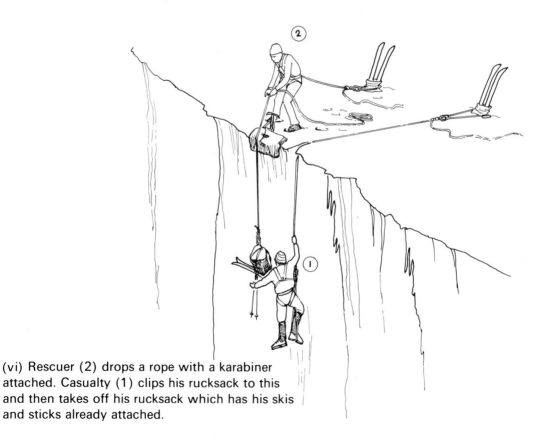

(vi) Rescuer (2) drops a rope with a karabiner
attached. Casualty (1) clips his rucksack to this
and then takes off his rucksack which has his skis
and sticks already attached.

Note: when the casualty falls in, his rope will cut into the lip of the crevasse. Due to his weight it will normally be impossible to get padding under it. Any further ropes which are used should be put over padding.

Methods of rescue
Five methods are discussed: (1) the straight haul; (2) a method for a long fall where the casualty can assist; (3) and (4) are two methods for the long fall where the casualty cannot assist, and (5) a method of self-rescue.

1. Straight haul: as already discussed, where the fall is short it may well be possible to haul the casualty straight out with a good strong pull. It may be necessary to take off his skis, sticks and rucksack, or it may be possible without doing this.

2. 'Raise the foot. Stand up': a method for the long fall where the casualty can assist.

The preliminary steps (i)–(vi) listed above will have to be taken.

Fig. 81   (i) Then a rescuer (2) drops a rope down with a loop in the end. The casualty passes this rope through his chest harness, and puts his foot in it. He can now take his foot out of his own foot loop.

(ii) On the command 'Raise your foot!', the casualty raises the foot with the loop as high as he can. (The person on the lip of the crevasse is in charge: he issues the commands and will have to encourage the casualty to really raise that foot.) At the same time the rescuers take in this rope as tight as they can and hold it or make it fast. (In the diagram No. (2) is holding it.)

(iii) On the command 'Stand up!', the casualty does that, helping himself by pulling with his hands on the foot-loop rope. If you have a mechanical prusiker (e.g. Jummar, Petzl or Clogger) it is a great help to the casualty to have this on the foot-loop rope, so that he can pull himself up on it. At the same time that this command is given, the rescuers (3 and 4) take in the casualty's original rope as tight as they can and hold it or make it fast.

The cycle of 'Raise the foot!' and 'Stand up!' is continued until the rescue is completed. At first, progress will be painfully slow as the stretch in the rope is taken up. Do not despair. As the casualty comes closer to the lip of the crevasse, there is less rope out and consequently less stretch, and progress will be faster.

3. For the long fall where the casualty cannot assist, and where there is plenty of spare rope and enough rescuers.

Fig. 82   (i) A rescuer (2) abseils down a spare rope, takes the skis and sticks off the casualty (1) and clips them onto the casualty's rucksack. He then ties an overhand knot in the rope below him and clips the casualty's rucksack into it.

(ii) A colleague (3) passes down a loop of rope with a karabiner and pulley attached. (2) clips this karabiner into the casualty's harness and then jumars back up the loaded rope.

(iii) The looped rope is belayed at one end, and the rescuers (3 and 4) haul in on the other end, with the benefit of this improvised pulley. At the same time the casualty's original rope is taken in by (5) and (6).

If the casualty is capable of assisting, even to a minimal extent, he can haul with his hands on the belayed part of the looped rope (marked X on the illustration). So this method can be used in place of the 'Raise your foot. Stand up' system: a loop of rope with a karabiner and pulley attached being lowered down from above, and the casualty attaching it himself. This system will resolve most situations and is therefore recommended.

4. *The 2:1 Bachman system:* for the long fall where the casualty cannot assist, and where you have no spare rope and a limited number of rescuers.

This is a most serious situation. Success will only be achieved through technical skill, strength and practice.

Fig. 83 (i) A rescuer reverse-prusiks down the casualty's rope. He takes off the casualty's skis and sticks, and attaches them to the casualty's rucksack, which he then puts on. He prusiks back up to the surface.

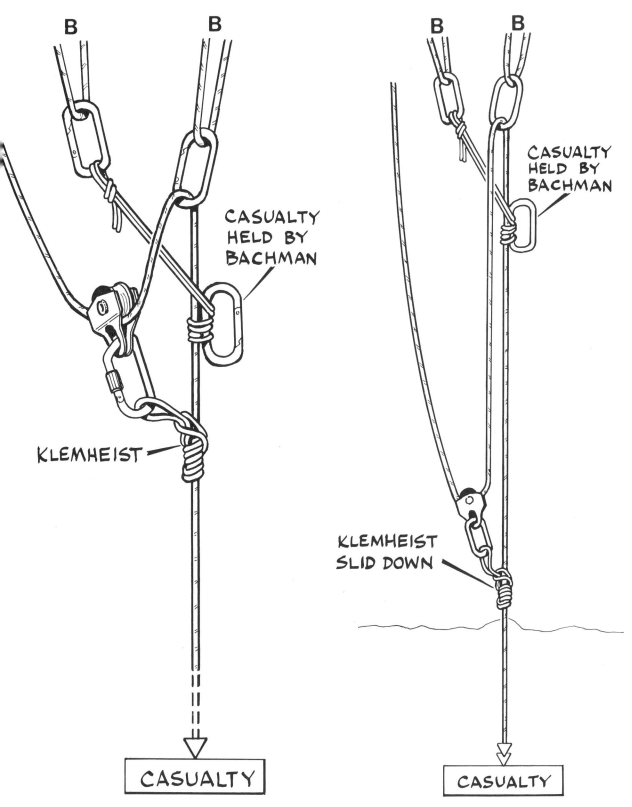

(ii) A 2:1 Bachman hoist is set up, using a reversed Bachman as a clutch. The casualty is held by the Bachman. ('B' is the belay point and will probably be skis.)

(iii) The casualty is held by the Bachman. A klemheist knot has been slid down the taut rope, in preparation for hauling, with a karabiner and pulley attached.

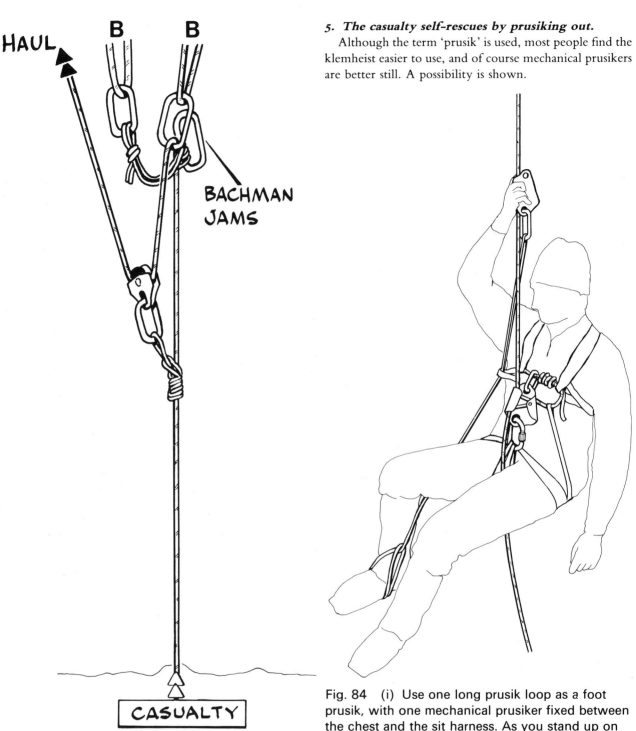

HAUL

B   B

BACHMAN
JAMS

CASUALTY

5. The casualty self-rescues by prusiking out.

Although the term 'prusik' is used, most people find the klemheist easier to use, and of course mechanical prusikers are better still. A possibility is shown.

Fig. 84 (i) Use one long prusik loop as a foot prusik, with one mechanical prusiker fixed between the chest and the sit harness. As you stand up on the foot loop, the rope slides through the fixed prusiker automatically. This is the easiest, and is recommended.

Prusiking up a weighted rope is much easier than up an unweighted one. One way of weighting the rope is to clip your rucksack plus skis and sticks onto the loop of rope forming below you. You will then no longer have the rucksack on your back, and will only be lifting half of its weight.

(iv) As the klemheist is hauled in, the Bachman jams against the fixed karabiner and acts as a clutch. This only works if the two belay points are close together.

When the haul rop is released in preparation for sliding the klemheist down again, the casualty will be held by the Bachman.

Useful Points

A fall into a crevasse may present a very serious situation indeed. The following points are offered as useful hints, applicable in most situations.

1. In heavily crevassed zones, have a long prusik loop already tied to the rope with the end of the loop tucked away in a convenient pocket. In the event of a fall, this can easily be brought into use as a foot loop.

2. Always have a lightweight snaplink karabiner hanging from one of the shoulder straps of your rucksack, ready for your skis and sticks.

3. Skis placed at a 45-degree angle make good belays, see page 23.

4. Bring belays as close to the lip of the crevasse as is safe, in order to reduce the amount of stretching of the rope.

5. To reduce stretch altogether, use pre-stretched ropes.

6. Be ready to lower clothing to the casualty. If he was stripped down for a hot day, he will soon become cold in his newly discovered deep freeze. As he cools down, so will he become progressively less able to help himself, and will soon reach the stage where he cannot perform the 'Raise the foot' and 'Stand up' method.

7. If during the rescue the casualty comes up under the lip of the crevasse, clip a karabiner attached to a rope into the hauling ropes and take this out to the other side of the crevasse. If the other side is higher, it will be possible to pull him out from under the lip, and if it is lower, it will probably be easier to take him out on the lower side.

8. Cut away the lip of the crevasse and pad it with rucksacks, skis or ice axes. Without this the hauling ropes will cut into the lip to such an extent as to make rescue almost impossible. The earlier in the season, the greater this problem will be.

Fig. 85   Lightweight pulley.

9. Lightweight pulleys make a world of difference, and two of these are useful items to carry.

10. And, finally, two most important points: there will be a tendency to panic, so somebody must assume control and the rest must keep quiet. Also, to be successful, these techniques all need practice.

SAFE HABITS TO ADOPT ON GLACIERS

The difference between the appearance of a glacier in March compared with how it looks in September is amazing. In March many of the crevasses will still be covered and invisible, whereas in September they will mostly be visible. It is quite useful, therefore, to look at photographs, even postcards, of the glacier taken in summer to get a good idea of where the crevasses are.

When choosing your line up or down a glacier, as far as possible avoid the sides of the glacier, in case of avalanches coming down from above.

When crossing crevasse lines, cross at right-angles, to avoid the whole party falling into the same crevasse.

Previous tracks may give an indication of a good line to follow, and in particular whether or not a bridge is safe to cross. Even though the tracks may have been blown in by wind, an occasional trace can often be picked out and be enough to be useful.

Rope-up in good time, and when moving through crevassed sections keep the rope tight. Wear a full body harness and practise crevasse rescue systems. A lot of risk can be avoided by skiing gently and carefully. It is essential to avoid falling over when skiing through a crevassed area, and those who cannot ski steadily down, in control, have no place in this environment. You must avoid shock-loading a hidden crevasse bridge, so avoid heavy jump turns.

If one person falls over, do not all rush to help, thus collecting in one place.

When you stop, do not all congregate around the same map, or get in close for a group photograph. It is amazing how often you see groups skiing well spaced out and then all getting together in a huddle when they stop.

Get in the habit of always having one ski on. For example, when taking off or putting on the skins, do one ski at a time, because you might be standing on a crevassed bridge.

Glaciers are much safer in the cold, so make sure of an early start in the morning. If you get delayed during the day and are confronted by a crevassed section in the afternoon, it might well be a wise thing to sit down and wait for the cooler temperatures of evening.

Finally, when the Föhn wind is blowing, it is usually best not to go at all.

Fig. 86 Skiing carefully on a crevassed area.

8 Navigation

I do not intend to look in detail at all aspects of navigation, as this is covered in other books referred to in the Bibliography, but rather to look at particular points relevant to navigating on skis.

In fine weather, with good visibility, all that is required is map reading, i.e. looking at the map and being able to picture the actual ground in one's mind. This pictorial image is created by the contour lines: the shape of the lines showing the shape of the mountainside, and the amount of spacing between each one showing the steepness. The process, of course, works equally well in reverse: particular mountain features are shown on the map and can be identified from it. By carefully reading the map you can pick out the route you want to take, and at any given moment can pinpoint your position. You may want to do the odd check with a compass or altimeter, but these are not essential.

In bad weather, however, it is a different matter altogether, with the compass and altimeter immediately becoming essential pieces of equipment. Navigation then becomes a difficult task, requiring great concentration and the application of a variety of skills. A complicating factor is that in bad weather on a crevassed glacier, one becomes preoccupied with avoiding crevasses – and rightly so. But this preoccupation can adversely affect the concentration which should be going into navigation.

MAPS

1. Shading: if you open a Swiss map (*Carte Nationale de la Suisse*) or an Austrian map (*Alpenvereinskarte*), you will probably be impressed by the three dimensional effect. The map is almost a photograph. The ridges and glaciers are very obvious. Much of this is due to shading. For example, the Swiss maps have the slopes facing north and west shaded lighter than those facing south and east.

2. Contour Lines: the interval between contour lines

varies. For example, in Britain and France it is 10 m (33 ft), while in Switzerland, Austria and Germany it is 20 m (66 ft). Forgetting this could mean finding the slope twice as steep as you expected.

3. Grid Lines: French maps have very few; Austrian maps none at all. This means that taking compass bearings is slightly more haphazard, and you cannot give grid references. Swiss maps have grid lines, but they use a different numbering system.

4. Magnetic Variation: this is much less than in Britain and for practical purposes is ignored.

5. Ski Routes: for the main areas you have a choice between a map with ski routes and one without. The ski routes are marked in red, and are recommended routes for winter and spring tourers. On the back of some maps (e.g. the Swiss 1:50,000 and the Austrian 1:25,000) are short route descriptions in guide-book form, giving approximate times.

6. Glaciers: the snout (tip of the glacier) may be a long way further back than indicated on the map – easily as much as 200 vertical metres (660 ft) or 1 km (½ mile) horizontally. An example of this is the Sulztal Glacier in the Stubai Alps of Austria.

7. Crevasses: crevasses which are marked on the map may not be there; and, more important, a glacier which is marked as being crevasse-free may become heavily crevassed. A year or two later they may have gone again.

8. Guide Books: a guide book may advise a summer route which goes up the glacier for a while and then takes to the rocks at the side. If the glacier has retreated, the rocks, which have subsequently been exposed, may be extremely smooth and unclimbable; and your 'easy glacier route' starts to take on different dimensions.

9. Huts: a hut which was once built by the side of the glacier may now be left perched well above it. The Konkordia Hut in the Bernese Oberland has a long section of ladders leading up to it.

ALTIMETER

A good skier can drop height so quickly, that, if he is not careful, he can get on the wrong side of a glacier and find his way barred by crevasses. What took five minutes to descend could take an hour to re-ascend. An altimeter shows your altitude all the time and is therefore invaluable in preventing that kind of mistake. In Alpine ski mountaineering I use mine far more than I use my compass.

Fig. 87   The Swiss-made Thommen altimeter is the best, although expensive. It is small, easy to read, very reliable and strongly made. Each calibration is 10 m (33 ft) and it is possible to be accurate to this degree. Full instructions come with the instrument, but the following points are worth noting.

Points to note in using an altimeter

1. As it works off barometric pressure, the altimeter is affected by changes in the weather. It must be continually adjusted by resetting it at known points. If you know, for example, that a trough of low pressure is coming through, be careful about this point.

2. For the same reason, if you go for more than 10 km (6 miles) horizontal distance or more than 500 m (1,640 ft) vertical height without resetting it, it may be inaccurate.

3. The speed at which you travel is important. If you are moving slowly, it could take two hours to cover 5 km (3 miles); and two hours is more than enough for pressure to change and for the instrument to become inaccurate.

4. The altimeter is affected by temperature changes. There is a complicated procedure for correcting this, but, provided you reset regularly on known points, this can be (and in practice invariably is) ignored.

5. Method of use. If, for example, you are going from A (height 500 m/1,640 ft) to B (height 800 m/2,620 ft), make sure that at A the altimeter is reading 500 metres. If it is not, adjust the setting so that it does. When you get to B, it will read 800 metres. When at B, a small adjustment due to barometric pressure or temperature may be necessary. Be sure to make this adjustment before continuing, because otherwise the inaccuracies may become cumulative.

6. In a hut or tent, you can use the altimeter overnight as a barometer. Either set it to zero or to the height of the hut. If, in the morning, the instrument shows the height of the hut to be higher than it actually is, the pressure has dropped. If it shows the height to be lower, the pressure has risen.

7. Some cheaper altimeters have calibrations every 50 m

(164 ft) or more. These are useless for mountain navigation, as the interval between calibrations is too great. A 10-
metre interval, as in the Thommen, is recommended.

NAVIGATING CREVASSED GROUND
We will now look at the different skills which might be
used to navigate over crevassed ground in bad weather in
three different situations – moving on flattish ground,
ascending steep ground and descending steep ground.

Flattish Ground
Going up a flattish glacier, the party will presumably be
roped-up and on skins. If descending, presumably at least
the front three will be roped.

Map Reading: the first thing is to look carefully at the
map and to plan the route. Areas to avoid are crevassed
areas and areas threatened by avalanches from above.
Points to go for as identifiable points are rock points or the
bottoms of rock ridges, both often spot-heighted; and
changes in gradient, shown by changes in the contour
lines. Such changes need not be great – indeed, just two
contour lines closer together or wider apart could indicate
a change in terrain which would be clearly identifiable.

Estimate of Time: when calculating an over-all estimate
of time, allow a fairly slow time for a party roped on skis,
say 2½ kph (1½ mph); and where there is some steady
ascent, try calculating on 3 kph (1·9 mph) plus half an hour
for every 300 vertical metres (980 ft). Such estimates
depend very much on the snow conditions underfoot, the
prevailing weather conditions, the fitness of the party, and
the weight of the rucksacks.

Compass Bearing: the compass bearing is an essential aid
in bad weather navigation in getting you from one known
point to the next. But it can be a difficult thing to do
accurately, and there is plenty of opportunity for error.
   It makes sense, therefore, to get someone to check that
you have worked out the bearing accurately, by asking
them to do it too. And be careful of any metal objects
which might affect the magnetic needle. The handles and
shafts of ski sticks do not normally do so, but the points
certainly do if held close to the compass. With practice one
can keep going while holding both sticks to the side in one
hand and sighting with the compass in the other.

Navigation Checker: when setting off, ask someone
with a compass to go third in the line to check your
bearing, leaving a gap of about 15–20 m (16–22 yd)
between yourself and the second person, and the same gap
between the second and the third. This third person can
sight his compass through the second to you, and can easily
see if you are wandering off the line. Rather than correct

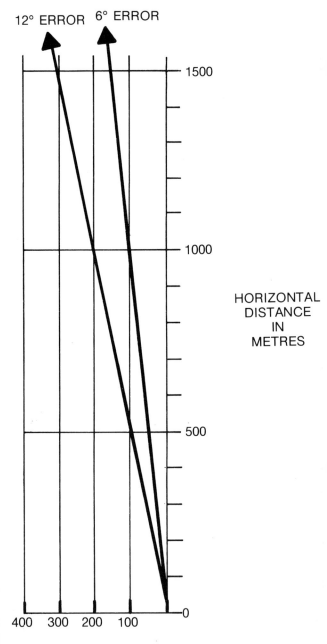

HORIZONTAL
DISTANCE
IN
METRES

ERROR IN METRES

Fig. 88   You might make an error of a few degrees
when taking the bearing off the map. Imagine the
situation – a blizzard, big gloves, cold fingers and a
slippery map surface. Another error may occur
when adjusting for magnetic variation. And then
there is the problem of following the bearing with
nothing ahead on which to sight the compass.

you every time you stray (which results in much shouting
and fairly slow progress), he can wait for you to look back
and then indicate with his arms.

Glacier skiing.

Heading from the Vignettes Hut to Col du
l'Evêque, Haute Route Day 7.

Ice avalanche falling from N. Face of l'Aiguille Verte over descent track from Grands Montets, Haute Route Day 1.

Walking out down the Murchison Glacier, New Zealand, in poor weather

Skiers being dropped on Tasman Glacier, New Zealand

Descent of the Stockji Glacier past the Matterhorn,
Haute Route, Day 7.

On the Lower Murchison looking up to Mt Cook.

Glacier skiing.

Glacier skiing.

Fig. 89 Signals for navigation checker:
Both arms raised: on course.
One arm extended: go that way.

Ascent of Steep Ground

Map Reading: just as for flattish ground, this is the most essential skill. Gradients are seldom uniform for any length of time: there will be small changes, clearly shown by the contour lines, in both steepness and shape. It is vital to identify these and to use them. These changes in slope are identifiable points, and you should move from one to the next.

Estimate of Time: an approximate estimate can be worked out, maybe at around 300 vertical metres (980 ft) per hour. It all depends on the conditions, the steepness of gradient and the fitness of the party. I think the fastest I have climbed on skins is:

> (i) Heidelberg Hut to Zahnjoch: 681 vertical metres (2,230 ft) and 4 km (2½ miles) horizontal in two hours;
> (ii) Jamtal Hut to Ob. Ochsenscharte: 812 vertical metres (2,660 ft) and 5 km (3 miles) horizontal in two hours.

Compass Bearing: it will be difficult to follow this accurately, as the climbing track will be zig-zagging around on either side of it. So the bearing is used as general guidance only.

Altimeter: again, an invaluable aid. This, combined with map reading and a general bearing, will enable you to move from known point to known point.

Descent of Steep Ground

The method of navigating is very similar to that used for ascending, with map reading and the use of the altimeter being the most useful skills. The descent will usually be as close to the fall-line as possible, in order to lose height quickly. Skiers develop a great feel for the fall-line: for example, when stationary, we automatically put our skis at a right-angle to it, so that we stand still; and as we get better, so we try to ski as near the fall-line as possible. This feeling or awareness can be put to the skier's advantage, because the fall-line is the aspect of the slope, i.e. the direction in which the slope is facing. Mountaineers on foot seldom have the same awareness of the fall-line.

Any change in direction of the fall-line can be registered as a change in direction or bearing, and any change in gradient can also be noted.

9 Ski Extrème by Anselme Baud

(Translated by Marie Francoise Gaff)
Introduction by Peter Cliff

INTRODUCTION

A good intermediate skier on Red runs will normally be skiing on slopes of around 20 degrees, and an expert on Black runs will seldom ski anything steeper than 33 degrees. I am referring here to the over-all gradient of the run and not to individual sections which may be steeper.

Sylvain Saudan was one of the pioneers of extreme skiing in the late 1960s, making the first ski descents of the Spencer Couloir, the Whymper Couloir on the Aiguille Verte, the Gervasutti Couloir on Mont Blanc du Tacul, and the South Face of the Jorasses. Anselme Baud and Patrick Valleṇant broke new barriers in the late 1970s, often together. The slopes they skied down are twice as steep as Red runs and sometimes twice as steep as Black.

Here are some of Anselme Baud's descents (first descents marked*).

	degrees
Aiguille du Tour, Couloir de la Table	40–50
Tête Blanche, North Face	50
Tour Ronde, Gervasutti Couloir	45+
Petite Aiguille Verte, Chevalier Couloir	50–55
Aig.d'Argentière, Upper Chardonnet Glacier	45–50
Aiguille de Blaitier, Spencer Couloir	51–55
Col de la Dent Jaune, North Couloir	43–53
Dents du Midi, Couloir Nord des Doigts	40–55
Les Courtes, North–North–East Face	47–49
Grandes Jorasses, South Face	40–45
Col Armand-Charlet*	45–55
Mt Blanc du Tacul, Gervasutti Couloir	50–55
Aiguille Verte, Whymper Couloir	47–55
Aiguille Verte, Couturier Couloir	45–55
Aiguille Blanche de Peuterey, North Face*	40–55
Aiguille du Midi, North-West Face	40–50
Aiguille du Midi, North Face*	up to 60
Mont Blanc, Arête de Peuterey*	up to 60

This is an aspect of ski mountaineering practised by only a handful of people, and most of us will never have the skill or the courage to join them. To find out why people ski in places where a single fall would be fatal, here is Anselme Baud's account of two of his major descents.

NORTH FACE OF AIGUILLE VERTE, COUTURIER COULOIR

'The ideal extreme ski descent could be that of the Couturier Couloir on the Aiguille Verte. This nearly perfect slope, falling down the North Face of that magnificent 4,000 m summit is a powerful magnet to mountaineers – sometimes only to help them dream.

The first time that I was with my skis at the foot of that couloir I had a strong desire to ski down it; and that must have been in the spring of 1967. A little later I climbed it; and at every belay from where I was securing, my friend the dream slowly wore off, leaving me with a great respect for that cold icy slope. I thought that I would never dare to descend it alone without a rope.

Three years later, during the guides' course at the École Nationale de Ski et Alpinisme at Chamonix, I met Patrick Vallençant again, and our common passion led us to the descent of the Aiguille Verte by the Whymper Couloir. Our experience of this descent, which gave us no problems, made us more confident. We thought seriously of the Couturier Couloir, realizing that we would have to prepare for it conscientiously, without rushing.

And, so, at the end of July 1973, we climbed a little more than halfway up the couloir, to the point where the slope reaches 55 degrees. We were too late to continue to the top, so we skied back down, making about three hundred turns, to the foot of the couloir. This experience left us feeling entirely confident for the next attempt, which we planned for the following Sunday.

In the meantime Serge Cachat-Rosset landed by helicopter on the summit and made the first ski descent of the couloir. At first we felt bitter to see this first descent escape us, particularly because of the method used. The following Sunday we climbed the couloir and arrived at the top at 0800 a.m. The snow surface was still very hard, and we found real pleasure in controlling our turns down the 55-degree chute. We nevertheless took time for photography; and one hour later, having crossed the bergschrund, we were looking back at our tracks and already planning our next project.'

At that time, the descent of the North Face of the Aiguille Verte was a big landmark in the development of extreme skiing.

First descent: Serge Cachat-Rosset on 2 August 1973, after landing on the summit by helicopter. Descent in four and a half hours.

Fig. 90   Anselme Baud at the start of Arête de Peuterey, Mont Blanc (first descent).

Second descent by Anselme Baud and Patrick Vallençant on 5 August 1973, in one hour, after first climbing the couloir.

Starting point: Argentière at the Grands Montets cable-car station.

Height differences: ascent: 1,350 m (4,400 ft) from the Argentière Hut to the summit or 1,000 m (3,300 ft) from the lower bergschrund to the summit. Descent: 1,000 m (3,300 ft) of couloir, or nearly 2,900 m (9,500 ft) if there is enough snow to ski down to Argentière.

Difficulty: ED for the whole route. The ascent: a long snow route where the difficulty is constant and with no rest point until the arête of the 'dôme'. Descent: the height of the couloir is the main difficulty, as well as possible changes in snow between the north-facing dôme and the north-east-facing couloir.

Slope angle: 51 degrees between 3,100 m (10,200 ft) and 3,800 m (12,470 ft); 55 degrees between 3,300 m (10,800 ft) and 3,600 m (11,800 ft); 45 degrees for the remainder, and less for the dôme.

Time: ascent: from the Argentière Hut to the start, 1½–2 hours. From the bergschrund to the summit, 3–5 hours. Descent: 1 hour.

Favourable periods: from March to the end of July, depending on the amount of snow on the north faces.

Route description:
Ascent: from the Argentière Hut cross the glacier to get to the left of the foot of the Grande Rocheuse spur. Go to the first gap which allows you to reach the base of the north-east Arête of the Grande Rocheuse 2,866 m (9,400 ft); bear right to the outfall of the couloir beneath the bergschrund. Start the couloir on the right from the highest point on the bergschrund, and climb up to the dog's leg of the couloir where you keep to the outside of the bend (approx. 3,500 m/11,480 ft). Return very quickly to the right, avoiding having to traverse too much. Carry on in the direction of the dôme without going over the rocks on the right.

On the dôme the slope is more or less regular, leading to the summit after several little ice walls and a final steep slope.

If you bivouac at the Aiguille des Grands Montets, take a route under the bergschrunds of the Petite Aiguille Verte, then off the Cordier Couloir, and so to the foot of the couloir.

Descent: follow the line of the ascent and get away from the left side of the couloir to avoid the difficulties of the dog's leg. At the Rognons Glacier, it depends on the amount of snow as to whether it is best to follow the climbing tracks down to the Argentière Glacier, or, alternatively, to cross beneath the bergschrunds of the triangle of rock on the left. Cross the Rognons Glacier high enough to avoid the many crevasses and rejoin the Grands Montets ski run.

ARÊTE DE PEUTEREY, MONT BLANC

'I had broached the subject of this extraordinary ski descent with Patrick Vallençant at the beginning of our ski trips together. It would be dangerous, if not careless, to go into this enterprise alone, not only for the descent itself, but especially for the return at the end of the morning through the crevasses and avalanches of the Envers.

We were to make a film of what seemed to us a unique first descent – right from the summit of Mont Blanc, the highest point in Europe. We also wanted to add a really good one to our collection of first descents; and even though, only a few days earlier, I had successfully done the first ski descent of the North Face of the Aiguille du Midi with Yves Dietry and Daniel Chauchefoin, I needed another complete one.

In early 1977, ski extrème was developing quickly but in different directions. The new enthusiasts were not satisfied any more with skiing down extremely steep and exposed slopes, but were also skiing down Alpine climbing routes with copious use of the rope in order to abseil down non-skiable sections. There was certainly a lack of ethics here (but this is open to discussion) and yet an irreversible step had been taken. In the same way that certain climbers got away with using expansion bolts on impossible slabs, nobody could forbid this sort of exercise.

When I first seriously took to extreme skiing, about 1970, I disagreed with the greed for adventure of those skiers who were landed by helicopter or by plane on the tops of slopes with no respect for the mountain. Then, with Patrick Vallençant, a guide but still an 'amateur alpinist' like me, we thought we had succeeded in making some acceptable rules to be followed on our descents. Without such rules amateur adventurers like us could, with the help of a long rope, ski down the Shroud on the Grands Jorasses, and why not the Walker Spur!

Unhappily that summer of 1977 saw two young Americans fall down the North Face of the Matterhorn as they attempted a ski descent! I suppose they did not know how to abseil. . . This proves that one has to be a good alpinist for this sort of undertaking.

Anyway, this first ski descent of the Arête de Peuterey made big demands on us in terms of effort and willpower. Two days previously we had succeeded so easily on the North Face of the Aiguille Blanche that we set off full of determination. However, the evening before the descent, clouds were still rolling onto the summit of Mont Blanc; and when I went to sleep, I was quite worried. At midnight the stars were shining and the faint light of the moon was enough to light the way.

The ski descent from the hut to the Col Moore was fantastic: a light fall of powder snow had fallen during the evening and we could see the crystals rise, glittering in the moon. To be out skiing at 0100 a.m., in such exceptional surroundings, makes it really worthwhile being alive. Without using a headtorch to the Pilier d'Angle, we needed less than half an hour to reach the bottom of the next long slope. The fresh snow of the previous days had been transformed into a crusted snow, and we sank above the knee at every step. Beneath the col the snow became more consistent, and two hours passed before we reached the upper plateau of the Freney. To get over the lower bergschrund of the Eccles Couloir we had to climb with our skis on our rucksacks. Higher up, the approaching dawn allowed us to make a way between the rocks embedded in the ice, to reach the summit of the Pilier d'Angle. From here a magnificent spectacle was in front of us: the sun rising in turn on Mont Maudit, the Grandes Jorasses, and l'Aiguile Verte. On the Italian side, from the Gran Paradiso to the Vanoise, the summits seemed to emerge from the blue depths of the valleys.

On the corniced arête the climbing became delicate and hard with the slopes falling steeply away on each side. Six hours had passed since the start and the slope to the summit was still rising in front of us. The 'wind of the four thousand metres' had hardened the snow, and our crampons were biting less and less on the hard crust, stripped of soft snow.

We arrived at last a few metres below the summit cornice, and there was a final icy patch which we could not have skied down. It therefore seemed pointless to carry the skis any higher, as we would only have to abseil back down over the cornice again.

Vincent Mercier, with Frederic Bourbousson, was ready to film from the Aiguille Blanche de Peuterey. We knew, thanks to the walkie-talkie, that the other team with the telephoto lens was also ready to follow the descent. The yellow, vertical flame of the Freney Pillar was pointing up below us, and the North Face of the Aiguille Blanche de Peuterey, one thousand metres below us, looked strangely horizontal.

We had both climbed several times before to the highest point of Europe, but only today were we conscious of the extraordinary position of that high window on the world. After seven hours of extremely hard climbing, loaded with all the climbing and skiing equipment, and on top of that a radio and 16 mm camera, we had worn ourselves out. Although the overhanging cornice looked very solid, we could not stay any longer contemplating this universe of light and colour.

A difficult task tested our morale: having to replace our crampons, sticking into the snow with all their points, with the skis, whose main feature is sliding and slipping. I believe I forgot even to think during those delicate manoeuvres. We were fully aware that even one slight mistake leading to loss of balance was totally out of the question. The slope below fell away to the left and seemed to blend into the Brenva Glacier – in fact, one thousand metres of vertical cliff separate the two! This is the Pilier d'Angle. On the right-hand side rocky ridges, cut by icy couloirs, swept down under the North and Central Pillars of the Freney.

The summit slope was 55 degrees with hard and fairly smooth snow, so the first turns were followed by long sideslips in order to lose some height. It was impossible to get the shaft of the ice axe in for security in order to take any film or photographs. Patrick was only able to film the beginning of my descent – I could not even feel my skis, which were chattering on the icy snow. I stopped for a longer time 300 metres lower down where it was possible to rejoin the start of the ridge of the Pilier d'Angle – this was less difficult because it was less icy. A small cornice separated the Brenva and Freney sides: the former very steep and of hard snow; the latter of corrugated snow, lacking in consistency and more dangerous.

The intense nervous tension to which we had been accustomed for a long time was now a faithful companion. As if to increase the difficulties, we were forcing ourselves to film and take photographs; the colours were too beautiful not to make the effort to stop, to secure ourselves with the ice axe and to take out all the equipment.

Above the Eccles Couloir there was a perfect funnel, emptying itself 400 metres lower down on to the upper Freney Glacier. It was difficult to keep in balance on the corrugated snow, which was breaking off in slabs. The slope, fortunately, was not more than 45 degrees at this point, fortunately because not only were the slabs breaking away under the skis, but also we could not recover our balance by using our ski sticks, as the points of the sticks did not grip in this snow. Twice my uphill knee touched the snow, and the recovery had to be quick and decisive.

These new difficulties were stiffening all our muscles, especially the leg ones, already on the verge of cramp, and so far we had only descended the first third of the route!

Lower down, the couloir presented some new problems – little rocks emerging from the hard snow (and often ice) would make us do short and abrupt turns. I admit to not finding much pleasure in skiing those 300 metres. However, this icy shute was also part of the same fight against fear. Like being caught in a mousetrap, we were fighting alone, both of us looking for the best route between the rocks in order to lose height. Only the lower part which joins the Col de Peuterey was excellent powder, and we enjoyed a schuss, crossing the col from north to south. We could at last relax, with our skis flat on this big plateau, although our minds were reliving the recent challenges. We knew that, technically, nothing could now stop us from finishing this unbelievable descent.

The north-east slope of the Col de Peuterey was waiting for us and the consolidated snow was excellent, cut with small furrows over which we could ski with no problem – all seemed easy. Despite the weight of the rucksacks and the tiredness which were slowing us down, we were experiencing some fabulous moments.

I quickly aimed for the base of the Pilier d'Angle, and found a very direct route for swiftly crossing the avalanche cones of the Envers of Mont Blanc. Sheltered under Pt Moore, I sat in the wet snow with no cares and made a big effort to rise when Patrick arrived a few seconds later. The unique handshake which linked us during that instant expressed our mutual feelings better than any words.

Meanwhile the tension was disappearing and we felt very tired, but at the same time very proud. Waiting for our two friends who were descending with crampons from the Aiguille Blanche, I was thinking of the long climb to the Col Moore, then the crossing under the Brenva, the ascent again to the Ghiglione Hut in soft snow at this late hour in the afternoon, the descent into the Maudit basin and finally the tracks which would take us to the top of the Col du Geant. Seldom have I felt fatigue so intensely, increased above all by the effort of concentration.

In fact, the next evening we set off again from Chamonix for the Aiguille du Midi, where we slept before doing the descent of the Gervasutti Couloir . . .'

First Descent: Anselme Baud and Patrick Vallençant on 31 May 1977.

Starting Point: Chamonix at the Aiguille du Midi cablecar station; or Entrèves in Italy, to take the cablecar to the Col du Géant.

Height Difference: ascent: 1,400 m (4,600 ft) if leaving from the Ghiglione Hut, to which is added 350 m (1,150 ft) for the ascent of the Brenva Glacier to the Col Moore, and

from there to the Ghiglione Hut. Descent: 1,400 m (4,600 ft) to which is added the descents below the Ghiglione Hut and from the Col Moore to the Brenva Glacier.

Difficulty: ED because of its long approach and its dangerous return and obviously because the slopes reach 60 degrees in the Eccles Couloir.

Equipment: high-alpine skiing equipment appropriate to an alpinist for a two-day route in that isolated part of Mont Blanc.

Time: ascent: $7\frac{1}{2}$ hours from the hut to the summit; descent: $1\frac{1}{2}$ hours from the summit of Mont Blanc de Courmayeur to the Brenva Glacier.

Favourable Period: May–June.

Route Description

Ascent: the ascent to the Ghiglione Hut can be made from:

(a) the Aiguille du Midi: follow the classic route of the Vallée Blanche as far as Pt Adolphe-Rey (approx. 3,500 m/1,500 ft); then work up under the foot of its south face and go on until you can line yourself up on the Col du Trident. Climb the snow cone under the north-west spur of the Trident; cross the bergschrund, and climb the steep slope up to the hut which is on the left behind a ridge (two hours).
(b) the Pt Helbronner: reach the foot of the Tour Ronde by the Col des Flambeaux and rejoin the previous route.

From the Ghiglione Hut descend the upper Brenva Glacier by a steep slope. Cross about the middle of the glacier to reach the Col Moore. Behind the col, descend as well as possible through the slopes beneath the Brenva Spur to reach the lower glacier. Cross quickly under the Envers du Mont Blanc, because the serac falls are frequent, irregular and extremely dangerous.

Start the ascent below the Col de Peuterey (sometimes with skins in good conditions) up to the steeper slopes, and cross one or more bergschrunds. Under the col, the slopes are steeper and the access to the Freney Plateau is sometimes made tricky by an impressive cornice. Cross the bergschrund by the snow-covered rocks. Gain some height by this irregular and snowy couloir (rocks).

Reach the funnel which is topped by the ridge coming down from the Pilier d'Angle; climb it on the right and take the Peuterey Ridge, which is not too steep at first.

Between the sides of the Freney on the left and the Brenva on the right, gain some height until you reach a point just below the first rocks, then go up a slope (50–55 degrees) on the right of the rocks; climb the last 200 m

(650 ft) leading up to Mont Blanc de Courmayeur.

Surmount the cornice on the left-hand side and go on to the summit (4,742 m/15,550 ft).

Descent: most of the relevant points are already covered in the text and it is not necessary to repeat them here. This route is exceptional today, and it will remain exceptional on subsequent attempts – which will not be too many. The descent from the Col de Peuterey could be done more often.

For good ski mountaineers this ski descent, a trip right into the Envers du Mont Blanc, is the finest, not only because of its situation, but also because of its isolation under the menace of the seracs and cornices. It was one of these cornices which fell in the winter of 1980 and killed three mountaineers, one of whom was the young Chamonix guide, Daniel Monaci.

TECHNIQUES

'Extreme skiing may be considered close to the ideal enterprise: the preparation with the outcome unknown; the efforts of the ascent; then the moments of calm and lucidity before the start; and finally the concentration before the action of the first turns.

The enthusiasm of youth must be balanced with a certain wisdom. Nevertheless, you reproach yourself sometimes for a lack of audacity. It is necessary, having completed an extreme descent, to question your motives for doing it in the first place? Was it just for pleasure, or for a kind of victory, or to satisfy your pride? Or maybe just for a few moments of happy memories while planning the next descent!

Snow conditions

Everyone knows the difference between skiing in soft powder snow and on hard snow. On the steeper slopes the fear of the big drop takes over; the mistake which would lead to the fatal fall; the nervous tension which stiffens the muscles and leads to the imbalance of the skier. In a ski-extrème descent you are close to the concept of solo climbing: no mistake is allowed.

You must, therefore, put all thought of the risks to one side. When your physical condition and technique are at their peak, you can take on the steep hard-snow slope. It is therefore on hard snow that you will find the greatest satisfaction in controlling fear, yet the risk will also be greater.

On the other hand, if your technique is insufficient or your equipment not quite adequate, it is better to give up a project which is too dangerous, even if you are already at the top of the slope.

It may happen that the snow does not melt as much as anticipated. This may be due to an icy wind or to the sun not coming out. If, despite this, you decide to start the descent, there is a simple way of trying out the slope: drive the shaft of the ice axe into the snow, and make a succession of short side-slips, bracing yourself against the head of the axe. This system is a little slow, but very safe. It allows you to test the performance of the skis, or even to get over a particularly steep and dangerous section. As soon as you are happy, all you have to do is slide the axe behind your shoulder under the strap of the rucksack. This method may bend the ethical considerations a little, but, on the other hand, it is better to avoid bad cramp in the legs. In any case, do not forget to weigh up the mountaineering risks involved.

A weaker skier with less training can start a descent on the rope. This requires a certain amount of skill and some speed in the manoeuvres. By letting out enough rope before a short turn, it really is possible to secure someone from above. On the other hand, it is more difficult from below, because in that situation a good belay is essential.

In conclusion, the differences between the various types of snow on any given slope considerably affect the standard of difficulty.

The turn

The objective is to make a short turn which avoids picking up speed, in which you do not lose balance, and which does not tire you with energetic movements.

The jump turn, which consists of jumping energetically off both feet at the same time is not suitable for use on very steep slopes. On the one hand it is very difficult to maintain a balanced and efficient stance when your two feet are not on the same level; and on the other hand an important jump could put you out of balance on landing. Also, consider the great effort needed for a jump turn.

The type of turn most used involves unweighting twice, combined with a transfer of weight from one foot to the other, and the use of both sticks. Preparation for flexion of the legs is done with most of the weight on the lower ski. Both sticks are planted; the uphill foot is lifted and replaced forcefully on the snow (sometimes pointing a little down the fall-line). At the same time go for the first unweighting: by the extension of the lower leg. This extension is possible thanks to the brief weighting of the uphill ski. Both skis are then unweighted by a quick and complete flexion of the knees, which allows the heels of the skis to reach the top of the slope.

Support on the two sticks is essential. It not only helps with the unweighting, but it also ensures the correct position of the upper body.

Once the skis are pointing down the fall-line, they are side-slipped, and the turn is controlled by edging.

The important thing is to get an efficient unweighting, and this is done by fluent and skilful technique which really just uses vertical movement. The downhill stick must be planted well down the slope. The skis are always well apart, the uphill one in front, to guarantee a balanced position, with most of the weight on the downhill ski.

I resorted to this type of turn on all my descents of couloirs and steep slopes – whether alone or with friends, among them Patrick Vallençant. The technique appeared to me to be very reliable and most suitable for steep slopes, narrow couloirs, and for bad, unstable and crusted snow. Also it demands the minimum of effort, and this is important on high mountains after the efforts of climbing a couloir.

I finish with a personal thought, but it is one which is shared by many others: always climb the couloir before skiing down it. It enables you to have a look at the slope, at the condition of the snow, at the exact route. It lets you warm up before having to ski down, and, above all, it lets you get accustomed to the slope. All these things reduce the risks and increase the chances of success. Finally, it is a question of ethics: to play the game without cheating, without the help of outside elements. To try and at least respect this ethic is important, because we can do so. Above all I believe it is better to be a mountaineer; to understand the behaviour of this element 'snow' on high mountains; to train on slopes which are not too dangerous in order to get confidence, and then to make a plan and to complete it with honesty.'

EXTREME SKIING IN SCOTLAND
Harry Jamieson made the first steep ski descents in Scotland, with descents, in the early 1970s, of the following Cairngorm gullies: Aladdin's Couloir, Pinnacle Gully,

Castlegates Gully and The Couloir in Coire an Lochain. Many other descents have now been made by a variety of people, but none more than by Martin Burrows-Smith, and, for interest, here is a list of his descents, many of them first and unrepeated:

Northern Cairngorms
Coire an-t-Sneachda, Jacob's Ladder, Forty Thieves, Aladdin's Couloir, Aladdin's Mirror, Central Gully Left Hand, Central Gully, Central Gully Right Hand, Crotched Gully
Coire an Lochain, Fiacaill Ridge, The Couloir
Stag Rocks, Diagonal Gully
Hell's Lum Crag, Hell's Lum Shelter Stone Crag, Castlegates Gully, Pinnacle Gully
Lochnagar, Black Spout, Left Hand Branch, Central, Redspot
Creag Meaghaidh, Easy Gully, Raeburn's Gully, Cinderella
Ben Nevis, No. 5 Gully, No. 4 Gully, No. 3 Gully

Glencoe
Aonach Dubh, No. 2 Gully.
Stob Coire an Lochain, Forked Gully
Beinn Dearg, Cadha Amadan
An Teallach, Lord's Gully, Hay Fork Gully

Recommended Tours and Tour Accounts

1 Scotland

INTRODUCTION

While seldom exceeding 1,300 m (4,000 ft), the mountains of Scotland show every type of landscape, from rounded desolate hilltops to secluded corries whose vertical walls provide the challenging ice climbing for which Scotland is justifiably well known. The last glaciers in Scotland existed around 10,000 years ago, but it would only need a mean drop of 2°C. for them to return.

There are two villains in the Scottish mountains: the wind and the warm fronts. The wind is your constant companion, and much as you might try to bend with it, the fact remains that if you are to get anything done at all in winter, you have to fight the wind – and fight it hard. On the summit of Cairngorm it hits Gale Force 8 almost every day, and Hurricane Force 12 every third day. That is an annual average, including the summer months. Winds over 160 kph (100 mph) are not unusual. As for the warm fronts, they come belting in from the Atlantic, bringing sudden warm spells which can rocket the freezing level from 300 m (1,000 ft) to 1,500 m (5,000 ft) in a couple of hours, melting the low-lying snow and ruining one's carefully prepared plans.

And so you keep bashing on, skiing on ice, heather and rocks until, one day, the sun shines, the snow is perfect and there is no wind. The ski mountaineering possibilities are then endless, from as early as November to as late as May, with the best month usually being March.

Since the weather is, on the whole, so harsh, local enthusiasts get used to going out in bad conditions, and this means that they have some memorable tales to tell.

One of the best ones for me was in the Cairngorms when searching for a missing ski mountaineer. The Cairngorm Mountain Rescue Team has a ski mountaineering group, and four of us from this group were to search a route which included the descent of the March burn, a steep stream falling 300 metres (1,000 ft) from the Cairngorm Plateau into the Lairig Ghru. The weather was poor (wind, snow and very cold), and visibility was dreadful. The burn itself was a steeply angled funnel of ice and snow, and fearing that we might inadvertently ski over a frozen waterfall, we came out to the side. This was not much better, and we had to abseil one section with our skis on.

We lost height slowly, trying to keep close to the edge of the stream, which was our only reference point.

Suddenly I found myself back in the stream having dropped over the cornice. I was on a steep funnel of snow and ice, with a big overhanging cornice rearing above me on both sides, and unable to see anything below me because of white-out – I could not see if there was a waterfall, I could not even see what was at my feet. Climbing back out over the overhanging cornice looked uninviting, so I had to go down. I radioed my intention to the others, who had no idea where I was – I had simply vanished.

The snow was just moist enough to make a snowball and I dropped it at my feet. It rolled for about three or four feet, and then disappeared in the white-out. I side-slipped down the three feet, and dropped another snowball . . . side-slip . . . snowball . . . sideslip . . . snowball . . . sideslip. Eventually I got to the bottom (with no waterfalls en route), and there was the most amazing sight of all. The wind had blown the snow up into two high walls, one on either side of the burn. They were so close together that a man could only just pass through. I shussed out between them, more than a little relieved to be reunited with my friends.

This illustrates how dangerous white-outs are. The definition of a white-out is that one cannot distinguish between the ground and the horizon. This may occur in conditions of high wind and driving snow, i.e. blizzard. It may equally well occur in very still conditions. The result is the same – appalling visibility. Ten feet in front of you there could be a vertical drop, flat ground or a steep wall – and you simply cannot see it. Throwing snowballs is one way of breaking up the white-out and allowing progress to continue.

A guidebook is published in 1987 giving details of eighty ski tours in Scotland. It is called *Ski Mountaineering in Scotland*, edited by Donald Bennett and Bill Wallace and published by the Scottish Mountaineering Trust.

CAIRNGORMS

Map: Ordnance Survey 1:50,000 Sheet 36.
The Cairngorms contain the second highest mountain in

Britain, Ben Macdui 1,309 m (4,300 ft), and three other mountains over 1,200 m (4,000 ft): Braeriach, Cairntoul and Cairngorm. Viewed from a distance, particularly from the south west, they look flat and uninteresting, but this is deceptive, as they are the largest area of high mountains in Britain, containing some of the finest cliffs, corries and lochs. They are very exposed to easterly winds and consequently get a lot of snow. Much of this will be blown around and away by subsequent westerlies, and this must be born in mind when estimating where the best snow will be lying.

A classic short tour is the Tops of the Northern Coirries, using the lift system on the way up Cairngorm, then to the top of Sneachda 1,176 m (3,850 ft), on to the top of Cairn Lochain 1,215 m (3,990 ft) and a good ski run back to the Coire Cass carpark. You can do it in three hours, and spend the afternoon piste skiing.

The classic long tour (and it is long!) is the Four Tops: Cairngorm, Ben Macdui, Cairn Toul and Braeriach. The ski descent from Ben Macdui down to the Lairig Ghru can either be by the Allt a'Coire Mhor or the Tailors' Burn – both are excellent, with a vertical drop of over 700 m (2,300 ft). The story of the Tailors' Burn is a sad one: three tailors had a wager that they could dance a reel on the same night in both Rothiemurchus (near Aviemore) and Brae-

mar. It was New Year's Eve. They danced the one in Rothiemurchus, but died in the snow at the foot of this burn on the way through to Braemar.

From the top of Braeriach one can return to the Coire Cass carpark via the Sinclair Hut and the Chalamain Gap. But more interesting variations are either by one of the ridges of Coire Ruadh and then north west into Glen Einich, or, from spot height 1,235 m (4,050 ft), ski down the magnificent slope north west into Glen Einich, which gives the greatest vertical height drop in the Cairngorms – 750 m (2,460 ft).

However, for something slightly different I recommend the following two tours:

Recommended Tours

(1) Cairngorm, Ben Macdui, Beinn Mheadhoin

Start from the Coire Cass carpark and use the lift system to get to Cairngorm, then to Sneachda 1,176 m (3,850 ft) and on to Ben Macdui, following more or less the line of the summer path. From the summit ski down briefly east and then north east to Loch Etchachan – a delightful descent on an easy-angled gradient. Climb via spot height 1,163 m (3,815 ft) to Beinn Mheadhoin (pronounced Ben Vane). The descent from here is superb – north north east down

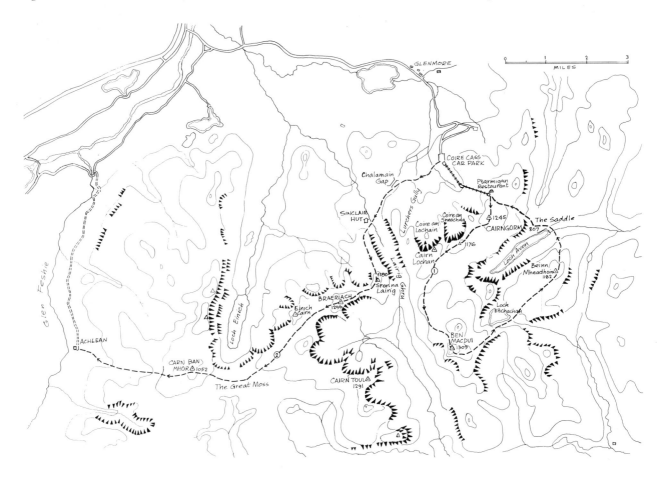

Fig. 92   The summit of Cairngorm.

through the cliffs to the end of Loch Avon (pronounced Arn), with a drop of 500 m (1,640 ft). The final ascent is long: up to the Saddle at 807 m (2,650 ft); north north west under the cliffs, and then north west round Cairngorm to rejoin the lift system at the Ptarmigan Restaurant. If you are late and this is closed, your consolation will be the descent to the carpark on deserted slopes.

(2) Coire Cass carpark, Lairig Ghru, Braeriach, Carn Ban Mhor, Glen Feshie

This is a fine traverse which can be completed in a day from either direction. There are, however, three advantages in doing it from east to west (i.e. from Coire Cass to Glen Feshie), namely: by driving to the carpark one has an initial height gain of 300 m (1,000 ft) over Glen Feshie; secondly, from Braeriach the ski descent south west to the Great Moss is better than the one north east to the Lairig Ghru, and thirdly, one finishes with a ski descent at the end of the day down to Achlean in Glen Feshie.

From the Coire Cass carpark traverse round into the Lurcher's Gully, climb in a rising traverse to the Chala-

main Gap, passing above the actual gap, since the boulders in the gap seldom have sufficient snow cover, ski south down to the Lairig Ghru, and up to the Sinclair Hut. Ascend the north ridge of Braeriach to Sron na Lairig, and on to the summit. As already mentioned, the ski descent from Braeriach is very fine with a vertical height drop of 400 m (1,300 ft). Traverse the Great Moss, which is the undulating and rather tiresome ground bordering the southern cliffs of Loch Einich, and then climb briefly to Carn Ban Mhor. Ski west down the stream to Achlean.

GREY COIRRIES

The traverse of the Grey Coirries is an excellent ski traverse, usually done from west to east so as to have the prevailing wind on one's back. The projected ski-lift development on Aonach Mhor will make the start even easier.

With Spean Bridge as a base, use a car to get you up the forest road to Creag Aoil, then go round the ridge, climbing the following en route: Aonach Mor 1,210 m (3,970 ft), Aonach Beg 1,236 m (4,055 ft), Sgurr Choinnich Beag 996 m (3,170 ft) and Mor 1,095 m (3,590 ft), Stob Coire Easain, 1,080 m (3,540 ft), Stob Choire Claurigh 1,177 m (3,860 ft) and Stob Coire na Ceannain 1,121 m (3,677 ft). Finish down the track on Allt Leachdach to the road at Corriechoille, and so back to Spean Bridge.

It is easy enough to break off at any time and head off down the Allt Coire an Eoin or the Allt Choimhlidh.

Map: Ordnance Survey 1:50,000 Sheet 41 Ben Nevis.

BEN ALDER

Ben Alder is a remote mountain lying to the west of the A9, with the usual access from Dalwhinnie and then down the north-west shore of Loch Ericht. Permission may be obtained from the estate to use their road as far down as Benalder Lodge, but even with this time-saving help it is still too far to visit the mountain in one day, and it is normal to spend one or two nights at either the Culra Bothy or the deserted Benalder Cottage – deserted, that is, except for the ghost of its one-time occupier, McCook. If sleep escapes you in the cottage, walk up the hill behind and see if you can find Bonnie Prince Charlie's cave – reputedly the only cave in which you can light a fire and not be asphyxiated, as the smoke escapes up a natural chimney.

Ben Alda is beautiful and well worth seeing and John Harding discovered that the best way to visit the mountain in a weekend from London was by taking the Friday-night sleeper to Corrour (south west of the mountain), and returning on the Sunday-night sleeper from Dalwhinnie (north east of the mountain). This not only gives a traverse of the mountain, but gets you back to London in time for work on Monday morning. The following account by John Harding first appeared in the *Eagle Ski Club Book*, 1983:

During the season, skiers are a familiar sight at Euston on a Friday night. Ski mountaineers less so. My reading for the northern journey was Paul Theroux's *The Old Patagonian Express*. His rail odyssey from Boston to Patagonia was characterized by discomfort, while ours from London to Corrour on the *Highlander* was close to luxury. Four tartan blankets apiece is upmarket of an S.N.C.F. couchette. We slipped out of Euston at 2055 hours and later that night Alan's brother Nick climbed aboard at Carlisle to complete our team.

The old magic of a Highland awakening never fades. At 0800 hours next morning, Saturday 12th February 1983, the three of us lined the corridor peering outwards to assess the weather and if Corrour would be above or

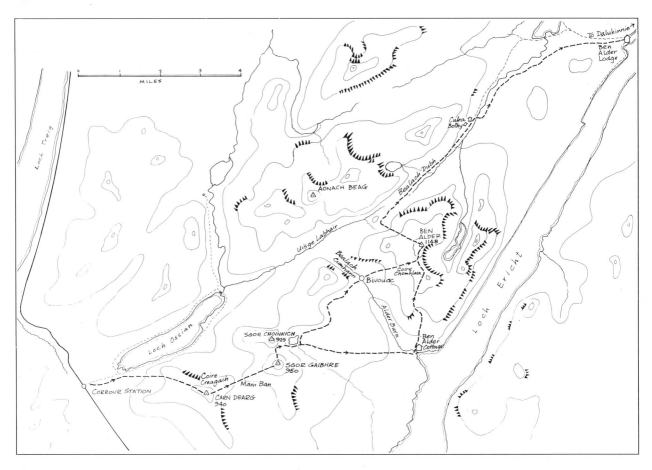

below the snowline. We need not have worried. Corrour Station, at 1,347 ft [410 m] the highest in Britain, fulfilled every expectation. Near to the railway line stags foraged in snow which stretched to an indeterminate horizon, there to merge with the cloud. Bundling ourselves out of a warm train onto a frozen platform, a brisk and bewhiskered figure in uniform greeted us: the man – Corrour's station master: the train – his day's main event. Yes, he would telephone the Grampian Hotel, Dalwhinnie, forthwith to confirm our high tea booking for Sunday night. No – he would not be paid for it: the call was by courtesy of British Rail. Echos from another Age of the Train long banished from the Southern line.

We skied off the platform at 0930 hours heading eastwards for the southern shores of Loch Ossian. Nick, experimenting with langlauf, was yards faster over flat and undulating ground but handicapped on the steeper stuff. The first objective was Carn Dearg, at 3,083 ft [940 m] a Munro* in its own right. But visibility was such that we saw nothing of or from that hill, save glimpses through veils of mist of the great cliffs of Corrie Creagach from near its corniced summit. That we reached after three hours at 1235 hours and thence made a tricky descent to Mam Ban, a high col which led by a laborious climb on foot to the top of Sgor Gaibhre – at 3,124 ft [950 m] our second Munro that day. Away to the north-east, under a lowering sky of shifting clouds, the great bulk of Ben Alder was just discernable, separated from us by a desolation of wintry moorland. Only the dark waters of Loch Ericht to the east broke the stark uniformity of the scene.

From Sgor Gaibhre we skied steeply down to the Bealach separating it from Sgor Choinnich, and then an exhilarating descent on good snow to a frozen lochan at its foot. But already the day was closing in. We had climbed two hills and covered nine miles, and were beginning to feel the weight of our rucksacks. Comfortable accommodation for that night was available at Benalder Cottage, deserted on the shores of Loch Ericht. But the cottage is haunted and to lose 500 ft to reach it clinched the argument.

Our bivouac was sited on a snowy platform just above the Alderburn and some way below the Bealach Cumhann. We dug through the snow to get water from the stream and settled down for a long northern night. Our tents were guyed by skis, poles and ice axes. By the light of a headtorch I boiled the water that alone is required in the preparation of Raven accelerated freeze dried boeuf bourguignon – that and an undiscriminating palate.

Some snow fell that night, but by morning the weather had lifted slightly. At 0835 hours we struck camp and headed upwards into the cloud by the western flanks of Corrie Chomhlain for Ben Alder's summit. This approach is the mountain's only significant weakness. Its precipitous north and east faces are probably inviolable to the skier. The upper slopes were steep, but with good snow and the sun occasionally breaking through, we made our summit after two hours and 2,200 ft [670 m] of climbing.

With cloud low, there were no great views to savour except to the north-west across the cleft of the Uisge Labhair, from whose depths rose the white pyramid of Aonach Beag 3,644 ft [1,110 m]. This impressive mountain had featured on our original itinerary but was a peak too far that day.

The summit plateau of Ben Alder is over 3,500 ft [1,066 m] high and covers some 400 acres. Our descent, initially due west and then veering to the north, took in neve, sastrugi and breakable crust in succession. From the Meall Slugain we made an exit via the Bealach Dubh, and thence to easier ground to skim across a bleak tract of moorland which in summer would give heavy going. Above Loch Ericht there were great herds of deer and here too, on the lochside, we made first contact with our own kind since leaving Corrour – two climbers also Dalwhinnie bound.

The rest is short in telling. Sixteen miles and nine hours from our bivouac site we reached the Grampian Hotel at 1730 hours for an extended high tea. As we had arrived, so we departed from another snow-bound platform at 2200 hours on board the *Highlander*, as its only passengers from Dalwhinnie.

Back in Bishopsgate E.C.3 next morning the past forty-eight hours seemed as a dream. Yet Scottish ski touring is nothing if not substance, for beneath those cold northern skies is country altogether wilder and more remote than anything in Europe outside Scandinavia.

Map: Ordnance Survey 1:50,000 Sheet 42.

(*a Munro is a Hill over 3,000 ft [914 m] as listed in Munro's Tables.)

2 The Bernese Oberland, Switzerland

Observant travellers on the train from Bern will catch a glimpse of distant peaks rising above the blue waters of Lake Thun. Every day throughout summer and winter thousands of visitors will look up from Grindelwald, Mürren, Wengen and Kleine Scheidegg at the towering faces and precipitous snowfields of the northern summits of the Bernese Oberland.

Best known is the Eiger (the Ogre), whose North Face dominates Grindelwald and Scheidegg like a giant tombstone – 1,800 vertical metres (6,000 ft) of rock, snow and ice – for many young climbers the ultimate and final theatre of challenge.

The Mönch is the Monk, standing firm and square, almost aloof to the dramas of his more famous neighbour. The most beautiful of these mountains is the Jungfrau (the Virgin), whose white flowing glaciers resemble the robes of a vestal virgin, protected by the symbolic ramparts of sheer rock faces and vertical cascades of ice.

When not hidden in wreaths of clouds, the Wetterhorn (the Peak of Storms) reveals the magnificent sweep of its final summit slopes.

While these magnificent mountains form the northern limit to the Bernese Oberland, the boundary to the south is drawn by the River Rhône whose source is the Rhône Glacier on the east side of the range, and which flows south west and then south, to become one of the largest and most important rivers in Europe, finally entering the sea at Marseilles.

Everything is impressive in the Bernese Oberland, especially the Gross Aletsch Glacier which, when combined with the Jungfraufirn, gives a 20 km (12 mile) glacier run, with the ice at the Konkordia Platz reaching a depth of 800 m (2,600 ft), the deepest in Europe.

One of the most impressive features is man-made: namely, the cog railway running from Kleine Scheidegg to the Jungfraujoch. The tunnel has been cut right through the Eiger. Two halts are made, giving the opportunity to look out of the station windows straight onto the North Face of the Eiger. There used to be a hotel at the Jungfraujoch (3,454 m/11,330 ft) and I remember spending a comfortable night there in 1970. Unfortunately, it has now been destroyed by fire. There is everything for the tourist up here: observation platform, exhibition, restaurant, telephone call-box, and a shop selling films, postcards

and miniature ice axes.

The ski mountaineering possibilities are endless. One of the easiest day tours is: Jungfraujoch by rail, ski down to the Konkordia Platz, climb up to the Lötschenlucke and ski down the Lötschental to Blatten. There are many excellent peaks, some of them over 4,000 m (13,000 ft), (Jungfrau, Gross Grünhorn, Fiescherhorn and Finsteraarhorn). Perhaps the area lends itself best of all to traverses, particularly from east to west.

One of the most important events in the history of ski

mountaineering was the traverse of the Bernese Oberland in January 1897 by Wilhelm Paulke. The route was from Grimsel, via the Oberaarjoch Hut, Grünhornlücke, Konkordia Hut, and down the Gross Aletsch Glacier to the Belalp Hotel. They had no guides, no crampons and no sealskins. It was an extraordinarily bold expedition, being the first traverse of the Alpine group on skis; and ski mountaineering can truly be said to stem from this date.

When Paulke and his party arrived at the Belalp Hotel, it was closed for the winter. This did not deter the triumphant party: they broke in and spent a good night, helped along by some excellent wine. The next day they skied down to the valley where the owner of the hotel told them, to their great surprise, that the wine which had tasted so good was in fact vinegar.

Although the Konkordia Hut existed in 1897 it was far from the comfortable hut it is today. All the huts are excellent, attended by a guardian during the ski mountai-

Fig. 94   Skiers on Konkordia Platz.

Fig. 95   Descent of Gross Aletsch.

neering season (usually from the end of March to the end of May). The food varies, depending on how recently fresh supplies have been flown in. Recently I spent three nights at the Finsteraarhorn Hut. When we arrived the guardian was looking tired, being single-handed, and he was short of food. We had two evening meals of rather undercooked pork-fat and noodles. But then, on the third day, the guardian's wife arrived by helicopter with fresh supplies, and that evening we had a magnificent roast with potatoes and vegetables. A speciality of the guardian at the Konkordia Hut is to add a little alcohol to the fruit salad.

There are two points which need special care in this area:

1. All big mountain masses create their own bad weather, and this area is no exception. With big permanent snowfields and many peaks over 4,000 m (13,000 ft), bad weather must be expected at any time of the year.

quadrants, but in practice the Jungfraujoch is by far the most popular starting point, the other routes being used mainly for descent.

North: the Jungfraujoch (3,454 m/11,330 ft) is reached by rail from Kleine Scheidegg. There are two rail routes to Kleine Scheidegg: either Interlaken, Grindelwald, Kleine Scheidegg; or Interlaken, Lauterbrunnen, Wengen, Kleine Scheidegg. This is an excellent starting point, giving access in a day to the following huts: Hollandia, Konkordia, Finsteraarhorn and Mönchjoch. It is possible to descend easily, but expensively, to Grindelwald or Lauterbrunnen by the Jungfrau railway, but note that the entrance to the tunnel at the Jungfraujoch is difficult to find in bad weather.

East: (1) if doing a traverse of the area, the route from the Grimsel Pass via the Oberaarjoch Hut to the Finsteraarhorn Hut is suitable.

(2) A popular descent route from the Finsteraarhorn Hut is via the Galmilücke and Münstinger Glacier to Münster.

South: (1) the Gross Aletsch Glacier offers a long and impressive ski descent. Taken from the Grünhornlücke, the descent is 15 km (9 miles) long, with a vertical height drop of 1,300 m (4,260 ft). As you shoot out from the Grüneggfirn, past the Konkordia Hut on your left, go into the 'tuck' position and enjoy a 6 km ($3\frac{1}{2}$ mile) 'schuss'. Keep to the right (west) side until about 2,200 m (7,220 ft), and then start moving over to the left (east) side. This is through some quite complicated terrain, and if you are breaking trail it is difficult to get the right line. Leave the glacier at about 2,000 m (6,560 ft) on a path leading up through the woods to the Rieder Furka – this can be quite tricky when banked up with snow. From Rieder Furka take the lift system down to Mörel, and from there go by bus, train or taxi to Visp and Brig.

This descent of the Gross Aletsch Glacier should be avoided in conditions of fresh snow, as the gradient is very gentle. Good hard snow is ideal in order to keep going without having to pole.

(2) The most direct descent from the Finsteraarhorn Hut is down the Fiescher Glacier. This is a serious glacier and the descent should only be undertaken by competent parties in good conditions. Ski down the left (east) side to about 2,800 m (9,190 ft), and then cross to the other side, coming close to the bank on the right (west) side at 2,600 m (8,530 ft). Ski down the gully between the bank and the glacier until about 2,300 m (7,550 ft), when it is possible to move out into the middle of the glacier again. A heavily crevassed zone starts at 2,000 m (6,560 ft), and the route keeps to the middle of the glacier through these crevasses. Move off the glacier on the right (west) side at 1,800 m (5,900 ft), climb up briefly and then descend to the path which leads to Fieschertal and Fiesch.

2. Navigation across the Konkordia Platz in misty conditions can be difficult: crossing it in almost any direction presents a featureless and flat traverse of 2–$2\frac{1}{2}$ km ($1\frac{1}{4}$–$1\frac{1}{2}$ miles).

Maps: *Landeskarte der Schweiz* No. 264 'Jungfrau'.

Access points

It is possible to gain access to the area from any of the four

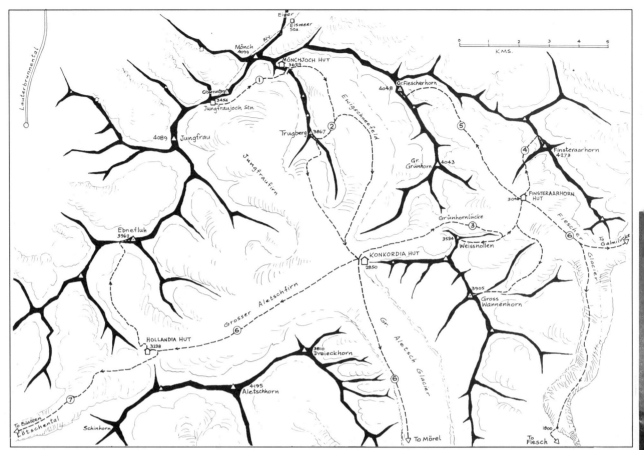

West: the descent of the Lötschental from the Hollandia Hut to Blatten is one of the finest ski descents in the Alps. The route itself is straightforward enough, but nevertheless there is one great danger: the north-facing slopes of the Schininhorn, Beichgrat and Breithorn (which are on the left during the ski descent) are very prone to avalanches. One is exposed to this danger for the whole of the descent, and it is for this reason that the Lötschental has the reputation of being one of the most dangerous valleys in the Alps.

Recommended Tour

Day 1. Jungfraujoch to Mönchjoch Hut: reaching the Jungfraujoch in the early afternoon, there is a short traverse on skins to the Mönchjoch Hut. This is quite a new hut, owned not by the Swiss Alpine Club but by the Grindelwald Guides. It is on the lower rocks on the west–north-west side of the Mönchjoch (3,629 m/11,900 ft).

Day 2. Mönchjoch Hut, ascent of the Trugberg, to Konkordia Hut: ski down east, then south west, down the Ewigschneefeld to about 3,465 m (11,370 ft). Climb on skins, a rising traverse, to the ridge. Leave the skis and go the rest of the way on foot to the Trugberg (3,867 m/

12,690 ft). The ski descent is easiest via the Ewigschneefeld and on to the Konkordia Hut. A much steeper descent is via the south slope, through banks of crevasses, to the Jungfraufirn, and then on to the Konkordia Hut.

There are 90 m (300 ft) of ladders up to the hut, and it is normal to leave skis at the bottom.

Day 3. Traverse of the Grünhornlücke, ascent of the Weissnollen to the Finsteraarhorn Hut: climb on skins to the Grünhornlücke; then ski down to about 3,000 m (9,840 ft) at the bottom of the ridge running east from the Weissnollen. This is a fine, although short, ski descent,

usually holding good snow. Leave rucksacks here and climb the Weissnollen, the descent of which can offer very fine skiing. Pick up the rucksacks and move on to the Finsteraarhorn Hut.

A very competent party can climb from the Grünhornlücke up the north-west ridge of the Weissnollen, a steep and direct way to the top.

Days 4 and 5. Ascents of peaks in the vicinity of the Finsteraarhorn Hut, of which there are many, the best

Fig. 97 Finsteraarhorn.

being the Finsteraarhorn itself (4,273 m/14,020 ft). It is usual to carry skis and wear crampons from the hut, certainly, as far as the Frühstückplatz (the Breakfast Place) at 3,616 m (11,860 ft), and sometimes right up to the Hugisattel (4,094 m/13,430 ft), but this depends on conditions. Leave skis here and climb the final, delightful ridge which is very exposed to the north east.

The Gross Fiescherhorn (4,048 m/13,280 ft): climb easily on skins to Pt. 3443.8 m (11,298 ft), which is at the foot of a rocky ridge. From here the ascent is much steeper and it is heavily crevassed. As one bends left (west), it gets easier. If going for the Hinter Fiescherhorn (4,025 m/13,205 ft), head south to the ridge and on to the summit. For the Gross Fiescherhorn, make for the ridge at Pt. 3,923 m (12,870 ft). Leave the skis here and climb the easy, but exposed, ridge to the summit.

The Gross Wannenhorn (3,905 m/12,811 ft): this is a very fine ski mountain, technically easier than the Finsteraarhorn and the Gross Fiescherhorn, and invariably holding superb snow for the ski descent. It is highly recommended. Ski down from the hut to pass close to Pt. 2,919 m (9,576 ft), which is at the foot of the rocky northeast ridge of the Gross Wannenhorn. Climb on skins more or less up the centre of the glacier to about Pt. 3,614 m (11,857 ft), and then bend right to the ridge. Skis may be left here, or, in good conditions, continue with them right to the top.

Day 6. Descent from the Finsteraarhorn Hut to the valley: the valley can be reached in one day from the Finsteraarhorn Hut by the long and impressive Gross Aletsch Glacier (first climbing the Grünhornlücke from the hut), or by the direct and more difficult descent of the Fiescher Glacier, or by the Münster route over the Galmilücke.

Alternative descent from the Finsteraarhorn Hut to the valley: from the Finsteraarhorn Hut climb on skins to the Grünhornlücke, ski down to the Konkordia Platz and then climb on skins to the Hollandia Hut. This latter ascent is long and tedious, despite the fine scenery on one's left. However, it does offer a relatively straightforward escape route in bad weather.

Day 7. From the Hollandia Hut the Ebnefluh (3,962 m/12,998 ft) can be bagged before lunch, but this may make the descent of the Lötschental more hazardous. Priority must be given to this descent as it is very avalanche-prone. In deciding whether or not to do the Ebnefluh, consider carefully the factors of temperature, snow conditions and time. The descent of the Lötschental is in itself straightforward, and in good snow conditions offers a superb ski descent, giving a fine climax to a week's ski mountaineering.

3 The Haute Route

The Haute Route must be the best known ski tour in the world. The Classic Route, from Chamonix to Zermatt and on to Saas Fee, is about 145 km (90 miles) long, crosses twenty-three glaciers and has a total ascent and descent of 10,000 m (33,000 ft) – by comparison Mount Everest is 8,848 m (29,028 ft) above sea level.

Why is the Haute Route so justifiably popular? One of the reasons must be that it is a traverse, which is always particularly satisfying on skis. In this case, one starts from Chamonix, the centre of alpinism in France, passes through probably the finest high-alpine scenery in the Pennine Alps, steps briefly into Italy, and descends under the North Face of the Matterhorn to Zermatt – the centre of all the early mountain exploration in Switzerland. A second reason for its popularity is that the scenery is really unbelievable. On the first day, coming out of the Grands Montets, the view is stunning: l'Aiguille du Chardonnet, l'Aiguille d'Argentière, le Tour Noir, Les Aiguilles Rouges, Mont Dolent and l'Aiguille de Triolet. As you ski down to the Argentière Glacier, the view on the right progressively opens up until you are right under the huge north faces of the Verte, Droites and Courtes. I have been there on sunny days, cloudy days and stormy days, and it is always dramatic, sometimes frightening. I have known more than one person reduced to tears by it.

But the Haute Route is not just a fine ski traverse through superb scenery. It is a great adventure – it always has been and it always will be. Once the reserve of only the strongest and most determined alpinists, today ski lifts, helicopters, huts and good equipment have opened it up to many more people. On a fine day maybe a hundred people or more will start from Argentière, and the same number again from Verbier. It is, nevertheless, a serious tour, demanding a thorough knowledge of alpinism, good techniques and a high level of fitness.

Due to its great popularity, there is now overcrowding at some of the huts at peak times. Despite this, it is difficult to imagine the popularity of the Haute Route ever decreasing. Its reputation has gone before it, and it is the yardstick by which budding ski mountaineers judge themselves.

History

The Haute Route was developed as a summer route on foot by Englishmen, notably by members of the Alpine Club. It was probably completed in 1861, because the first detailed description of it appears in the 1862 edition of *Peaks, Passes and Glaciers* and is by F. W. J. Jacomb.

(Although currently more popular on skis, it can still, of course, be done on foot and as such is a very worthwhile expedition.)

The first major attempt on it using skis was in 1903. On 16 January a party, consisting of Joseph Ravanel 'Le Rouge' (because of his red beard), Alfred Simond and Dr Payot, left Argentière accompanied by Camille and Jean Ravanel and Jules Couttet who between them carried photographic equipment weighing 19 kg (42 lb). Their route took in Col du Chardonnet, Fenêtre du Saleina, Cabane d'Orny, Orsières, Val de Bagnes, Cabane de Chanrion, Otemma Glacier and the Col de l'Evêque. Here they were forced back down to the valley by bad weather. They travelled by road to Les Haudères, crossed the Col d'Herens and skied down to Zermatt. It was a magnificent achievement, linking Chamonix and Zermatt for the first time on skis. But they had avoided the crucial section of the south side of the Grand Combin, and this was not to be resolved for another eight years.

A month later, in February 1903, Dr Helbling and Dr Reichert crossed on skis from the Val de Bagnes to Arolla via the north side of the Grand Combin. They continued to Zermatt via the Col d'Herens.

In 1907 the first ski ascent of the Grand Combin was made by Marcel Kurz, Prof. F. Roget and M. Crettox. And in 1910 the Adler Pass was crossed for the first time on skis by a party which included Oscar Supersaxo, an early member of the famous Saas Fee guiding family. And so the Zermatt to Saas Fee section was complete.

Finally, in 1911 – the same year in which Amundsen reached the South Pole on skis – Marcel Kurz, Prof. Roget and guides skied from Bourg St Pierre over the Plateau du Couloir and Col du Sonadon, down the Mt Durand Glacier to Chanrion, and on to Zermatt, making the first winter ascent of the Dent Blanche on the way. They were the first people to find the key to the south side of the Grand Combin, and, considering Prof. Roget was over fifty years old at the time, it was an extraordinary achievement.

And so the Classic Haute Route was completed – not in one glorious expedition by a single individual, but as a result of several attempts in which four of the early pioneers of ski mountaineering – Marcel Kurz, Prof. Roget, Dr Helbling and Dr Payot – all played a part.

It is interesting to note that the easier variation, namely the Verbier Start, was not done until as late as 1926 when Marcel Kurz skied from the Mont Fort Hut over the Rosablanche and on to the Dix Hut.

Standards and Difficulties

All the problems of high-alpine ski mountaineering are present, even if, due to a spell of fine weather, some of them might appear to be temporarily dormant, for example: avalanches, crevasses, bad weather, complex route finding, difficult snow conditions and high altitude. Many

Fig. 98   Marcel Kurz (above) and Prof. F. Roget
(right).

people have cruised over the Haute Route, following other
people's tracks in glorious weather, using neither the rope
nor the compass. Several days of fine weather at Easter
may result in a track from Chamonix to Saas Fee the size of
a motorway. But the weather can change quickly and five
minutes of wind can blow the tracks in. Many experienced
alpinists, including the author, have had forced bivouacs
on the Haute Route.

It should never be underestimated. It is a tour for
experienced ski mountaineers who have the skills of high-
alpine ski mountaineering, whose equipment is tried and
tested, and who know the standard of fitness required.

Direction

Considering all the following factors, most parties choose
to do the route from west to east, rather than from east to
west.

(1) Ski descents. When going from west to east the
following are the best ski descents: Val d'Arpette, Mt.
Durand Glacier, Col de l'Evêque and Col de Valpelline.
From east to west they are: Adler Pass, Col de l'Evêque
and Col du Chardonnet. The ones from west to east are
longer and generally done in better snow conditions.

(2) Any short, steep sections are better ascended on foot
rather than taken in descent, because it is not only easier
and quicker to climb up them, but also, if descended on
rope, valuable vertical height is lost which could have been
enjoyed on skis. From west to east the following are
climbed on foot: Fenêtre du Saleina, Plateau du Couloir,
Col du Mont Brulé and the Adler Pass – a total of roughly
950 m (3,116 ft). From east to west, only the following are
climbed on foot: Fenêtre du Chamois and the Col du
Chardonnet – a total of roughly 250 m (820 ft).

(3) The lift systems can be used to gain height easily and
effortlessly. From west to east, these are: the Grands
Montets cablecar, the Gornergrat railway and the Stockhorn cablecar, giving a total height gain of 3,800 m
(12,500 ft). From east to west you can use the Felskinn
cablecar and the Schwarzee cablecar, giving a total of
2,170 m (7,100 ft). So west to east has a net gain of 1,630 m
(5,350 ft).

(4) Perhaps the crucial factor is the Plateau du Couloir.
When taken from west to east it is climbed on foot, early
in the morning, from a hut conveniently placed directly
below it. From east to west the Plateau du Couloir will not
be reached from the Chanrion Hut until midday or early
afternoon, which is an unhealthy time to be descending
such a steep south-facing slope.

Maps and Guidebooks

Cartes Nationales de la Suisse 1:50,000 with ski routes: 282 Martigny, 283 Arolla, 292 Courmayeur, 293 Valpelline and 284 Mischabel.

The 1:25,000 series covers the area Bourg St Pierre to Saas Fee, of which No. 1346 Chanrion is probably the most useful.

High Level Route, Eric Roberts. Published by West Col., Meadows Close, Goring, Reading, Berkshire, RG8 0AP, England (in English).

Haute Route, Hartranft and Koniger. Published by Berg-verlag Rudolf Rother, Munich, West Germany (in German).

The Classic Route

A daily schedule is suggested, but this is obviously open to many variations depending on the actual route taken and on the fitness of the party.

Day 1: Chamonix (Argentière) to the Argentière Hut

From Argentière take the lift system to the Grands Montets. From here there is a magnificent view of the Chardonnet Glacier. Ski down the piste for a short way and then head right (south-east) onto the Rognons Glacier. The sudden move from the safety of the marked ski run onto the crevassed Rognons Glacier, dominated as it is by the North Face of the Aiguille Verte, makes an impressive and slightly daunting start. This section is fairly dangerous due to numerous crevasses and the ice avalanches which come down off the North Face of the Verte.

It is safer, particularly in bad weather, to descend from the Grands Montets, at first on the piste, to the rock at 2,980 m (9,777 ft), bearing 50 degrees true, then 72 degrees true to the couloir which is bounded on the left by a moraine. Traverse out right at about 2,600 m (8,500 ft) and head south-east onto the Argentière Glacier.

Then climb easily on skins to the Argentière Hut.

Day 2: Argentière Hut to Trient Hut

Ski down the right (north-east) bank of the Argentière Glacier and then climb on skins up the Chardonnet Glacier which is fairly steep in its middle section but flattens easily at the top. The descent of the Col du Chardonnet, on its north-east side, is short but steep with a bergschrund at the bottom. It will invariably require the use of a rope, a normal practice being to abseil down with skis on. Rock belays are scarce, so a ski belay is usually used, and the last person either skis or climbs down.

Ski easily round the foot of the Grande Fourche and then climb on skins to the Fenêtre du Saleina, probably doing the last 30 m (100 ft) on foot. An easy traverse on skis leads to the Trient Hut, a traditional stone-built Swiss hut.

Day 3: Trient Hut to Bourg St Pierre

Make a late start, about 8 a.m., so that the snow is in good condition for the descent of the Val d'Arpette. Ski down the right (east) side of the Plateau du Trient, until it is possible to traverse across a steep slope to the Fenêtre du Chamois. This is one of the key sections of the Classic Route, the descent of its north side usually involving a 100 m (330 ft) abseil, for which there is a good flake belay at the top and another one halfway down. This can be avoided by skiing steeply down the right (east) side of the Trient Glacier, crossing the bergschrund at the bottom, and skiing easily to the Col des Ecandies. Traditionally the route went over the Fenêtre du Chamois, as this bergsch-rund used to be impassable, but now it is usually well bridged and it is therefore quicker via the Col des Ecandies. If you have the time, however, the Fenêtre du Chamois is fun!

Given good snow conditions, the ski descent of the Val d'Arpette to Champex can be a delight, to be lingered over and always remembered. And what better way to do this than over a drink at the little auberge at the road-end. Whether or not you stop there, you really must stop at the Swiss Alpine Club hotel and restaurant in Champex, about halfway down on the right. While you relax over a long drink and piece of home-made cake, they will arrange a taxi for you to Bourg St Pierre – buses are also available.

Bourg St Pierre is a charming little village, incon-gruously nestling beside the Great St Bernard highway, complete with motels and juggernauts loaded with Italian cars heading for the markets of Europe. Away from this, in the old village there are delightful little chalets offering cheap accommodation and a small café serving fondue.

Day 4. Bourg St Pierre to Valsorey Hut

A rather long and tedious ascent is made to the Valsorey Hut (guidebook time is four and a half to five hours). The summer path is followed as far as the Chalet d'Amont, but leave it here, as it is very avalanche-prone higher up. Instead climb up through the Valsorey Gorge. From the top of the gorge the hut is visible and it looks quite close, but it takes a deceptively long time to reach it, and the last 400 m (1,300 ft) can provide a test of one's fitness. The final slope (to the west-northwest of the hut) has avalanched on a number of occasions, as well as being very vulnerable to avalanches from above. If in doubt, at 2,600 m (8,530 ft) go straight up the snow slope towards the rocks below the hut, keeping to the right, then climb back left, on the rocks to the two cairns, and then straight up to the hut.

Day 5: Valsorey Hut to Chanrion Hut

This is the big day of the Classic Route, the key section, finally resolved in 1911 by Marcel Kurz and Prof. Roget. Other days are longer, for example Day 7 from the

Vignettes Hut to Zermatt, but none have the delicacy of the traverse to the Plateau du Couloir, none have the feeling of commitment which can be felt on the Col du Sonadon, and, in bad weather, none have such difficult route-finding as the descent of the Mt Durand Glacier.

It is invariably best to go on foot, with crampons, from the hut, with the skis on the rucksack. The traverse to the Plateau du Couloir is straightforward, but exposed, and the final section may be guarded by a cornice and may be icy. It might be best to rope-up for this.

The descent of the Mt Durand Glacier can give some excellent skiing, some of the best of the Haute Route. At about 3,200 m (10,500 ft) there is a large icefall across the centre of the glacier. The normal descent route is to ski straight down from the Col du Sonadon, being wary of the crevasses, and to traverse right at about 3,300 m (10,830 ft) above this icefall. An alternative route, which has fewer crevasses, is to ski south from the col to the pass just south of Pt 3,526 (11,568 ft) and then to ski east south east down a steep slope to join the normal route at the right (south) end of the big icefall.

Care must be taken not to follow the glacier to the bottom, as the final section is very steep and difficult, but to traverse off, right, to Pt 2,735.7 (8,975 ft). From this point the best snow is usually close to the summer path, but, at about 2,400 m (7,874 ft), make a traverse to the right (east), ski down a steepish slope and traverse close under the rocks on the right and down to the bottom.

The Chanrion Hut is tucked away on a small plateau in the middle of some undulating ground. It can be difficult to find in bad visibility, and the 1:25,000 map is useful as it shows all the huts and chalets of La Paume. Pass close to the Chalet Neuf and the Chanrion Hut is 200 m (650 ft) further on.

Day 6: Chanrion Hut to Vignettes Hut

The standard route is up the rather tedious Otemma Glacier. While this is a good way of moving huts in unsettled weather, a far more interesting route is up the Brenay Glacier to the summit of Pigne d'Arolla 3,796 m (12,454 ft). It is a straightforward glacier with one steep section, between 3,000 and 3,200 m (9,842–10,500 ft), which is taken on the left (west) side, usually on foot. The scenery is superb and Pigne d'Arolla, while one of the easiest peaks in the Alps, is well worthwhile, not only for the magnificent views, but also for the good ski descent to the Vignettes Hut.

Alternative Route: if an extra day is available, it is well worthwhile crossing from the Chanrion Hut to the Dix Hut via the Col de Lire Rose, Col du Mt Rouge and Col de Cheilon. It is a straightforward day except in avalanche conditions when it should definitely not be done, as the south slope to the Col du Mt Rouge is prone to avalanche.

There have been some nasty accidents on it, at least one being fatal.

The second day of this alternative is the delightful crossing from the Dix Hut to the Vignettes Hut by ascending the Tsena Refien Glacier, climbing Pigne d'Arolla and skiing down to the Vignettes Hut.

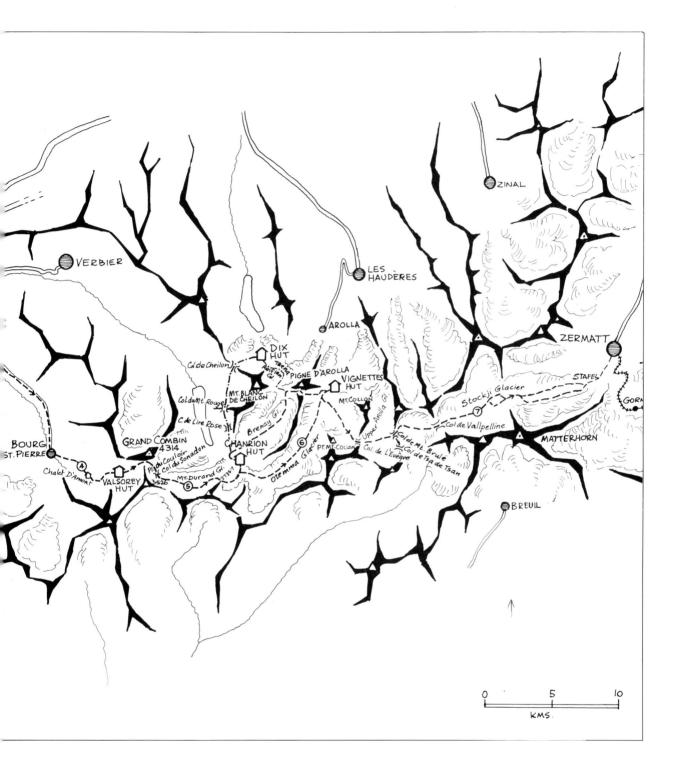

Day 7: Vignettes Hut to Zermatt

This is a long way with a distance of about 30 k (19 miles) and three high cols to cross – l'Evêque 3,392 m (11,128 ft), M. Brulé 3,213 m (10,541 ft) and Valpelline 3,568 m (11,706 ft). The hut should be left early, probably still in the dark between 3 and 4 a.m., in order to reach the Col de Valpelline before midday, in time for reasonable snow conditions on the descent to Zermatt.

When skiing down from the hut, keep your skins inside your clothing so that they are warm and therefore stick well for the ascent to the Col de l'Evêque. With luck you should get a view from this col of the sun rising on Mt

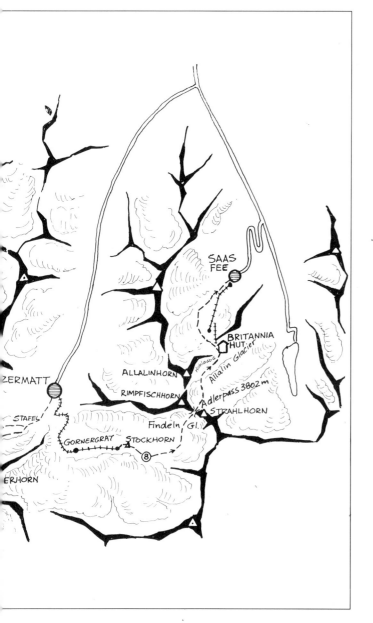

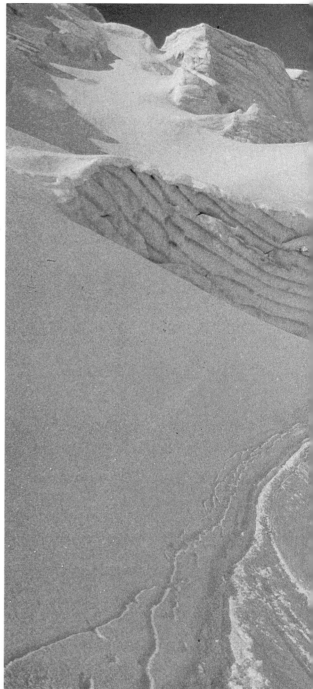

Blanc, but do not dawdle too long here as there is a long way to go, starting with a superb ski down from the col in the magnificent scenery of the Upper Arolla Glacier.

Care must be taken to identify correctly the Col du Mt Brûlé, as it can be mistaken for the more obvious col to the right which is the Col de Tsa de Tsan. The final slope up to the col is steep and may have to be done on foot.

Ski easily down to the Upper Tsa de Tsan Glacier, and, at the point where skins are put on again, it is usual to enjoy the first rest of the day – this is actually in Italy, but there never seems to be much sign of Customs Officers. The ascent to the Col de Valpelline is much longer than it looks (guide book time one and a half to two hours).

During the ski descent to Zermatt snow conditions will progressively deteriorate, and the top section of the Stockji

Glacier must be skied with care as it is heavily crevassed. At about 2,600 m (8,530 ft) there is a choice. The normal route goes down the left (north) side of the Zmutt Glacier and then crosses to the middle of the glacier to Stafel, and for much of the time it may be possible to ski down the track made by people climbing up to the Schönbiel Hut. Without a track, the descent can be slow and tedious. A faster alternative is to cross to the right (south) side taking as high a line as possible under the North Face of the

Fig. 100   Traversing right at 3,300m (10,830 8ft) on the Mt Durand Glacier.

Matterhorn. Having been in the shade for longer, the snow will be harder, and this route is therefore much faster. However, it is open to avalanches from the North Face of the Matterhorn.

The Furri cablecar offers a quick and easy descent to Zermatt, while purists and late arrivals will enjoy the walk down the path, amid the first spring flowers and the smell of the pine woods. A haven for ski mountaineers lies in the centre of Zermatt in the Hotel Bahnhof, run by Paula Biner. Her brother, Bernhard, was a highly respected Zermatt guide who frequently guided English-speaking clients. Since his death in 1965, Paula has continued to offer a warm welcome to mountaineers, and, in recognition for all she does for British ski mountaineers, in 1981, she was elected an Honorary Local Member of the Eagle Ski Club, the premier ski mountaineering club in Great Britain.

Fig. 101. The final steps onto the Col de Valpelline slowly reveal one of the finest views in the Alps, starting with the top of the Matterhorn appearing as a small pyramid on the horizon, and finishing as one finally reaches the crest of the col with the full panorama of all the magnificent 4,000 m (13,000 ft) peaks of Zermatt.

Day 8: Zermatt to Saas Fee

Take the Gornergrat railway, followed by the two-stage cablecar to Stockhorn. A half-hour walk, carrying skis, leads to the top of the Stockhorn 3,532 m (11,588 ft). The ski descent of the Findeln Glacier can give excellent spring snow on the section between 3,400 and 3,200 m (11,150 and 10,500 ft). The long and steep Adler Pass is, at 3,802 m (12,474 ft), one of the highest cols in the Alps and the highest crossed on the Haute Route. The top section is steep, and sometimes icy, but it is seldom realized that the steepest section of all is actually at the very bottom – at 3,200 m (10,500 ft) when climbing from the Findeln Glacier onto the Aletsch Glacier. Due to the movement of the glacier, it has become steeper over recent years and should now invariably be done on foot.

Skis can be left at the Adler Pass, and the Stralhorn 4,190 m (13,746 ft) climbed: a straightforward and convenient four thousander. The ski run down the Allalin

Glacier and across the Hohlaub Glacier is easy-angled and pleasant. The Britannia Hut is a convenient stopping place and enables the Allalinhorn to be climbed the next day, but it is quite normal to ski on down the pistes of Saas Fee, so crossing from Zermatt to Saas Fee in one day.

Variations

(1) Grande Lui: from the Col du Chardonnet on Day (2), instead of crossing the Fenêtre du Saleina, ski down the Saleina Glacier to the Saleina Hut. On the next day climb on skins to the Col du Saleina on the east side of the Grande Lui. Ski down past the À Neuve Hut to La Fouly. Climb up the Val Ferret and cross the Col des Planards, and then ski down to Bourg St Pierre to join the normal route.

Although this misses the Fenêtre du Chamois, it does provide a direct way through to Bourg St Pierre without a road section, and therefore has a lot to recommend it.

(2) Verbier Start: this route is easier than the Classic Route as it misses the Fenêtre du Chamois and the Plateau du Couloir. For this reason it is often favoured by guides guiding unknown clients. Although the route is easier over all, while traversing above the Lac des Dix there can be a long and very serious exposure to avalanche risk.

Day (1): Verbier to Mont Fort Hut. Using the Verbier lift system, ski easily down to the Mont Fort Hut.

Day (2): Mont Fort Hut to Prafleuri Hut. Cross the Col de la Chaux and the Col de Momin, traverse round the north side of the Rosablanche (climbing this en route if desired), and then ski down the Prafleuri Glacier to the unwardened Prafleuri Hut (Swiss one-franc coins needed for the electricity meter).

Day (3): Prafleuri Hut to Dix Hut. Climb to the Col des Roux, ski steeply down to La Barma and then along the side of the Lac des Dix – the debris from large wet-snow avalanches may prove an awkward obstacle. Climb up to the Dix hut.

Day (4): Dix Hut to Vignettes Hut – already described. Rejoin the Classic Route at the Vignettes Hut.

Many do the first two days of the Classic Route and then, on Day (3), go by road from Champex to Verbier and continue from there. Some parties go from the Mont Fort Hut through to the Dix Hut in a day, which is a very long and rather tedious trip, taking the dangerous slopes above the Lac des Dix in the afternoon – the most dangerous time.

We should not forget all the hard work of the early pioneers in finding a way round the south side of the Grand Combin, that is the Haute Route. If you find an easy option which avoids the main difficulties, you may have some good ski mountaineering and you may have a nice time, but you will not have done the Haute Route.

(3) Courmayeur Start: this is a very interesting and direct route, seldom done. It rejoins the Classic Route at Bourg St Pierre for the Plateau du Couloir. I first came across it in 1972 when on the British Alpine Ski Traverse. The senior monk at the Great St Bernard monastery recommended it, and it proved to be excellent advice. We did it east to west, but here it is described from west to east.

Day (1): Courmayeur to Great St Bernard Monastery

Go by road to Entrèves at the foot of the Val Ferret, and then up the Val Ferret as far as La Vachy 1,642 m (5,387 ft). Climb on skins south east to Malatra and continue on the right (south) side of the stream (the summer path is on the other side), to about 2,530 m (8,300 ft), when a rising traverse can be made to the left (north-east) above the rocks and on to the Col Malatra 2,928 m (9,606 ft).

Ski down the foot of the rocky ridge running south-east from Mt Tapie, following the line of the summer path. Traverse across at about 2,480 m to pass below the rocky ridge running south-east from Bella Comba. Climb north and then north-west, between this ridge and the stream on the right to about 2,750 m (9,022 ft), and then head north-east to the unnamed col at 2,816 m (9,239 ft). Ski east down the Comba La Tula to cross the Col St Rhemy 2,560 m (8,399 ft). Ski down north-east and east to pass the huts at Pra di Farco, and then down to the old road and so up to the monastery.

Traditionally, free shelter was given to passing travellers by the monks, but in this modern age it is, understandably, no longer free. Nevertheless it is still well worthwhile staying here, not only for the chance to meet a real brandy-carrying St Bernard dog, but also to drink the monks' tea which is accompanied, not by milk but by red wine!

Day (2): Ski down the old road to the Super St Bernard ski lift. Continue by road to Bourg St Pierre, and so rejoin the Classic Route.

4 The Vanoise, France, by Jeremy Whitehead

This is probably the finest area in the French Alps for the average-standard ski tourer, and it also offers much for the more serious ski mountaineer. It receives an abundant snowfall, is easy of access and is well provided with huts. The relief is mostly not too steep, so that large numbers of the peaks and passes are accessible to the skier. Few of the summits rise to much above 3,600 m (11,800 ft), and most of the huts are around 2,400 m (7,870 ft), so ascents are never too long.

The skiing of Savoie is well known because of the chain of major resorts situated along the upper valley of the Isère, which the French know as the Tarentaise. South and west of the Tarentaise is situated the Vanoise National Park (PNV) which extends down to the Haute Maurienne, or upper valley of the Arc. The park is a sanctuary for animal and plant life, and no development is allowed inside its boundaries. Thanks to these restrictions, the Vanoise remains an admirable area for the summer wanderer and the ski tourer, while the Haute Maurienne, too, retains much of its rustic charm.

This is an area where a great variety of tours is possible. There are simple valley traverses and circuits possible even at Christmas, as well as high-glacier traverses, such as those of the Haute Maurienne and the Glaciers de la Vanoise. There is serious ski mountaineering to be found on the Tarentaise frontier chain, Mont Pourri and its satellites and the Grand Bec de Pralognan. If you can climb the Grande Casse and ski down the Glacier des Grands Couloirs – 365 m (1,200 ft) at 40 degrees – you have arrived as a ski mountaineer! But it is for the novice or intermediate tourer that the area is best suited, with many of its glaciers easy and almost crevasse-free, and slopes which can be skied almost anywhere in good snow conditions.

A glance at the admirable Didier and Richard map of the Vanoise will show how many combinations of routes are possible, as well as giving the positions of the huts. The best approaches into the area are from the east at either Tignes or Val d'Isère, from the north via Moutiers and the Pralognan valley, or from Modane in the south which gives access to the Haute Maurienne.

A recommended tour through the south-eastern part of the area can be taken starting at Termignon, easily reached by bus from Modane. It takes you through the Rocheure valley, the most remote in the park. Later you will see a little of the character of the Haute Maurienne. It is for ski tourers of medium standard, and is designed for those anxious to do a peak each day. It will be found not too stranuous, and allows two nights at each hut, so that ascents can be made with light sacks. It does not take you on extensively crevassed glaciers, but a rope and a couple of axes should be taken for security on some of the ridges, as well as crampons for everyone. The best time is from early April to mid-May.

At Termignon there is a *gite d'etape* (dormitory accommodation) where you can spend the night, and you should carry provisions for the first four nights, as the huts, while fully equipped, are unguarded.

After that the huts are normally guarded, but you should telephone to confirm this and to assure places. The best map to use is the IGN 1:25,000 violet series No. 237 Haute Maurienne, and the routes are described in the Didier and Richard guidebook No. 111: *Massif et Parc National de la Vanoise*.

Recommended Tour

Day 1: Ascend to Refuge Plan du Lac.

Day 2: Col de Lanserlia and Pointe de Lanserlia 2,909 m (9,544 ft) returning to Plan du Lac. An easy day for training and acclimatization.

Day 3: Pointe du Grand Vallon 3,136 m (10,288 ft) with descent to Rocheure Valley and ascent to Refuge de la Femma. An equipment depot can be left while on the mountain, to be picked up on the descent.

Day 4: Pointe de Méan Martin 3,330 m (10,925 ft). An easy ascent with a short scramble to finish. The summit pyramid is rockier than the maps seem to indicate.

Day 5: Ascend Pointe de la Sana 3,435 m (11,270 ft), leaving the sacks near Col des Barmes de l'Ours, and descend to Val d'Isère. Reach Refuge de Prariond, either direct or by taking a half-day lift pass to reach the Pisaillas Glacier and by crossing Col Pers. This day will be too long for many, who will prefer to cross the Col de Rocheure 2,911 m (9,550 ft) to Val d'Isère. The Val side of this pass is steep and prone to windslab.

Day 6: Visit Col de la Galise 2,987 m (9,800 ft) or climb Pointe de la Galise 3,343 m (10,968 ft). The latter is a magnificent viewpoint, but has one very steep slope, short and sometimes hard-frozen.

Fig. 102   Refuge de la Femma, Rocheure valley.

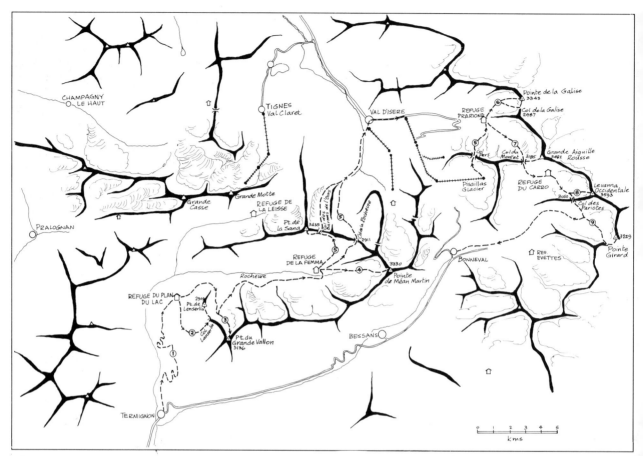

Day 7: Traverse Col du Montet 3,185 m (10,449 ft) to Refuge du Carro. Sacks can be left at the col to make an ascent of Grande Aiguille Rousse 3,482 m (11,424 ft).

Day 8: Ascent of Levanna Occidentale 3,593 m (11,788 ft). A short ascent with a finish on foot. A good chance to sunbathe at the hut.

Day 9: Traverse Col des Pariotes 3,050 m (10,006 ft) and ascend Pointe Girard 3,259 m (10,692 ft). Descend direct to Bonneval. The summit slopes are steep and need confidence to ski if the snow is hard. It is usually possible to ski most of the way to Bonneval.

Such a tour can only give an indication of what this district has to offer. You still have the rustic charm of the Champagny Valley, and that of Poturin. Then there is the Peclet-Polset massif with its classic Glacier de Gebroulaz, the Averole Valley and hut with a range of ascents, and the remote cirque of Le Clou. After that there are the links with the Gran Paradiso area in Italy to be explored, via the Col de Bassagne or Col de Rhemes-Golette.

Maps: Didier and Richard No. 11.

Fig. 104   Touring party in descent.

5 The Dauphiné, France, by Jeremy Whitehead

This area, known to the French as the Massif des Ecrins, or Les Disans, is very different from any other area of the French Alps. Here you find steep rocky peaks, joined to form high ridges, with deep, steep-sided valleys in between. You have none of the broad, easy passes of the Bernese Oberland, Pennine Alps or Vanoise, but abrupt narrow gaps, often with steep and rocky sides, which are not ski passages at all. Ski routes of any sort have to be looked for; there are few easy ones, and this is essentially a district for confirmed and experienced ski mountaineers who can judge conditions correctly.

The ideal time to visit the Dauphiné is in May, when you can expect the big avalanches to have come down already and spring snow conditions to be found. My trips have been in April when bad weather is apt to occur. With so few easy options, much time can be spent hut-bound, and one needs patience (and a good book in the rucksack!). However, when conditions are good, the ski mountaineering is superb.

The huts in the Dauphiné tend to be without wardens or cooking facilities, so it is necessary to carry the full paraphernalia of stoves, fuel, pans, plates and cutlery as well as your food. Careful planning is necessary to avoid carrying too much weight. The Refuges du Glacier Blanc and de l'Alpe may be wardened over the Easter period, and others at weekends in May, so it is wise to ask locally.

The main starting points are La Grave in the north, Vallouise in the south east and La Bérarde in the centre of the region, although Valgaudemar in the south has its attractions, and is less frequented. Access may have its problems, for the road to La Bérarde is sometimes closed beyond St Christophe and that in Valgaudemar beyond La Chapelle. It is sometimes not possible to drive from Vallouise to Allefroide (deserted in winter). The skier in Dauphiné has to be prepared for a long walk in.

La Grave has the advantage of offering easier ascents to the north, such as Pic Blanc du Galibier and Aiguille du Goleon, as well as the classic Dôme de la Lauze, now spoilt by lift access. Vallouise, too, has some easier tours to limber up on, and offers an escape to the pistes of Puy-St-Vincent should conditions be unfavourable. At La Bérarde, once you reach it, there is the CAF Centre which is,

in principle, open and, in any case, has a winter room. A small hotel there is sometimes open, but you cannot buy provisions. At La Grave and Vallouise there are *gites d'etape* (dormitory accommodation) as well as hotels and provision shops.

The classic ski summits in the Dauphiné are the Dôme de la Lauze, the Brèche de la Meije, Col du Clot des Cavales, La Grande Ruine, Les Rouies and the Dôme de Neige des Ecrins. Other routes can be found in the Didier and Richard guidebook No. 106, *Massif des Ecrins-Haute Dauphiné*. The Didier and Richard 1:50,000 map of the same title is useful for planning, but on the mountain the IGN 1:25,000 violet series maps are essential (nos. 241, 242 and possibly 243). Be sure to obtain the second edition sheets, which are marked with the ski routes.

It is only in recent years that skiers have worked out a continuous traverse through the whole of the Dauphiné, and most involve at least one night in a bivouac. The route described is one which has become classic, and takes you through the highest part of the region. When we did this in April 1974, we were fortunate to have perfect weather and snow conditions. Although we omitted the summits, the descents, each different in character, were a fascinating exercise in route finding. I count these as perhaps my finest four days on skis.

We took the traverse from Vallouise to La Grave, so that descents were on north- or west-facing slopes, but many prefer to take it in the reverse direction. The descents are uniformly steep, and require a good standard of skiing and judgement of the snow. The full range of ski mountaineering equipment is essential. It would be unwise to attempt this tour before mid-April, and May is probably the best month.

Recommended Tour

Day 1: Vallouise-Refuge des Ecrins or Refuge Glacier Blanc. The road is usually open to Ailefroide or beyond. If not, you will have a long day, or must spend the night in the diminutive Refuge Cézanne.

Day 2: Dôme de Neige des Ecrins 4,015 m (13,172 ft) – Refuge des Ecrins. This is often in poor condition and may be too much for an unacclimatized party. Roche Faurio 3,730 m (12,237 ft) offers a good alternative.

Day 3: Traverse of Col Emile Pic, with ascent to Refuge Adèle Planchard. A start from Refuge des Ecrins should allow time to climb Pic de Neige Cordier 3,613 m (12,150 ft) on foot, or Roche Emile Pic 3,585 m (11,762 ft) on skis. The descent is not marked on either map nor described in the guidebook. Keep always to the right to find the easiest route. The re-ascent to Adèle Planchard can sometimes be shortened by climbing a couloir north west of Pt 2,472 m (8,110 ft).

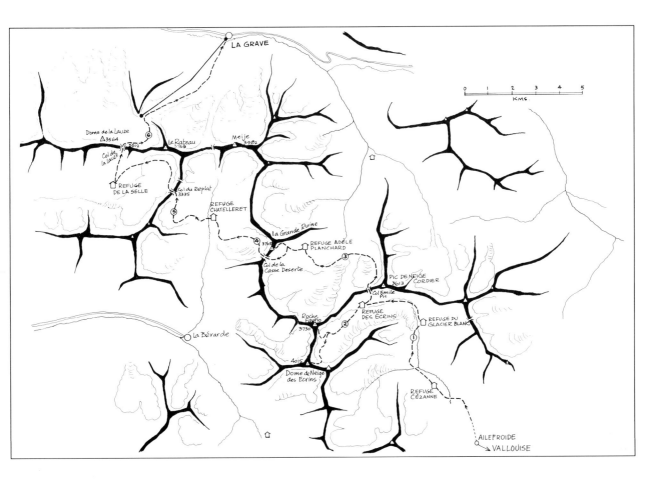

Day 4: La Grande Ruine 3,765 m (12,352 ft) and traverse of Col de la Casse Deserte to Refuge Chatelleret: a classic ascent to one of the finest viewpoints in the district. The east side of the col is steep and may require crampons, and there is a big crevasse on the descent to the west that is sometimes awkward.

·Day 5: Traverse of Col du Replat 3,335 m (10,941 ft) to Refuge de la Selle. There is a steep ascent to a curious gap between the two Têtes du Replat. In descending, keep well over to the north bank of the Glacier de la Selle to avoid the icefall.

Day 6: Traverse of Col de la Lauze 3,512 m (11,522 ft) to La Grave. This starts with a continuously steep ascent, which we were able to make in crampons. The descent is now usually well tracked, and offers fine views of the north flanks of La Meije and Le Rateau.

If the traverse is taken in the reverse direction, you can profit by using the cablecar up from La Grave. As descents will be on south- and east-facing slopes they will have to be well timed. It would be worthwhile to vary the second day by crossing the Brèche du Rateau and ascending to the Brèche de la Meije before descending to the Refuge Chatelleret. Another advantage is that you would tackle the Dôme de Neige when more fit and acclimatized. The best descent from Refuge Glacier Blanc is to traverse the Col de Monêtier to Monêtier-les-Bains, or to traverse Pic du Rif to Vallouise.

Map: Didier and Richard No. 6.

6 The Ötztal, Austria

As an area to visit for one's first experience of mountaineering, downhill skiing or ski mountaineering, I can hardly think of a better one than the Ötztal. For all these sports it has magnificent facilities, ideally suited to the novice or intermediate.

In summer there are easy hut-to-hut tours, some involving straightforward glacier travel; a great selection of mountains climbable by easy rock ridges; and a few typical Tyrolean north faces – snow and ice routes at 50–55 degrees and around 300 m (1,000 ft) long. The downhill skier can enjoy traditional Tyrolean hospitality in places like Sölden, Hochsolden, Vent and Obergurgl and provided you do not overindulge in the traditional hospitality, the Austrian Ski School is one of the best in the world. For the ski mountaineer there are many easy peaks of around 3,500 m (11,480 ft) with some good glacier skiing.

The area is very well served by excellently appointed huts (most of which are owned by the German Alpine Club). In March, April and May the main ski mountaineering routes are generally well tracked, so route-finding is seldom a major problem. In any case, the peaks are relatively low, the glaciers are straightforward, and the weather is generally good.

Access to the area is easy: one can arrive in the afternoon at Sölden, Vent or Obergurgl, and still be in a hut for that night.

The huts need a special mention, as they are some of the best in the Alps: invariably with excellent food, draught beer and good wine – sometimes even served by a waitress! A straightforward meal (*Bergsteigeressen*) is always available in the evenings – cheap, and strictly no choice. If you feel like steak and chips, it will probably be available, but expect to pay more for it than you would in the valley. For those who like a hot bath at the end of the day's skiing – well, you might just be lucky!

The Hochjoch Hospitz is an extraordinary old hut, hardly changed at all since first built in 1927, with a creaking wooden staircase, thin taps and huge steel bowls in the corridors for washing, and, in the winter room, a temperamental and very smoky wood-burning stove.

In April 1975 I was there with a party and we were caught by a snowstorm. In these conditions the hut is a real trap, but we passed the time pleasantly, playing bridge, drinking the guardian's Jager Tee, and sleeping. Jager Tee is bad for bridge, but good for sleeping. The recipe is: into a mug put two tots of schnapps, two tots of rum, and one glass of red wine. Fill up the mug with hot tea or water, and add sugar to taste.

After two days the snow stopped. The safest way out seemed to me to be over the Guslar Joch to the Vernagt Hut and down to Vent. The alternative was the summer path which is the most direct route between the hut and Vent. It is called the Titzentalerweg, after the man who engineered it. According to the map it appeared to pass through a very steep gorge, and I had discounted it as a possible way out, particularly in view of the avalanche risk.

Then the word went round the hut that three Germans were going to descend that way. I had a talk with the warden, who confirmed that this was so, and advised me that we would be fine if we followed the Germans who were not only very experienced alpinists, but also knew the way.

Talking to the three Germans I soon gathered that they had not been down the path before, and that their local knowledge was no better than mine. Also I got the impression that we were probably a stronger party than they were. I went back to the warden. He was adamant that the route would be fine.

'Follow the summer path. A bit steep, *ja*; but no problem . . .'

'What about the avalanche risk?' I asked.

'If you leave now, there is no problem of avalanches.'

I did not quite follow this, but hut wardens can speak with a lot of authority. Maybe I had missed something obvious. In retrospect I think I had – he had probably run out of food, and wanted rid of us. I went outside and watched people starting the 700 m (2,300 ft) climb to the Guslar Joch. That looked dreadfully hard work. So we set off with some trepidation down towards the gorge, with the Germans following.

The path itself was, of course, buried under several metres of snow, but I tried to stay as near the line of it as possible, as the guardian had been adamant that we had to enter the gorge on the line of the path. It was 2½ km (1½ miles) from the hut to the start of the gorge. On the way there was an enormous amount of deep new snow. It was rather warm and very quiet. We were well spread out, in view of the obvious avalanche risk, and I listened to the reassuring bleep of my Autophon. I began to regret ever leaving the hut . . . but then, the guardian had said it would be all right.

We came to the gorge, the sides of which were so steep that only a small amount of fresh snow had managed to stick on them. So maybe the avalanche risk was less here, except from above, of course. The one place where the fresh snow had drifted in large quantities was on the path, to such an extent that there was no visible trace of it. There were only two signs to guide us: one was the fact that every so often the snow would suddenly collapse under one's weight, and I presume this was when we were on the

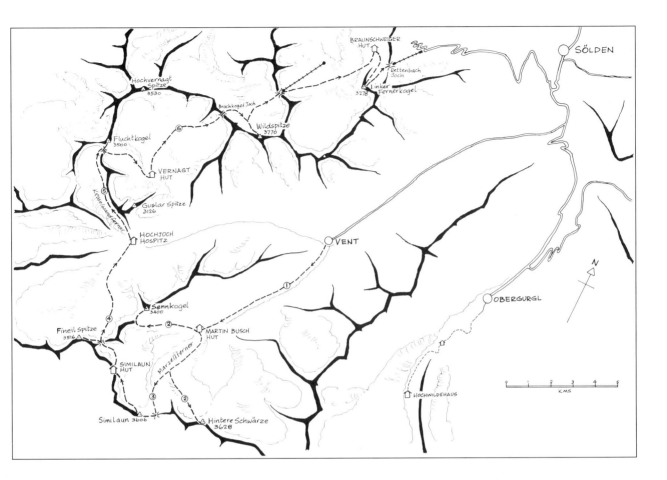

greater depth of drifted fresh snow; and the other was the intermittent tracks of a small animal, which I trustingly thought would keep to the line of the path, and which I found strangely reassuring.

We were soon high above the gorge, and the slope was terrifyingly steep. We edged slowly along, each of us secretly wishing he was somewhere else.

One section was so steep and exposed that we joined the three climbing ropes together and ran out a fixed rope of 137 m (450 ft), with everyone clipped onto it by their chest harnesses.

The guardian was right: we did get down safely. After a lot of back-slapping and arm-pumping from the three Germans, who by this time were like life-long brothers, we skied on down to Vent and celebrated our continuing life in the cosy bar of the Vent Hotel. While we were there the guardian telephoned to see if we had made it – so maybe he had been worried after all! Nevertheless, it was a nice gesture.

The morals of the story are many, not least: do not descend the Titzentalerweg in winter!

Access: the nearest airport is Innsbruck. A good rail service goes down the Inn Valley, with convenient stations at Landeck, Imst and Ötztal. Buses connect these stations

with villages up the valleys, of which the following are the most convenient – Sölden, Vent and Obergurgl.

Maps: *Alpenvereinskarte* 1:25,000 series. 30/2 Weisskugel-Wildspitze, 30/1 Gurgl, 31/1 Hochstubai.

Recommended Tours
The maps already referred to are so good that it is not necessary to give any detailed route description.

Tour (1)

Day 1: Vent to the Vernagt Hut.

Days 2–4: From the Vernagt Hut there are some excellent peaks which can be done in a day, e.g. Guslar Spitze 3,126 m (10,256 ft), Fluchtkogel 3,500 m (11,483 ft), and the Hochvernagt Spitze 3,530 m (11,580 ft). During these days, you will get to know the area, equipment and fitness problems can be resolved, and you need only carry a light rucksack.

Day 5: Vernagt Hut–Brochkogel Joch–Wildspitze (3,770 m/12,369 ft)–Mittelberg Joch–Braunschweiger Hut.

Day 6: Braunschweiger Hut–Linker Fernerkogel (3,278 m/10,754 ft)–Rettenbach Joch–Sölden.

Tour 2.

The Ötztal lends itself to an excellent traverse or round tour. The longer version of this starts from Obergurgl and goes via the Hochwilde Haus to the Martin Busch Hut. The slightly shorter version is to start from Vent, as follows:

Day 1: Vent to Martin Busch Hut.

Day 2: A day tour from the Martin Busch Hut, e.g. the Sennkogel 3,400 m (11,155 ft) or the Hintere Schwarze 3,628 m (11,903 ft).

Day 3: Martin Busch Hut–Marzellferner–Similaun Joch––traverse the Similaun 3,606 m (11,830 ft)–Similaun Hut.

Day 4: Similaun Hut–Fineil Spitze 3,516 m (11,535 ft)–Hochjoch Hospitz.

Day 5: Hochjoch Hospiz–Kesselwandferner–Ob. Guslar Joch–Fluchtkogel 3,500 m (11,480 ft)–Vernagt Hut.

Day 6: Vernagt Hut–Brochkogel Joch–Wildspitze 3,770 m (12,369 ft)–Mittelberg Joch–Braunschweiger Hut.

Day 7: Braunschweiger Hut–Linker Fernerkogel 3,278 m (10,754 ft)–Rettenbach Joch–Sölden.

7 The Stubai, Austria

The Stubai mountains are part of the Austrian Tyrol, lying between the Ötzal to the west and the Zillertal to the east. Being so close together, the Ötzal and the Stubai have many features in common: mountains between 3,000–3,500 m (9,800–11,500 ft), excellent huts, easy access and many fine glaciers which, on the trade routes, do not present too many difficulties. It is an ideal area in which to cut one's teeth.

Many of the mountains can be approached from more than one hut, which means that hut-to-hut traverses, combined with a peak, are a feature of this area. In fine weather there are invariably tracks on the more popular routes.

The Stubai Glacier lift system has brought downhill skiing to the area around the Dresdner Hut. There are the usual pros and cons of such developments. Ski mountaineers may wish to use it for training at the beginning of the tour, or in order to gain access to one of the huts. But mostly it spoils the isolation which ski mountaineers seek

and enjoy. My own feelings are either to use the lifts or to keep well away from them. It has always seemed to me rather perverse (not to mention masochistic) to flounder up on skins right by the side of a mechanical lift system, rather as if pretending it is not there.

Access: possible from several directions, with the north-east being the most popular.
North: Gries in Sellrain and Lusens.
North-east: Neustift and Ranalt in the Stubaital.
East: Gschnitz and Pflersch.
South-east: Maiern in Ridnauntal.
West: Sölden and Langenfeld in the Ötztal.

Maps: *Alpenvereinskarte* 1:25,000 No. 31/1 Hochstubai (with ski routes).

Recommended tours
The first tour is recommended for those visiting the area for the first time and for those fairly new to ski mountaineering. By spending a few days at the Franz Senn Hut, you can get a feel for the area without the commitment of a hut-to-hut traverse. The second tour is a traverse or round tour of the Stubai, taking a line over the highest cols and climbing the main mountains.

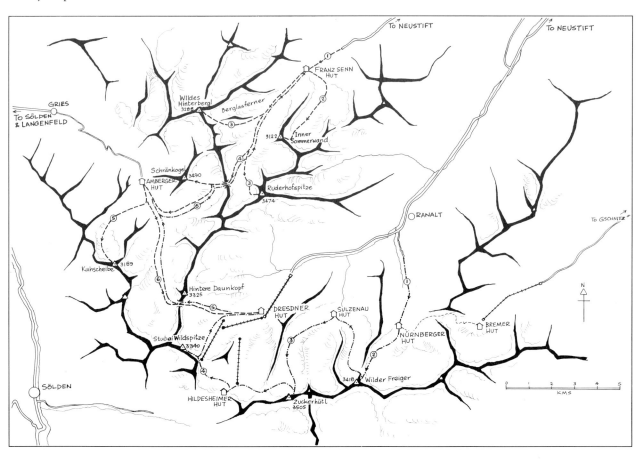

Tour (1)

Day 1: Neustift to the Franz Senn Hut 2,145 m (7,037 ft).

Days 2 and 3: There are several peaks which can be done in a day from the Franz Senn Hut, e.g. Ruderhofspitze 3,479 m (11,414 ft), Inner Sommerwand 3,142 m (10,308 ft), Schränkogel 3,490 m (11,450 ft) and the Wildes Hinterbergl 3,288 m (10,787 ft) (up via the Turm Schart and down via the Berglasferner).

Day 4: Franz Senn Hut to the Amberger Hut 2,135 m (7,005 ft), climbing the Schränkogel 3,490 m (11,450 ft) on the way.

Day 5: Amberger Hut–Kuhscheibe 3,189 m (10,462 ft)–Amberger Hut.

Day 6: Amberger Hut–Daunjoch–Hintere Daunkopf 3,225 m (10,581 ft)–Dresdner Hut.

Day 7: Dresdner Hut to the valley, using the lift if there is little snow.

Round Tour

Day 1: Neustift–Ranalt–Nurmberger Hut.

Day 2: Nurnberger Hut–Wilder Freiger 3,418 m (11,214 ft) (a beautiful mountain with the largest glaciers in the Stubai and superb views)–Sulzenau Hut.

Day 3: Sulzenau Hut–Sulzenauferner–Zuckerhütl 3,505 m (11,499 ft) (Sugar Loaf – the highest peak in the Stubai)–Pfaffenjoch–Hildesheimer hut 2,899 m (9,511 ft).

Day 4: Hildesheimer Hut–Stubai Wildspitze 3,340 m (10,958 ft) (fine pointed peak), or the Schaufelspitze 3,333 m (10,935 ft) (easier)–Dresdner Hut 2,302 m (7,552 ft).

Day 5: Dresdner Hut–Daunjoch–Hintere Daunkop 3,225 m (10,581 ft)–Amberger Hut.

Day 6: Amberger Hut–Schränkogel 3,490 m (11,450 ft)–Franz Senn Hut.

Day 7: Franz Senn Hut to the valley (Neustift).

Fig. 108 Climbing the Chardonnet Glacier, Switzerland. North Face of Les Droites behind.

The Gran Paradiso, Italy, by John Cleare

If you are an Italian, then the Gran Paradiso, culminating point of the Eastern Graians massif, must be an important peak to you, for it is the highest – indeed the only – 4,000 m (13,000 ft) mountain entirely in Italy. But it is no less worthy if you are a foreigner. An impressive mountain hung with fine glaciers, surrounded by a chain of other shapely peaks, the Gran Paradiso rises to 4,061 m (13,323 ft), from a beautiful area designated and protected as a National Park, a rare combination in the modern European Alps!

The Parco Nazionale del Gran Paradiso is the only region in the Alps where the once common steinbock or bouquetin survive in large numbers – there are some 5,000 head – besides large numbers of chamois. Often the creatures are relatively tame and are a common sight both in summer and winter. Ironically, the reason for today's great wealth of flora and fauna is the origin of the park as the exclusive hunting preserve of the Italian kings.

The Paradiso will interest the ski mountaineer in particular because its location in the Val d'Aosta Region in the far north-west corner of Italy, jutting into the Piemonte plains as an offshoot of the main Alpine watershed, allows easy winter access from the Geneva/Chamonix area – through the nearby Mont Blanc tunnel. More important, perhaps, it stands in the rain shadow of the high Dauphiné, Tarentaise and Maurienne ranges of the south-western Alps and often enjoys fine weather when everywhere else is socked in.

That was the reason I first visited the Paradiso early one May. Rain poured from leaden clouds clinging to the Chamonix rooftops, the streets were awash, and our projected ski ascent of Mont Blanc was impossible. Apparently conditions elsewhere in the Alps were as bad. We decided to drive down to Aosta to eat *gelatti*, drink the wine, and absorb the culture.

Through the tunnel in Courmayeur the rain was less ferocious, and above the famous Roman gate of Aosta the sky was blue. Grivola, northernmost peak of the Paradiso range, rose, a white pyramid, above meadows already lush and green. Such opportunities must be snatched greedily and by evening we were enjoying an excellent dinner in the little *albergo* at Pont 1,960 m (6,430 ft), hardly even a hamlet, where the mountain road disappeared into the snowdrifts at the head of the narrow Val Savarenche,

below the western slopes of the Gran Paradiso itself. Outside in the gloaming large-horned male steinbock butted each other in an age-old combat ritual.

The classic ascent in the range, in either summer or winter, is naturally the Gran Paradiso itself. The regular route, on foot or on skis, is up the glacier-hung western flank, graded in summer as *facile* and 'highly recommended'. It was said to be a fine ski route. We decided to go for it if the weather lasted.

The Rifugio Vittorio Emmanuele 11, below the west flank of the Paradiso, is only 762 m (2,500 ft) above Pont, so there was no great hurry in the morning. We skied over flat meadows alive with new-born streams bubbling through the drifts, following ski tracks into a wide couloir leading through a band of pine woods and into a steep craggy hillside. The couloir narrowed and the tracks led out right to a series of zig-zags on what must be, in summer, a fine foot path.

Once off the trail, it would be easy to become crag-bound hereabouts. In places the snow was patchy and we had to carry our skis. Then wider and more gentle slopes led to open moraine landscape from which rose a line of shapely ice-clad north faces – Ciarforon, Becca di Monciair and Cima di Breuil.

In this impressive situation stands the *rifugio*, a modern structure of curved aluminium – a three-story Nissen hut – offering 'restaurant and hotel service', bunks for 110 visitors and floor space for plenty more! It was busy when we arrived and full by the evening, but we were made very welcome. We appeared to be the first British visitors of the season, although there were skiers from all over the Alps, drawn, many told us, by the area's reputation for better weather, which all confirmed was terrible elsewhere.

We were away from the hut by 6.30 a.m., into a misty and overcast morning, with almost 1,340 m (4,400 ft) to climb. Our route was obvious for we were by no means the first party on the mountain. A gentle ascent northwards, round the base of the crags above the hut and over a large moraine, led into the hollow below the snout of the Ghiacciaio del Gran Paradiso, invisible under uniform snow slopes. We saw not a crevasse as we skinned up the glacier which steepened as our route curved rightwards beneath a line of cliffs. The snow was excellent, crisp and firm. In such conditions, with no objective dangers and the body working smoothly to a steady rhythm, the mind is free to wander and wonder.

After some 610 m (2,000 ft) we bore left again above the cliffs. Wider slopes and terraces fell away leftward to a deep glacial hollow beneath the formidable-looking south-west face of the now cloud-wreathed Paradiso itself. On the right a line of crags and pinnacles marked the crest of

Fig. 109   The Vittorio Emmanuele II Hut.

Fig. 110   Approaching Il Roc 4,026 m (13,209 ft) high on the Gran Paradiso.

the west ridge of the Becca di Moncorve. Now we were in the wind. I shivered at the suddenly cold sweat on my back. A few snowflakes swirled around us.

There were a few obvious crevasses up here, but we felt the rope was unnecessary, and some three hours after leaving the hut we found ourselves skiing gingerly along a narrow snow arête – obviously the key section of the ascent – leading onto the final glacier plateau. At the far end a party, already descending, waited for us to pass. Ahead loomed the great pinnacle of Il Roc 4,026 m (13,209 ft), with snow flurries sweeping over the saddle between it and the final rocky summit ridge.

In the scant shelter of Il Roc we paused to review the situation. We were just 35 m (114 ft) below the well-known Madonna on Paradiso's top. A short steep slope above us, cut by a bergshrund, led to the summit rocks.

We zig-zagged warily into the lower glacier valley and then swooped down it, only noticing when we paused to draw breath that down here the snow had stopped. It had taken us five hours to reach Il Roc. It took us two hours to get down. By 2.30 p.m. we were warm and dry and drinking beer in the Vittorio Emmanuele Hut as the first gusts of snow rattled the windows.

Ski mountaineering is most enjoyable when combined with a tour or traverse. There are several good ski routes in the Gran Paradiso Range, but not all the glaciers are easy. The best tours seek to avoid the worst crevassed areas, to delight in the great descents offered by glaciers like the Gran Paradiso, but, of course, this is not always possible.

The classic trip is the traverse of the range from south-west to north-east, from Val d'Isère in France to Cogne in Italy, a five-day journey that can be broken in several places, is not always straightforward, but crosses superb and little-frequented country. The comfortable Prariond Hut above Val d'Isère is the starting point and the first stage crosses the frontier at the 2,978 m (9,770 ft) Col de la Vache above it. The route down into the head of the Italian Nivolet Valley is awkward, for two steep snow couloirs are the only way through lines of cliff. It takes over seven hours to reach the unguardianed Chavasso Hut.

An easier stage leads to the Vittorio Emmanuele Hut via the Punta Foura and the glaciers around the head of the Vallone di Seiva above Pont. From the hut both La Tresenta (3,609 m/11,841 ft – five hours return) and the Gran Paradiso can be climbed. The lengthy third stage is usually combined with the Paradiso ascent, and, on the descent from 3,353 m (11,000 ft) contours round the western glaciers of the massif to reach the little Sberna Bivouac below the west ridge of Herbetet.

Now follows another crux section round the northern flank of the Gran Zerz, before a good run leads down to the Vittorio Sella Hut. The principal difficulty is locating couloirs to cross the rocky ridges that radiate from Herbetet and Gran Serz. There are several routes down to Cogne from the hut and a powerful party might even include, on foot, the fairly serious east-north-east rock ridge (summer grade III+) of Grivola (3,964 m/13,022 ft) – the second highest and arguably the most magnificent peak in the range.

Certainly the Gran Paradiso area has much to recommend it for a spring skiing visit: high and interesting, easily accessible from other well-known ski mountaineering areas, less frequented by the British and with possibly better weather – and all in joyful Italy!

Map: *Kompass* 1:50,000 No. 86 'Gran Paradiso + Valle d'Aosta'

Guidebook: *Guide des Raids à Ski*, Pierre Merlin (Publ. Denoel, Paris)

Through the mist and the falling snow we could see several large parties jockeying around those last rocks. We decided not to join them: the day was too cold and life too short. The Madonna could wait.

The descent was superb for the snow conditions were so good; a thin layer of new powder on crisp spring snow. I approached the arête apprehensively, but it went easily, even though the narrow delicate section led immediately into a series of steep tight turns on the edge of all things.

9 Ski Touring in the Pyrenees by J. G. R. Harding

The Pyrenees, extending some 450 km (280 miles) from the Atlantic to the Mediterranean, divide France from Spain and are Europe's second-largest range of mountains. Whereas the Alps were always a crossways, the Pyrenees have presented a physical barrier marking the frontier between Gaul and Hispania, Christendom and Islam, northern and Latin Europe.

Stronghold of the Basques and all manner of half-forgotten montagnard cultures, the Pyrenees retain a wildness and separateness now sadly gone from so much of the Alps.

The Pyrenees measure their high mountains in 3,000 m (10,000 ft) rather than 4,000 m (13,000 ft) peaks. There are almost ninety of these, with Aneto, the crown of the Maladetta, the culmination. But mere height is only one measure of mountain character. Verticality is another and this characterizes the High Pyrenees. The axis of the main range broadly follows the frontier, but there are any number of transverse and lateral ridges forming massifs or individual peaks. In the limestone areas the mountains are sculpted into enormous cirques, split by canyons and deep valleys. The French Pyrenees, arising abruptly from the plain of Gascony, can only be reached via deep gorges or *garves* which, higher up, give way to valley basins bounded by steep peaks. The Spanish Pyrenees, which include the highest massifs of Maladetta and Posets, descend gradually to the plateau of Aragon and Navarre and are spilt by transverse valleys creating their own communities isolated from one another and often from the world outside.

The Pyrenees boast the highest ice cave and biggest limestone cirques in Europe – that of Gavarnie is 10 km (6 miles) across and 1,800 m (5,900 ft) high – and the deepest cave in the world. No generalizations can properly describe such a variegated area but characteristic of the Central Pyrenees are both granite peaks with jagged ridges and limestone precipices, aiguilles, cirques and canyons. Here too are vertiginous gorges and prodigious waterfalls but, above all, a multiplicity of lakes, some large but mainly small, like the beads of a necklace, that thread the valleys.

Pyrenean weather is oceanic rather than Alpine. this imparts its special character. Summer is generally settled but in winter, with Atlantic squalls and depressions dominant, the weather can alternate dramatically from day to day, from the best to the very worst. The climate changes from west to east, and markedly from north to south.

On the French side, heavy precipitation produces magnificent forests of both oak and pine. The Spanish side, dry and torrid in summer, presents a wholly different southern face where the dwarf pines of the upper treeline add enchantment to the landscape.

There are many fine summer climbs in the Pyrenees, but at this time the mountains are parched; they assume a new character as winter mountains. Although glaciated areas are few, winter snow cover is extensive and transforms the benign peaks, passes and valleys of summer into demanding ascents, serious obstacles and hazards. The touring season spans January to May and even June in the highest massifs. If averages exist, April tends to be unsettled and March offers the best snow conditions. But in the Pyrenean winter no wholly predictable pattern of weather can be guaranteed.

As a consequence of its weather, the Pyrenees have an unenviable reputation for avalanches, particularly in the steep-sided French valleys, among which Gaube, Ossoue, Couplan, Moudang and Rioumajiou are notorious. Local weather advice is available from local guides bureaux, or the excellent Pyrenean gendarmerie, in most major valley centres, e.g. Aspe, Cauterets, St Lary, Bareges and Luchon.

The system of huts is less well developed than in the Alps. This lends a certain charm to ski touring but detracts from comfort and complicates logistics. The larger French huts, owned by either CAF, PNP (Pyrenean National Park) or privately, are adequately described in the various guidebooks and indicated on IGN maps. But not all are open in winter and some winter quarters are cramped and primitive. The better huts are not necessarily within the compass of a day's easy touring, but can be supplemented by shepherds' summer quarters, or *granges*, and any number of *cabanes* which are usually rude concrete structures. In Spain, standards are even more variable. Some huts, particularly in Catalunyd, are unexceptionable, others mere hovels. Whether in France or Spain cooking equipment and bedding should be carried and bivouac equipment is essential on the main range tours.

Maps

There is a wide variety of French maps to choose from including:

(a) IGN 100 m series: 4 maps. Useful to get an overall picture of the range, valley centres, roadheads and for general route-planning.

(b) IGN 50 m series: 22 maps providing a good overall picture of land forms and terrain, but poor on hut detail, outdated in some respects and with no ski routes marked.

(c) IGN R P 50 series: 9 maps now cover the whole range. Up to date, with huts and principal walking routes clearly marked, but cartography somewhat less well defined than standard 50 m series. Best buy overall.

SKI TOURING IN THE PYRENEES   127

(d) IGN Tourist 25 m series: maps 274, 275 and 276 cover the PNP. Principal ski routes marked. Best buy for PNP area.

The Spanish maps are generally inferior to the French and frequently unreliable. However, for touring in such areas as Posets, Maledetta and Ribagorca and the Spanish *Editorial Alpine* series is indispensible.

Guidebooks

An extensive Pyrenean bibliography exists but modern English guidebooks are a comparatively new phenomenon. West Col Publications has produced four guides, intended mainly for walking climbers, but useful in some respects for ski touring. These are *Pyrenees West, Pyrenees East, Andor/Cerdagne* and *Pyrenees High Level Route*. Another useful book in this category is Kev Reynolds's *Mountains of the Pyrenees* (Cicerone Press, Britain).

In French, there are four FFM ski mountaineering guides covering the principal ski routes of the western and central Pyrenees: (1) *Pays Basque, Aspe et Ossau* (2) *Balaitous, Marcadau* (3) *Cauterets, Vignemale, Gavarnie* and (4) *d'Argeles to Val d'Aran*. These guides, together with the CAF's *Haute Route d'Hiver des Pyrenees*, are all edited by Ollivier and indispensable for serious touring. They are not readily available in Britain or the USA, so application should be made to the Librarie Parisienne, 14 rue St Louis, 64000 Pau, France. In Spanish the Club Alpi Catula (Paradis 10, Barcelona (2)) produces a wide range of mountaineering guide books.

SKI TOURING

In the Alps, ski mountaineering was the precursor to modern ski racing. In the Pyrenees, both were later developments. The High Level Route (Haute Route) on ski, from Chamonix to Zermatt, itself following an 1861 Alpine Club summer route, was first completed in 1911. By contrast Charles Laporte's classic Pyrenean traverse from Canigou to Pierre St Martin, the equivalent of a major Alpine ski traverse was only achieved in 1968. The Pyrenees cannot rival the scale, variety and accessibility of the Alps and have nothing that readily compares with the High Level route. Lacking major glaciation there are few continuous downhill runs that compare in length. But, as the Alps have developed, so have the attractions of lesser ranges been enhanced.

The more ambitious Pyrenean tours, particularly those along the main range, are essentially mountaineering on skis and not to be undertaken lightly. The terrain tends to be steeper than the Alps, with a greater range of ascent and descent in the course of a day. Route-finding across remote and complicated country can be handicapped by inaccurate maps. The scarcity of good huts in some areas necessitates self-sufficiency and heavy packs, while the fickle Atlantic climate conspires to produce prolonged bad weather, uncertain snow conditions and high avalanche risk. Overall, expect nothing for certain and accept that the plans so carefully laid at home may have to be changed en route to take into account weather and conditions.

But it is this very remoteness, lack of facilities and uncertainty which lends the range its special flavour and casts a spell over its devotees. Except in the vicinity of the major valley bases, it is still unusual to meet other touring parties.

Although the entire range lends itself to touring, the track bounded by the Lescun Cirque to the west and the Val d'Aran to the east is the area broadly corresponding to that covered by the FFM guidebooks. Access to the range is best from the French side, whether by road, rail or air. Pau and Lourdes are the principal railheads: Cauterets, Gavarnie, Bareges, St Lary, Luchon and Vialla the main valley bases and ski centres. Other useful roadheads include Lescun, Urdos, Gabas and Heas. Apart from the Val-d'Aran, access to and from the Spanish side, with its deep transverse valleys and less-sophisticated road and rail network, poses any number of problems. Thus, although Benasque is an obvious base for exploring the Posets and Maladetta massifs, access to Benasque from France, by public transport, involves a complicated and time-consuming journey. While it may be easy enough to escape southwards into Spain in the event of bad weather on the main range, the difficulties of then returning to France within a reasonable timespan can be daunting.

Probably the best introduction to touring in the Pyrenees is the Neouvielle Reserve, easily accessible from either Bareges or La Mongie to the north, or St Lary to the south. This is a delightful area of granite peaks, rolling upland snowfields, dwarf pines, myriad lakes and a smattering of decent huts. Cauterets provides another useful introductory centre with the Wallon Hut – unusual in the Pyrenees in providing a year-round warden (*patron*) service – giving access to the Vignemale and its satellites and other ski peaks. The complete Pyrenean High Route is a formidable undertaking of thirty-four stages but any number of sections, with variations, can be worked out, including such circuits as Urdos to Gabas, Gabas to Cauterets and a tour of the Gavarnie area well served by the Sarradets, Espurgettes and Goriz huts. The charm of the Pyrenees is to work out one's own itineraries, for there is still much in this area to be explored by ski mountaineers.

10 The Moroccan Haute Route by Hamish Brown

That Morocco is a skiing country comes as a surprise to many, but at one time it boasted the highest ski lift in the world (3,273 m/10,738 ft), at Oukaimeden (still a pleasant, quiet resort), and in Jebel Toubkal 4,167 m (13,671 ft), has the highest summit in all North Africa. The weather in the High Atlas tends to be superior to that of the Alps, while 30 km (19 miles) north of the mountains lies magical Marrakech in the exotic, colourful world of a differing culture. No wonder ski touring has become a regular part of the Atlas scene.

The High Atlas range sweeps down from the coast right across the country, a barrier to the desert south, peopled by rugged Berber tribes who have never been conquered for long by outsiders. It is a harsh world with habitation only made possible by the snows of winter which melt to water the valleys and plains to the north. (If snow fails it means deep hardship.) Only two roads, spectacular feats of engineering, cross the highest part of the Atlas. The Toubkal Massif, lying between these roads is the popular area for climbing, trekking and skiing. There are several 4,000 m (13,000 ft) summits; most are good ski ascents, expeditions being made from the three CAF huts.

Considering the Moroccan (Moorish) influence on Europe, we have been strangely slow in realizing what a fascinating country lies just across the Straits of Gibraltar. Marrakech is only a simple air flight away and a ski holiday in the Atlas will cost no more than one in Europe. Marrakech is thoroughly geared-up for tourists and I recommend the Hotel Foucauld on the edge of the Medina. It is helpful and serves good local food. *Grande taxis* can be hired for the 60–80 km (40–50 mile) trip to the hills (expensive), or a local bus taken to Asni, 1,165 m (3,822 ft), and then a communal taxi hired from there (ridiculously cheap). This lands one at Imlil where there is a comfortable CAF hut, 1,740 m (5,709 ft), at the end of a motorable road. One of the helpful guardians speaks English, and mules, guides and porters, etc., can be hired there at fixed rates.

At the head of that valley lies the Neltner or Toubkal Hut, 3,207 m (10,522 ft). Over a pass and up the valley to the west is the Lepiney Hut, 3,050 m (10,006 ft). Over another pass and up the valley to the east is the Tachddirt

Hut, 2,314 m (7,592 ft). East again, over a col, is the resort of Oukaimeden, 2,660 m (8,727 ft), which has a motorable road to it from Marrakech via the Ourika Valley. A few days of piste and local touring there are recommended before tackling the big peaks. The dry heat and altitude can violently affect the unacclimatized, and so a fortnight is advisable for an Atlas visit – as a minimum.

Most skiers simply rush up to the Neltner to 'do' Toubkal and perhaps one other peak. The Atlas deserves better, and a 'Haute Route' of some character has now evolved, largely pioneered by a few local (French) enthusiasts. This has variants, but the best route is described here. Parties have to be largely self-supporting, for two bivouacs are involved and the huts are more basic than alpine-style huts. They do have custodians and the Haute Route can be made easier by organizing porters to take up food for use en route, rather than carrying it all the whole way yourselves.

Food is best purchased in Marrakech (Gueliz Market) and special lightweight items brought from home. Imlil's supplies are erratic, but some locals have opened shops and sell surplus expedition food and even ski equipment. Ropes, ice axe, crampons and harscheisen are essential. Early starts are important for the sun can be punishing to both humans and snow conditions. (Aim to descend by midday.) This tour is a serious one and a careful eye should be kept on the weather. Storms, although infrequent, can be ferocious. March and April are the best months. Depending on the season south-facing slopes can be bare of snow, which is why the route is followed in the direction described, giving the maximum downhill opportunities.

Maps: Maps can be difficult to obtain. There is a 1:50,000 'Jebel Toubkal' sheet (NH-29-XXIII-1a) and a 1:100,000 IGN series sheet 'Oukaimeden–Toubkel' (NH-29-XXIII-1), while West Col do a *kamcarte*, along with their English-language guidebook *Atlas Mountains*. (This essentially gives summer descriptions and is weak on winter or ski information.) I buy any maps I can find in Morocco, or try suppliers or shops like Stanfords, West Col or Cordee in Britain. It is worth taking both maps for neither is entirely adequate for such complex country. Route-finding skills will be well tested. With the landscape lacking contrasting tones, it is often difficult visually to separate ridges and heights and distances will always demand more time and effort than expected. The French language *Skis Dans le Haut Atlas de Marrakech* by Claude Cominelli is very useful. There is also *La Grande Traversee de l'Atlas Marocain* by Michael Peyron, covering the whole Atlas. I have only seen those on sale at Imlil and Oukaimeden.

Fig. 111   Jebel Toubkal (4,167 m/13,665 ft), the highest summit in north Africa, showing ascent route of the Ikhibi Sud valley.

Recommended Tour

Day 1: from Imlil walk up to the Tizi (pass) Mzic, 2,489 m (8,166 ft), and traverse to Tamsoult and the icy gorge beyond. Leave early. Mules can usually reach the gorge and porters can carry from there to the Lepiney Hut at 3,050 m (10,006 ft). (Check key/warden arrangements at Imlil.)

Day 2: climb to the pass above the head of this grand valley, the Tizi Melloul, 3,860 m (12,664 ft) 3½ hours. (The valley head cirque is turned right of the icefall.) From the pass descend the other side for 1½ km (1 mile). (Time may not allow ascents of peaks unless returning to the Lepiney.) Turn up eastwards to the Tizi n'bou Imrhaz, 3,875 m (12,713 ft) (Tizi n'Ouanoukrim on 1:50,000) and the col between Akioud n'bou Imrhaz and Ras n'Ouanoukrim, 4,083 m (13,396 ft) (this is the north top of a pair, the other, Timesguida n'Ouanoukrim, 4,088 m (13,412 ft) is the second highest peak in the country). Do not descend the corrie but bear left under Akioud to cross the col between it and Tadaft (Morocco's answer to the Inaccessible Pinnacle). Then a good corrie descent follows, with a gun-barrel shooting one out into the main valley not far above the Neltner Hut.

Day 3: ascend the steep slope opposite the hut, then bear left, round and up into the Ikhibi Sud hanging valley. When this opens to a basin, climb up to the right skyline (foul scree in a poor season) and follow it to Toubkal, 4,167 m (13,665 ft), with one short narrow section requiring care. Follow the north-east ridge down to an obvious levelling-off or col (Imousser peak beyond). Very steep gullies (the crux of the tour) fall to the east (towards Tissaldai, 2,094 m/6,870 ft). Choose one.

After 100 m (320 ft) the angle eases and skis go on for a classic long descent. Bivouac overnight at Azib n-Tarhba-lout, 2,400 m (7,874 ft): not named, but west of the height shown as 2,547 m (8,356 ft) or 2,530 m (8,300 ft), at the confluence with Tichki's southern drainage. (*Azib* means goat shelter.) This is a very remote area with no ready escape route. Settled weather is advisable. (An alternative Day 3 and Day 4 is given below.)

Day 4: the Tichki–Tinilim ridge is part of the main spine of the Atlas. It is a long pull up to the Tizi-n-Terhaline 3,300 m (Tizi-n-Ounrar on 1:100,000), but the descent makes up for it. Descend via the Azib Tifni or over Pt 3,426/7 (11,240 ft) east of the col. The traditional bivouac site is the Azib Likemat 2,650 m (8,694 ft), well down this valley, which has impassable gorges further on and a great feeling of remoteness.

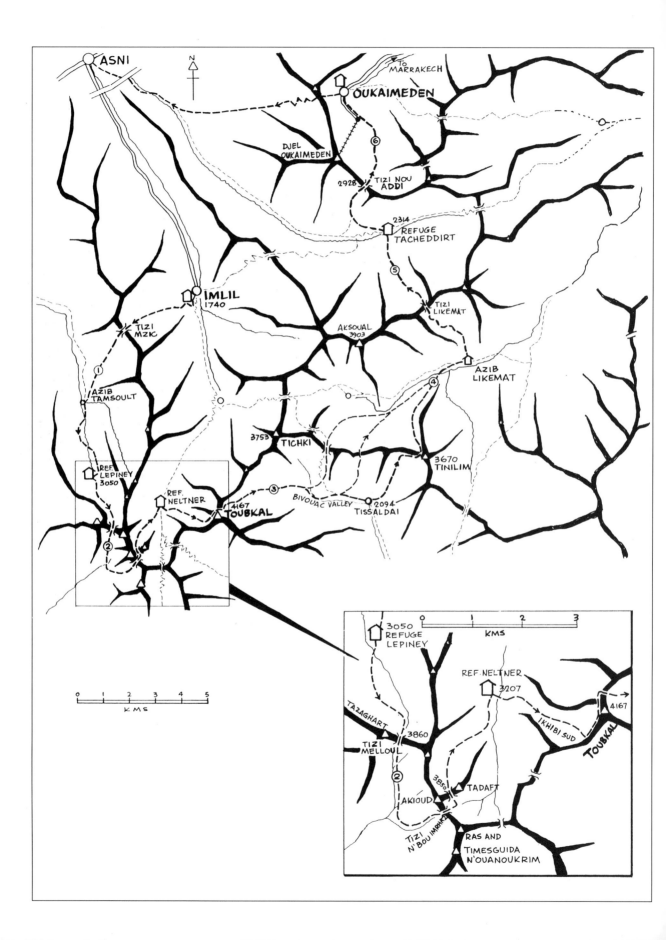

ASNI

N

TO MARRAKECH

OUKAIMEDEN

DJEL
OUKAIMEDEN

6

2928   TIZI NOU
ADDI

2314   REFUGE
TACHEDDIRT

IMLIL
1740

5

TIZI
MZIC

TIZI
LIKEMAT

AKSOUAL
3903

1

AZIB
LIKEMAT

AZIB
TAMSOULT

4

REF.
LEPINEY
3050

3753   TICHKI

3670
TINILIM

REF.
NELTNER

3

BIVOUAC VALLEY

4167

TOUBKAL   2094
TISSALDAI

2

KMS

KMS

3050
REFUGE
LEPINEY

0   1   2   3

KMS

REF. NELTNER
3207

4167

TAZAGHART

IKHIBI SUD

TOUBKAL

3860

TIZI
MELLOUL

2

3850   TADAFT

AKIOUD

TIZI
N'BOU IMRHZ

RAS AND
TIMESGUIDA
N'OUANOUKRIM

Fig. 114   A=Tizi Melloul; B=Tizi n'bou Imrhaz;
C=the Akioud-Tadaft col.

Day 5: a similar sort of day with many hours of skinning (or walking!) to reach the broad Tizi Likemat, 3,540 m (11,614 ft) (there is a path if clear of snow). An excellent run down to the valley follows, with the hut perched on the far side, on the northern edge of Tacheddirt village.

Day 6: a rising track (seldom skiable) leads to the Tizi nou Addi (Eddi), 2,928 m (9,606 ft), beyond which lies Oukaimeden, 2,660 m (8,727 ft), with its CAF chalet hotel and several tows and lifts. Cross early to enjoy a few descents (on and off piste) from the summit of Djbel Oukaimeden, 3,273 m (10,738 ft), a magnificent viewpoint. 'Chez Ju Ju' does good food and bunkhouse or room accommodation if the CAF chalet is full, for example in the school holidays.

Day 7: a car could be arranged for the descent to Marrakech, but a better finish is to walk down to Asni, 1,165 m (3,822 ft), sending the skis with porters. It is a complex route. The Hotel du Toubkal at Asni does excellent food in a palatial setting. You will have earned it. There is also a youth hostel which is open to non-members.

Alternative

Day 3: traverse Toubkal, ascending by the Ikhibi Sud and descending by the Ikhibi Nord. Then ski down to overnight at Sidi Chamarouch 2,310 m (7,579 ft), a shrine which Moslems only may enter, but there are huts for bothy accommodation.

Day 4: a long climb leads to the Tizi-n-Tagharat 3,456 m (11,338 ft). Do Tichki 3,753 m (12,313 ft) if there is time before the long descent via Azib Tifni to Azib Likemat. Splitting this marathon day is preferable, by spending the night at Azib Tifni and perhaps skinning to Tzi-n-Terhaline; or even reaching Adrar Tinilim 3,670 m (12,041 ft) before descending to Azib Likemat.

11 New Zealand Ski Touring by Bruce Clark

(Since writing this chapter, Bruce Clark was tragically killed in an accident during a mountain rescue exercise in New Zealand.)

Most ski touring in New Zealand is done in the South Island's Southern Alps, a range of mountains stretching from Fiordland in the south to Arthur's Pass in the north. With thirty mountains over 3,000 m (10,000 ft), and hundreds of glaciers flowing east and west off the main divide, the Southern Alps are an ideal playground for the ski mountaineer. Mt Cook 3,764 m (12,349 ft), New Zealand's highest mountain, lies more or less in the centre of this mountain chain, a mere 35 km (22 miles) from the Tasman Sea, a proud mountain towering over the land, its head thrust above the clouds: *Aorangi* the Maoris called it, meaning 'cloud piercer'. Most of the winter snows come from the north-west, often firm and windblown on the west side of the divide, but lighter and softer on the east. Winds from the south bring the light fluffy stuff that skiers dream of, usually with a clearance in the winter, giving days of excellent skiing.

The season varies depending on the number of early winter storms, but usually goes from late June to the end of September, with good spring skiing from the end of September to early November. The best time is August, but with the inevitable crowded huts and ski tracks everywhere. However, by wandering farther afield it is certainly not hard to find absolute solitude.

Touring in New Zealand's high mountains has many facets, from hut-based activities with their pleasant day trips, to the more demanding multi-day adventures using snow caves and tents, carrying everything with you. However, the most popular form is to fly into an area with a week or so's food, using a hut or snow cave as a base to do day trips and so enjoying the climbing and skiing to the full. Evacuation is mostly on ski to lower levels, followed by a day's walk to the nearest road. Some parties have been known to fly out as well.

Alpine skis with touring bindings and skins are the most popular type of equipment, along with ski mountaineering boots which are suitable for walking, climbing and skiing. The use of cross-country skis with metal edges and three-pin bindings is increasing in popularity. Used with heavy-duty boots and skins their advantage is in their lightness, the skier producing graceful telemark turns. Avalanche awareness is high amongst New Zealand ski mountaineers, and most parties carry Pieps avalanche transceivers and lightweight snow shovels in case of emergency.

There are many areas suitable for touring in New Zealand, but most activity is centred around the Mt Cook National Park. The Mt Aspiring National Park is also most popular, but tours here are of a more serious undertaking because of the lack of huts.

MT COOK NATIONAL PARK

Areas include the Tasman, Murchison, Fox and Franz Josef glaciers. Air access is from Mt Cook Tourist Village by fixed-wing aircraft or from Fox Glacier township on the west coast by skiplane and helicopter. There are huts in all of these areas providing stoves, fuel, cooking utensils and mattresses only – you provide the rest.

MOUNT ASPIRING NATIONAL PARK

Road access is from Wanaka via Matukituki River and from Queenstown via Rees and Dart Valley. Then by helicopter from the road end to areas like Volta, Bonar and Whitbourne glaciers. There is a New Zealand Alpine Club hut on the Bonar Glacier, which has bunks for six but all the other areas require snow caves or sturdy tents.

AREAS NORTH OF MT COOK

Godley Glacier: access by four-wheel drive vehicle from the road end at Lake Tekapo, and then by foot or helicopter from Franz Josef Township on the west coast to the head of Scone Glacier.

Garden of Eden and Allah Ice Plateaux: air access by fixed-wing plane or helicopter from Mt Cook Tourist Village, Mesopotamia and the west coast.

Recommended Tour

Murchison Glacier: NZMS Topographical Map 1:63,360, Mt Cook S79, Waiho S71.

This area is situated on the east side of the main divide in the Mt Cook National Park. Many of the skiable slopes face east and south, providing excellent soft-snow skiing. It is sheltered from the prevailing westerly wind and consequently has better weather than most of the other touring areas in the park. Murchison Hut 1,860 m (6,102 ft) is owned by the New Zealand Alpine Club and has accommodation for twelve. Access is by ski plane from Mt Cook Village onto the glacier 200 m (660 ft) below the hut.

Day 1: arrange your plane flight as early in the day as possible so that, after arriving at the hut a half-day trip up to Starvation Saddle can be made in order to familiarize yourself with the area. Some parties arrange to leave most

Fig. 116   Tasman Saddle Hut, Tasman Glacier and Mt Cook.

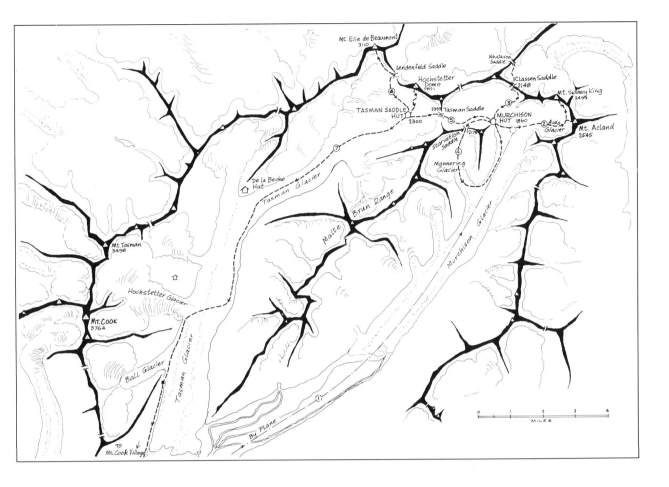

of their equipment on the glacier landing-site and, with day packs, fly up to the Tasman Saddle and ski the head wall of the Murchison Glacier before establishing themselves in the hut at the end of the day.

Day 2: ski down from the hut to the bowl of Murchison Glacier and, using skins, climb up Ada Glacier to the foot of Mt Acland. Turn left and climb through a crevassed area until the upper slopes beneath the summit of Sidney King are reached. The best ski run follows the line of ascent. Alternatively, a climb of Mt Acland 2,545 m (8,350 ft) can be made with a ski ascent to 2,100 m (6,890 ft), and roped climbing to the summit. Both north and south ridges provide excellent scrambling.

Day 3: from the glacier below the hut, head in a north-east direction to the slopes east of Classen Saddle 2,148 m (7,047 ft). Some trouble could be experienced getting off the Murchison Glacier due to crevasses, but this depends on the season. Once the ridge crest is gained, head north-west to Classen Saddle. If there is time, a run down the Classen Glacier is well worth the effort or a climb up to Whataroa Saddle can be made for a view of the west coast. Return to Murchison Hut by way of your ascent.

Day 4: from Murchison Hut sidle west, losing 150 m (490 ft), into the bowl of the glacier, and climb on skis up to Starvation Saddle. This route takes you through steeper and sometimes crevassed slopes just off the bowl of the glacier. The Mannering Glacier offers some of the best skiing in the area with south-facing slopes, as it receives good powder snow and little sun. Most parties ski down to the flat part of the glacier (1,830 m/6,004 ft) and return to the saddle the same way. In good snow years, a round trip can be made by skiing the length of the Mannering to the Murchison Glacier and climbing back up to the hut.

Day 5: pack up all your equipment and drop onto the glacier. Using skins, climb up the centre of the glacier, veering in a semi-circle to the left. Using the easier left-hand slopes, climb up the glacier head wall to the Tasman Saddle and ski west to Tasman Saddle Hut, 2,300 m (7,546 ft). The afternoon can be spent making runs off Hochstetter Dome or down the Tasman Glacier on slopes to the west of the hut.

Day 6: climb on skis past Hochstetter Dome to Lendenfield Saddle. If conditions allow, a ski ascent of Mt Elie de Beaumont can be made by skinning up the Anna Glacier. Parties have experienced trouble with large crevasses and icy conditions near the summit. The descent route varies depending on where the best skiing is, but few route-finding difficulties should be encountered. Avoid skiing below the hut, which could necessitate a lengthy climb on skis at the end of the day.

Day 7: carrying all your equipment, ski down through bowls to the west of the hut. Alternatively, flights can be arranged to carry out heavy packs if desired. The ski down the glacier is straightforward, staying in the centre of the glacier all the way to opposite the De La Beche Hut, where you veer left and stay on the glacier ice until opposite the Hochstetter Icefall. Head south-west onto the white ice of the Hochstetter and follow it to the foot of Moraine on the Ball Glacier. Move towards Moraine Wall, on the far side of the Ball Glacier, to meet the track at the Ball Shelter. This last day is the longest and often requires a pre-dawn start. If you are able to ski to the end of the white ice on the Tasman Glacier, you should have little trouble reaching the road end in a day.

Fig. 117   Looking across Fox Glacier to the Tasman Sea.

12 Greenland by Derek Fordham

Wind, snow, space, a feeling of well being – these are surely the ingredients of any ski mountaineering expedition. Add to them the midnight sun drifting its pale shades over endless unnamed and untrodden ranges fading into the incredible distances and infinite solitude of the Arctic landscape and you have the essence of an Arctic ski expedition.

Comradeship is forged better in such conditions than in the incestuous well-trodden valleys of the Alps where every ski track, hut or other party diffuses isolation. To approach such paradise requires total commitment. An Arctic expedition is no holiday, however successful the outcome. No one summed it up better than the Norwegian explorer Roald Amundsen when he said: 'In the Arctic one should be prepared for the worst then whatever happens will be better.'

Such thoughts were with us on Mont Forel in East Greenland one May as we lay in our sleeping bags watching the tent fabric forced inwards under the onslaught of ferocious gusts of windblown spindrift; the physical assault accompanied by a wild, unrestrained cacophany of noise.

A few days previously, after long delays due to bad weather, we had chartered a Greenlandair helicopter to fly five of us and some 150 kg (330 lb) of equipment from Kulusuk airstrip to the icefield under the North Face of Mont Forel at the start of the expedition, the planning for which had begun in earnest some eight months earlier.

The coastal mountain ranges of Greenland offer endless possibilities for exploratory ski mountaineering, and for those who take on the months of preparation, there are the rewards of travelling unsupported through some of the most remote and unexplored mountain fastnesses in the world. The price for reaping these rewards is high; in Greenland there are none of the established facilities for ski mountaineers which exist in the Alps. Permission to undertake one's proposals must be obtained from the Ministry for Greenland and, once obtained, papers, confirming that the specified insurance against search and rescue costs has been effected, must then be submitted to the Ministry before the expedition commences.

Fig. 118   Storm at Forel Camp.

Search and rescue can be expensive, if not impossible, in many areas of Greenland and each expedition must review its proposals and equipment with this in mind. Food, although available in the stores which are found in most settlements, is seldom of a type suitable for expeditions, and, as with other facilities, has been brought in at great expense for consumption by the indigenous population. Any expedition should therefore aim to be entirely self-sufficient and, indeed, the authorities may well insist on this. The only sensible exceptions to this rule are liquid fuels, such as paraffin and petrol, and ammunition, all of which are easily obtained in most settlements, although the import and use of firearms, as with radios, is subject to strict controls.

Paperwork cleared, we had assembled our equipment several months prior to the expedition: cross-country skis with metal edges, clothing and tents to keep us warm in high winds at −30°C. and below – everything as light as possible.

One of the great fascinations of exploration in such areas is the definition of an objective and the associated study of the records and exploits of earlier explorers whose efforts in reaching these regions will never be paralleled. In May 1931, Alfred Stephenson and Lawrence Wager, of Gino Watkins's British Arctic Air Route Expedition, attempted Forel from the north and after a sterling attempt, which was Stephenson's first essay at mountaineering, failed about 100 m from the summit. More than fifty years later, our plan was to attempt the same, or similar, route from the lonely icefields which border the Inland ice cap to the north of Mont Forel.

We had made two attempts on the mountain before the weather struck. Our first followed Stephenson and Wager's route and the sun, the intense, clear blue Arctic sky and the white slopes twisting upwards through the solid, brown, rock buttresses combined to give a feeling that success was ours. In the wan light and freezing temperatures of a May Arctic evening, we turned back, planning to complete the final 100 m or so the next day. It was the last we saw of that side of Forel!

Blizzard after blizzard swept nightmarishly over our camp for the next week. The second attempt, forced ahead during what appeared to be a break in the weather, took us close to the top of the east ridge. The wind, rising to a physical presence, with the summit almost within reach, signalled a warning to retreat. We struggled down for hours through a solid wall of whirling spindrift. Back at the wind-racked tents, one frostbitten ear and two seriously frostbitten fingers remained with us as mute and painful reminders of our ordeal.

David's fingers and the appalling weather, with gusts reaching 50 knots, hurling snow and spindrift at the tents, decided the outcome of our expedition. I planned to leave for the coast as soon as possible.

It was not until two days later that the wind abated enough to allow the tents to be struck and our return journey to begin. It was a hollow feeling to leave our camp without success to spur our long return. Silently we shouldered packs weighing between 20–25 kg (44–55 lb) and skied across the sastrugi sculpted plain under the icy north-west flank of Forel, its gully-scarred buttresses facing out over the nunataks to our last sight of the distant hazy horizon of the Inland ice.

Thirteen years previously I had skied past Forel at the start of a long ski expedition which finished 1,100 km (684 miles) of ice desert away, at Sarqaq on the west coast. This time I was leading my party eastward, thwarted by the same forces of nature which had granted a measure of success all those years ago.

Fresh snow and whiteout on the Bjorn Glacier forced an early camp the next day on the edge of a large crevasse field.

Thirty-six hours later, navigating by compass, we groped our way down the Paris Glacier aware only of tantalizing glimpses of the sun and high peaks as clouds formed and reformed about us. No sign of life, not even the ubiquitous raven, disturbed the awesome isolation of this giant's realm.

A crucial moraine, identified from the helicopter as avoiding a difficult ice-fall, was located. We wound amongst its string of cyclopean blocks until the Femstjernen lay ahead of us, perspective and distance distorted by the glistening silver light filtering through layers of distant dark clouds. Our moraine and those parallel to it spread out like fingers grasping the icy plain and then, boulder by boulder, were swallowed into its frozen heart.

Tired thighs and aching shoulders forced our skis across this frozen plain, in whose exposed jaws we had no wish to camp. Two hours later we skied into a small bowl and established camp, 28 km (17 miles) of difficult travelling and the Femstjernen behind.

The next days were sunny and clear – real Greenland days – and we skied down the Glacier de France and took the first right to an unnamed, unexplored pass, delighted to find the tracks of an Arctic Fox that had, a few days earlier, crossed the col we were to claim for our own. We enjoyed a fine unroped descent before tackling the long hot climb to the foot of the Conniats Pass.

Several hours later, Rupert and I, convinced we could see the rock buttress below which our food boxes were depoted, selected a steep, direct route up through the ice fall. The others, less enthusiastic about tackling the large icicle-filled caverns we were skirting on cross-country skis and cable bindings, suggested an alternative. Secure in our conviction that the route would go, we pressed on. The others reluctantly followed.

We skied higher and higher, kickturning mostly, in firm snow lying on the ice, as a tremendous mountain pano-

rama opened up, often framed by the deep icy blue of the
crevasses we were negotiating. We belayed over the last
thin patch and skied expectantly over the crest – only to
find the ground falling away in front of us. We were off-
route!

Like two rather chastened eagles we sat on our perch
watching the sun moving slowly westwards over the
remote ranges beyond the Midgaard Glacier and wonder-
ing what we would say to the others when they arrived.

They were very good about it. They kept their no-
doubt succinct thoughts about our competence to themselves, despite having to remove skis and climb down a
short distance before we could continue.

Golden evening light flooded the mountains a few hours
later as we located the marker flag and food boxes on the
pass and, camp established, Rupert and I cooked dinner as a
penance for our over-confidence. Reclining in our sleeping
bags with the stoves purring and plenty of food in the tent,
Rupert confided, 'I still think it was an excellent mountaineering route through the ice-fall.' I found it hard to
disagree!

The next days were a jigsaw of cloud, whiteout, wind
and spindrift, each succeeding the other in an endless
pattern of swirling white.

On the Haabets Glacier at night our slender cross-
country skis slid metallically over the surface in the pale,
almost unreal midnight light, the mountains reduced to
stark silhouettes outlined against the pink and green Arctic
sky. Night time travelling is for me associated with a
strange isolated quality, each person skiing encapsulated
within his own thoughts, horizons, physical and intellec-
tual, limited by the cold rim of a parka hood.

So it was as we descended the Haabets towards the
lightening skyline of a new day. The backdrop of the high
interior mountains sinking, perhaps forever, behind us.

Once we were well established on the Knud Rasmus-
sen's Glacier the following day, our pace quickened, the
skis alternately clattering on icy crust and ploughing
through slush, the herald of the advancing spring. The
boxes had become our unspoken goal for the day, and far
down the long slope of the lower glacier a spot of orange
waved bravely. We reached them in deteriorating weather
at the end not only of a long day, but also our journey, and
at the beginning of a further two days of almost continuous snowfall and wind.

Tentbound again, the ritual of eat, sleep, read and talk
began and we made inroads into the last of the ration
boxes, the packing of which, months earlier in Greenwich,
with 4,200 calories per man per day of lightweight food,
seemed to have taken place in another world an eternity
away.

The spoon paused in front of my open mouth. Something stirred over the now much diminished rustle of the
wind. Rupert turned off the stoves. Neither of us wanted

to be the first to speak. The regular beat increased in
volume until there could be no mistake. 'The helicopter!',
and the expedition, in various stages of undress, exploded
onto the snow.

Crouched against the rotor-driven spindrift the crew
waded through the snow towards us. Suddenly others had
intruded into our world. The ephemeral bond which had
held us in our isolation was broken as quickly and casually

Fig. 119   Climbing to the Conniats Pass.

as it had been formed.

The last we saw of Greenland was the dirt strip at Kulusuk streaking under the wing of the Chieftain and Ole, the station chief, a solitary figure waving goodbye. At 250 m (820 ft) we entered cloud and once again the weather was master.

That was the end of just one of my many Arctic journeys. All different they have had for me one overrid-

ing common factor, and perhaps, as you ski for endless untracked miles under the pastel skies of the Arctic night, you too will lose part of yourself, as I and many others have before you, to that special magic of the Arctic, and a part of your heart will lie forever in that frozen and hauntingly beautiful land.

13 Ski Mountaineering in the United States by Lito Tejada-Flores

Paradoxically, ski mountaineering is both a popular and an unknown sport in the United States. I mean simply that the expression 'ski mountaineering' has never quite caught on here, perhaps because of confusion over whether it refers to skiing through mountains, or climbing mountains on skis. At any rate, Americans do a lot of both. Yet considering the size of the wild and protected regions – far larger than the whole of the Alps – it is not surprising that backcountry skiers often feel they have barely scratched the surface of this white universe. And it is true. The exploration component of ski touring and ski mountaineering, that sense of skiing where few or no others have skied, is an important part of the sport over here. But comparing American ranges with the Alps is like comparing apples and oranges.

THE AMERICAN DIFFERENCE

Terrain and climate give the American touring skier a very different playground to his European cousins. Major ranges in the west are generally quite high, but remarkably free of glaciers. The Colorado Rockies, for example, contain over fifty peaks of more than 4,200 m (14,000 ft), yet they extend as far south (in latitude) as Tunis or Algiers, and the timberline climbs to around 3,200 m (12,000 ft). Thus, except for the glaciated peaks and volcanos of the Pacific Northwest, the classic Alpine décor of crevasse and schrund wall is absent on most American ski mountaineering jaunts. As if to compensate, the more extensive high-altitude forests tend to shelter new snow from the ravages of sun and wind, preserving perfect deep-powder skiing for days and days after each storm.

Another major difference is the almost total absence of mountain huts in the American West (the only major exception is along the 10th Mountain Trail, named after the 10th Mountain Division of World War II fame, in Colorado where a linked-hut system is being extended across the backbone of the Rockies from Aspen to Vail). So, like snails, American ski mountaineers must carry their camps on their backs. A multi-day tour is far more of an undertaking, requiring more planning and possibly a stronger back than, say, the Chamonix–Zermatt Haute Route. Of course, this is a factor in summertime mountain travel as well, and as a result ultra-light camping gear and, above all, a great variety of freeze-dried foods are more available in the United States than in Europe. Long ski trips, however, require a good deal of strategy and cunning as well as a strong back. The typical solution for multi-week tours is to cache food and gas at different points along the route the summer before. In this way, long elegant tours along the entire length of ranges like California's High Sierra (sixty days of skiing!) and Wyoming's Wind Rivers have been realized in fine style. The need for light-weight kit, plus the American's insatiable appetite for anything new, have led to the most important difference between ski mountaineering on the two sides of the Atlantic – the emergence of a whole new style of skiing, telemarking. The telemark turn, of course, is neither new nor American. But in the United States it has been rediscovered, refined and applied with a vengeance to the most improbable range of skiing conditions.

The telemark turn is far more versatile and functional than anyone who has not mastered it might imagine – and, most important, it allows one to ski through (and down) the ruggedest mountains with amazingly light three-pin Nordic gear. True, telemark skis are wider than cross-country track skis and have metal edges; boots are ankle high, relatively stiff and sometimes double, but bindings are featherweight and the whole set weighs less than half the typical Alpine touring kit.

Telemark equipment, like the technique, is evolving from one year to the next. A major factor in this evolution has been a national telemark race circuit, and, just as in Alpine skiing, each new refinement of technique or equipment has been quickly applied in a touring context. Telemarking is physically more demanding than Alpine parallel skiing, and also seems to demand and develop better balance. It is, however, a rather easy and forgiving technique in any deep snow, from true powder to rotten spring glop. The biggest challenge is to apply it to very icy and steep surfaces, but even here the limits of the telemark are being pushed back year by year. However, this technique has not exclusively replaced Alpine skiing in the backcountry, though I would estimate that over half the mountain touring skiers in America are now skiing on Nordic equipment.

A REGIONAL SURVEY

I have already spoken of the West. The north-east offers classic cross-country aplenty, but there is very little serious ski mountaineering simply because there are very few serious mountains. Here in the United States, big mountains are synonymous with the West, and for the ski mountaineer that is where the action is. Without covering

Fig. 120   Carrying your camp on your back

every range and subrange in this limited space, I should begin by splitting this vast region in two: the Far West and the Rocky Mountains.

In the Far West we can distinguish two subregions: the California Sierra, a long friendly range with gentle, forested western slopes and steep granite escarpments on the east, and the Pacific Northwest, an area of isolated volcanos and dense coastal ranges. The entire Far West has a maritime climate which means lots of rather damp snow, falling at relatively warm temperatures (only a little below freezing). As a result, avalanche danger throughout the Far West is seldom extreme for long periods, diminishing rapidly in one or two days after most storms. While California skiers talk fondly of their terrible 'Sierra cement', I must say that snow in Washington is probably the wettest, mushiest stuff in the world.

The Rocky Mountain region, stretching from New Mexico in the south, up through Colorado, Wyoming, Montana and Idaho, is another story. Here a continental climate obtains: winter temperatures are very cold, the snow marvellously dry and light, and avalanche hazard can often be extreme for long periods in midwinter. This last negative factor is due to the typical early-season build-up of depth-hoar (unstable layers of temperature gradient snow crystals), plus low, low temperatures which can keep windslab in a state of hair-trigger brittleness for weeks at a time. Thus, in certain areas of the Rockies, high-mountain touring is far safer in spring than in midwinter. Utah's Wasatch Mountains, a subrange on the west slope of the Rockies, are justly famous for the deepest and lightest snow in America. Colorado is known as the home of the telemark revolution and backcountry skiers, these three-pin revolutionaries, have achieved a mastery of this technique that can scarcely be equalled elsewhere.

Finally, although the northern Rockies can be as remote, steep and rugged as you like, the immense rolling wilderness around Yellowstone Park is an ideal setting for any number of long Nordic-style tours which do not demand advanced downhill techniques, telemark or any other.

When it comes to ski mountaineering, the interior ranges of British Columbia and the Northern Rockies of Alberta probably offer the most spectacular possibilities in all North America: not as cold, nor as difficult of access as Alaskan ranges, their tracts of uninhabited mountain wilderness are vaster than anything in our 'lower 48'.

Recommended tour

Aspen and Crested Butte the two popular downhill resorts in central Colorado. In summer, it is a long drive from one to the other, skirting all the way around the massive spine

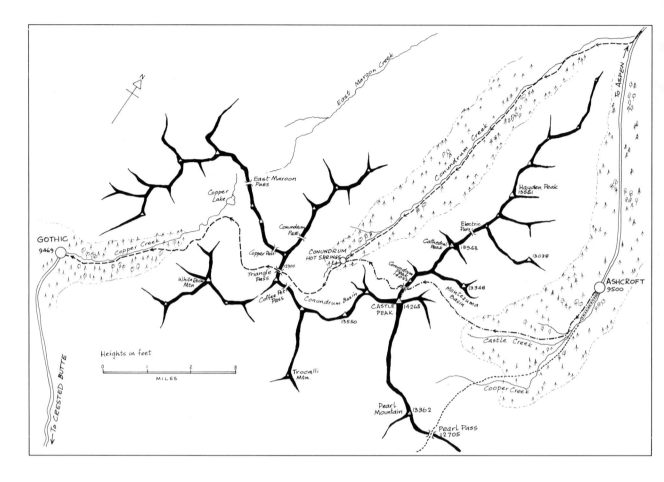

of the Elk range which separates them. In winter, you cannot reasonably get from one to the other except on skis – preferably on telemark skis. It is a two-day trip, a classic in anyone's book, complete with alternate routes, high summits to climb en route, grandiose views, nearly endless open slopes above timberline for figure-eighting and other aesthetic excesses on skis, and some of the best tree slaloms I have ever ever seen in the mixed spruce and aspen forests on the Crested Butte side. Best of all, there is an unforgettable overnight campsite for this two-day trip: Conundrum Hot Springs, a surrealistic oasis of green grass and steaming water, smack in the middle of big snowbanks and bigger peaks.

The route is straightforward: up Conundrum Creek from Aspen, some 14–16 km (9–10 miles) of easy skiing to the hot springs, an evening of sybaritic relaxation in the granite pool, an early-morning crossing of 3,932 m (12,900 ft) Triangle Pass and obvious ski lines down to the microscopic village of Gothic, a few miles outside Crested Butte. (USGS 7.5 minute topographic maps are the standard guides for this and most American ski tours – almost as good as the *Landeskarte der Schweiz*.) The best variation on this route is to start from the Ashcroft Valley near Aspen (also the starting point for the more popular, but less interesting, Pearl Pass route to Crested Butte). From Ashcroft, head up the Castle Creek drainage and climb up through Montezuma Basin to the shoulder of Castle Peak. The 4,348 m (14,265 ft) summit is only a few minutes' scramble away; as a special bonus you get a few thousand feet of really hair-raisingly steep telemarking down the other side of the peak to the hot springs. The skiing in the wide open basins between the hot springs and Conundrum Pass is so good that on one trip we got side-tracked into skiing there all day. We eventually came to our senses and only crossed the pass at six in the evening, finishing the tour in Gothic around midnight. Well worth it!

Our only companion that magical day was a lone coyote, loping over the pass ahead of us and disappearing into the sunset. That grand isolation is American ski mountaineering in a nutshell. Touring skiers here are few and far between; the mountains many and massive; the combinations endless.

A Ski-Tour in Alaska by Rob Collister

We set off that morning light-heartedly, revelling in the knowledge that we were fifty miles from the nearest road and off to climb our first peak. Leaving the tents up, we climbed on skins round a small ice-fall and up into a side basin of the Yanert glacier. The sun was shining and we carried only light day sacks. There was a sense of being on holiday after the hard graft of the previous week.

Almost immediately, however, the atmosphere changed. Gusts of wind swept down the basin, teasing at first, but quickly becoming vicious. The dry, loose powder that had lain so passive up to now, swirled aloft into stinging, blinding curtains of spindrift. David and Mike cached their skis beneath the bergschrund and swam slowly up a short but steep slope of bottomless powder. It was too cold to wait around, so Richard and I contoured round our little mountain to try our luck on another ridge. By now we could see nothing and relied for a sense of direction on the angle of our skis across the slope. Hoods up, heads turned away from the blast, we plodded on until we reached a col where, in a lull, we could dimly discern an easy rock ridge leading upwards. At that moment, Richard lost his balance and fell over. A boot released from its binding and while he struggled to relocate it, he dropped a mitt. That settled it. Summit or no summit, this was no place to be with nothing but Damart gloves on your hands. We groped our way down, skins still on the skis. My glasses were hopelessly iced up, but I needed them to protect my eyes and had to peer over them myopically to take advantage of the occasional lull.

Mike and David caught us up having reached the summit on their side. For a few minutes we became disorientated and strayed into a zone of crevasses. Visions of an epic began to loom before us. Wearily we climbed back uphill, then with relief recognized a glacier trench we had followed on the way up. Soon afterwards we dropped out of the wind and its attendant cloud of drift, and could see where we were. Off came the skins and we skiied rapidly back to camp, where there was scarcely a breath of wind. As we pulled clots of ice from our eye-lashes, we congratulated ourselves on a choice of camp site and joked that it had been like a good day on Cairngorm – which was not, I suppose, wholly facetious. Soon we were inside the tents, brewing up. Although our faces were burning, we were all chilled through, and Mike was anxiously warming white,

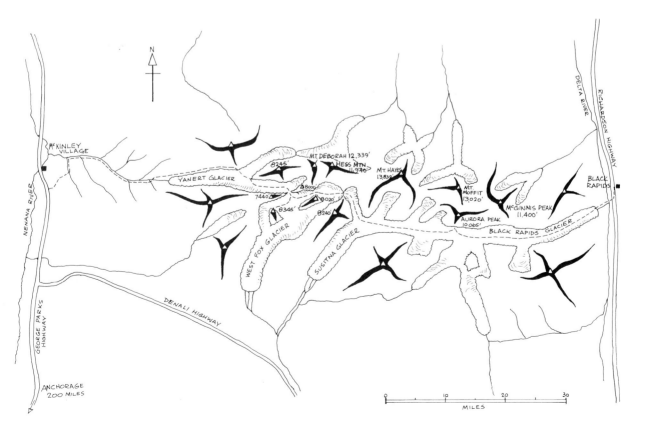

frozen toes.

We are not going to be let off so easily however. The water had not yet boiled when the first exploratory gusts came looking for us. Within minutes we had to extinguish the stoves, and thanked our stars that we had good tents and plenty of snow on the valances. All too soon this illusion of security was dispelled. In the blasts, the roof of the tent all but touched our noses as we lay in our sleeping bags, anxiously eyeing the fabric. The tent began to assume a distorted shape and we guessed that a pole had bent. One corner of the flysheet began to flap wildly, and we could feel the groundsheet lifting beneath us. The tent, it seemed, was ready for take-off. Crawling out into the frenzied cloud of drift, I found more by feel than sight that the valance had been completely stripped of snow and the polythene food bags had slid off. In fact, the snow all around was being eroded away by the minute, leaving each tent perched on a pedestal. There was nothing we could do now to secure them and they were not going to last indefinitely.

The wind's battering violence made it hard not only to move but even to think, but clearly something had to be done. More by luck than judgement, we were camped a few feet from a convenient bank, where snow had drifted over a morained ridge. While Mike and Richard knelt inside the tents, holding up the hooped poles, and no doubt holding their breath as well, at times, David and I stumbled and crawled over to the bank and frantically started to dig.

Two hours later as it was growing dark, we had made a cave just big enough for ourselves and our belongings. Carefully, we dropped the tents, one at a time, aware that it would be only too easy to lose one. Eventually we were all inside and the entrance blocked. After the maelstrom outside, it was miraculously still and silent. For a while spindrift continued to pour through the chinks, but these were sealed at last. We were cramped and, when the snow in our clothing melted, very dan.p. Fingers throbbed as they came back to life. But we were safe from anything the elements could throw at us.

That was a turning point in our traverse of the Hayes range. It was as though our credentials had been accepted, our entry to the high places approved. From that time on we could do no wrong . . .

The Alaska range is split in two by the George Parks Highway (and a railway line) connecting Anchorage and Fairbanks. West of the road is the McKinley National Park. East of the road lies the Hayes Range, lower and less well-known, and blissfully free from rules and regulations. It is bounded in the East by another road, the Richardson Highway, 160 km (100 ml) away as the crow flies. We knew the range to have been traversed at least once, from East to West by way of the Gillam glacier, North of Hess and Deborah. Indeed, near the snout of the Yanert, we met a party of two who had just completed that same journey. Our route, through the heart of the range had probably not been skiied before as a traverse, but most sections must have been covered before by someone. To put our efforts into perspective, a few weeks after our return to Britain we heard that a party from the U.S. nordic ski-squad had traversed the range in sixty-nine hours. Nevertheless, the area is not heavily frequented. From the Yanert snout we saw not a soul till the Black Rapids glacier, when a plane landed beside Mike as he was poling along on his own. The pilot wanted to borrow a map!

Now after one more day in which the wind blew itself out and we recuperated, we could enjoy ourselves. The weather became perfect, the soft snow had been replaced by wind-hardened sastrugi, and we had eaten enough to be able to move food and gear in single monster loads instead of relaying. Over the next week, we slipped into a routine of both skiing and climbing every day. There was no shortage of small peaks of modest difficulty for us to attempt. Windslab put a curb on our ambitions and we retreated from one route after setting off a small avalanche, but between us we reached the top of six mountains of 2–3,000 m (7–10,000 ft). These were days full of conscious pleasure and exhilaration as we skiied beneath magnificent peaks like Deborah and Hess, or thankfully dropped our packs and moved fast and light to the summit of the day's objective.

The key to our traverse was a 2,133 m (7,000 ft) col west of Hayes that was short but steep on both sides. We fixed a rope to help haul ourselves up, carrying skis as well as everything else; and for the descent in failing light on the far side, two of us preferred crampons to skis. Having crossed the col we had a not unwelcome lie-up day in heavy snow. Then the weather cleared on cue to present us with a marvellous descent in feathery powder down onto the Susitna glacier. A gentle climb brought us to the watershed where we paused to climb Aurora Peak by its long south-west ridge. Poling and skating energetically on a hard, fast surface, we descended the Black Rapids glacier in good style and crossed the gurgling river to reach the Richardson Highway at a sign that read:
FOOD   PHONE   GAS . . .   1 MILE.

Six of us from the Eagle Ski Club had left George Parks Highway at Mile 229 eight days before, with Bob Crockett of Anchorage and his dog team, the Chugach Express. The following day we were joined on the Yanert River by two other mushers with the rest of our food and gear. When the teams left us two days later we were on a shelf overlooking the snout of the Yanert glacier. Progress had not been as fast as we had hoped, but it had been interesting travelling with the dogs and infinitely more satisfying than an airlift. At this point Paddy and Steve had turned back, to our deep regret and their bitter disappointment. Both had frost bitten fingers, the result of an

Fig. 123   Yannert River.

incident with a petrol stove, and Steve's toes were injured too. Fortunately neither suffered permanent damage. From the snout, three days of ferrying loads through Deep Soft, and one day of lie up when it put down yet more snow, had brought us to the point where we could take a day off and try a climb.

The Big Blow was a salutory reminder that Alaska is a serious place. All our reading in back numbers of the American Alpine Journal had warned us that sudden violent winds are a feature of the mountains here. Yet on only three days in three weeks could we not travel. Although we were undoubtedly lucky to have quite such good weather, past records indicate that March, April and May are the most settled months in the year. From a skier's point of view, May is too late. The rivers are breaking up and snow disappearing fast from tundra and moraine. In an admittedly very mild year, we found overflow a problem on the Yanert even at the beginning of April. Overflow is caused by water seeping up through the ice to form a surface layer of water several inches deep. At night this freezes to form sheets of smooth glare-ice, difficult to travel on. Using skins we found it even more of a problem when the ice melted in the afternoons. The last few miles

of our traverse were very bare of snow. We were only able to ski all the way thanks to a raised skidoo track. The weight of the machine had compressed the snow sufficiently to withstand the thaw that was melting the rest away. All in all, March might be a safer month than April to be sure of good snow conditions low down.

March, however, is even more likely to be cold. Our arrival in Anchorage at the end of March 1986, coincided not only with the eruption of Mount Augustine and the first snow since November, but with a cold snap that lasted about a week. For the first few nights, the mercury in our little REI thermometers had dropped off the bottom of the scale at $-30°$ by 6 pm, and must have reached $-40°$ at night.

Towards the end of our journey we were skiing in shirt sleeves, but those first few days were colder than expected and our equipment, suitable for springtime in the Alps, was only just adequate.

An agent or friend in Anchorage is valuable for a trip of this nature. We were indebted to Bob Crockett. As well as providing the dogs at a very reasonable price, he organized the hire of a van, and its return to Anchorage, at the start of our journey, and he drove all the way up to Black Rapids

Fig. 124   Summit of Unnamed Peak.

to bring us back to Anchorage at the end.

We used alpine boots and skis whereas nearly all Americans would use light telemark skis, with metal edges and three pin bindings. We took the heavy gear partly because it was what we owned and were familiar with, but also because, had conditions been suitable, we could have attempted steeper climbing than is possible in nordic boots. As it turned out, with so much slab about, we climbed nothing that would not have been feasible in bendy boots. Although skiing sastrugi with a heavy pack on nordic skins would have been trying, to say the least, overall we would have travelled faster with the nordic gear.

14 The Ascent of Mustagh Ata, China by John Cleare

The wind sweeps, sharp and mean, across the roof of China. Its buffeting is ceaseless and its icy fingers probe between my ribs to chill the sweat on my back. I shiver involuntarily. I should feel elated up here at 7,546 m (24,757 ft) on the summit of Mustagh Ata, but I cannot. I am the expedition leader and I know that I must not relax until my team is home and dry – and safe – 3,700 m (12,000 ft) below.

Grim and Colin crouch beside me on the outcropping of black rock that is the top. It is the only rock in a desolation of snow and ice and streaming cloud. Grim is a schoolmaster in New England and Colin a heart-surgeon in Nevada. Fumbling through four pairs of gloves I break a bar of Kendal Mint Cake, carried ten thousand miles for this occasion. Colin munches hungrily at his chunk beneath the surgical mask he is wearing – an original protection against frost-bite. 'An old English mountain custom,' I explain. 'Hillary and Tenzing ate it on the summit of Everest!'

Bob arrives. He is shouting ecstatically but his words are whipped away by the wind to be lost in the void behind us. He removes his skis and struggles up awkwardly in his plastic boots to join us. Bob is an anaesthetist in Los Angeles. Now Johan approaches. He skis in apparent slow-motion, head down as if to avoid the cloud wreaths that scud so close above us. At fifty-seven he is the veteran of the party, another Californian medical man. He is not fast but he is very determined.

Between the snow and the cloud I can see the white ramparts of the Kongur Shan to the north. Clearer, to the south and barely 160 km (100 miles) distant, the horizon is rimmed by the saw-teeth of the western Karakorum. This is the Crossroads of Asia ... *Bam-i-Dunya* – the Persian 'Roof of the World' ... the frontier where once the Raj met Afghanistan and the empire of China and the Tsar. Here was played the 'Great Game', still played today but by different adversaries ...

But this is no place to linger. It is 2.30 p.m. on 17 August 1982, and time to head downwards. The summit plateau is plastered with iron-hard sastrugi – plates of windblown snow two or three feet thick. Skiing over them is a penance and a sprained ankle here could spell disaster. Tingling with adrenalin I lead off towards the first of our bamboo marker wands, a black hairline against the white horizon.

This was no ordinary expedition. For nine of the eleven members it was a holiday. Successful people, too busy with demanding professions to organize their own expeditions, they had bought a five-week 'package' organized by Mountain Travel USA, a world leader in 'adventure tourism'. Two members were women and there was only one other Briton. But for myself, and my deputy leader Steve McKinney, a climber and professional speed skier, the expedition was a job of work.

Mustagh Ata is an isolated and awesome mountain rising above the ancient Silk Road of Marco Polo in China's far western Xinjiang Province, beside the Soviet border. Together with neighbouring Kongur, it exceeds the height of Pik Communism in the Russian Pamirs less than 320 km (200 miles) distant across the frontier. Young-husband had ridden beneath it during his epic 1897 ride from Peking to Delhi and had recorded its name – 'Ice Mountain Father'. Sven Hedin, in 1894, and Sir Aurel Stein, in 1900, had both attempted to climb it, and in 1947 Shipton, Tilman and Gyalzen Sherpa had actually reached some 7,300 m (24,000 ft) before retreating. Finally a large Sino-Soviet expedition reached the summit in 1956. The third ascent was made by Ned Gillette's small American Ski Expedition in 1980 – and to date Mustagh Ata is still the highest mountain ascended and descended entirely on ski.

The friendly Chinese Mountaineering Association were pleased to grant us permission to attempt the mountain. They were able, for a price, to arrange the transport of both ourselves and our equipment from Beijing to a roadhead on the Karakorum highway beneath it, and from thence on camels to Base Camp, but above that we were on our own.

Virtually no maps are available of this sensitive region and the best I could obtain was a small segment of the restricted half-million scale American military air chart, xeroxed up to 1:100,000. Although very rudimentary (it was contoured every 300 m/1,000 ft) it did hint at the main glacier tongues and, most important, it gave me a shrewd idea of direction. *National Geographic*'s account of Gillette's expedition had been useful, and I had discussed the climb personally with members of both parties, but much of the delight of expeditioning is exploring things for yourself ... within the parameters of one's available time.

From the north and east Mustagh Ata appears most intimidating, while the gentler western flank is broken by a series of deep ice-filled chasms from which great glacier tongues pour into the surrounding desert. Flanked by awesome black cliffs, the wide ridges between these chasms offer obvious ski lines upwards, always providing that routes through the ice falls that band them can be found.

As leader of such an expedition, my responsibilities were

Fig. 125   Descending on skis from Camp II on
Muztagh Ata.

daunting. Previous ascents had been made by very accom-
plished mountaineers, while my team of fee-paying clients
was an unknown quantity. I had decided early on that my
slim chance of success, in the all too short twenty-one days
I was allocated on the mountain, lay in strict acclimatization to altitude and careful placing of camps. We would
'climb high – sleep low', placing five camps at 600 m
(2,000 ft) intervals and spending three nights at each,

meanwhile carrying loads to the next campsite. And then
only 500 m (1,700 ft) to the top ... the main dangers
would be the weather and sickness: the difficulties would
be logistics and route-finding. There are no Sherpas to help
you in China.

Our first set-back occurred early on. An anguished
American stumbled into our road-head camp. He was
leader of the Colorado Ski Expedition who were on the

mountain a month ahead of us. His two summit climbers were missing – presumed dead. It was a bitter blow to our morale. Suddenly Mustagh Ata was real, huge and mean. The holiday spirit evaporated.

Later, we learned that one man eventually returned, badly frostbitten and alone. Their high camp was a full 900 m (3,000 ft) below the summit, yet their unacclimatized companions were unable to support them. Lost in whiteout conditions – it seems that they had no compass – they had endured several terrible bivouacs before one man had disappeared . . . it was a grim lesson.

Camels carried our equipment across the desert to Base Camp, a sheltered hollow in the moraines at 4,450 m (14,600 ft). Here our three Chinese staff – liaison officer, interpreter and cook – kept house while we established Camp 1 on the snow line 670 m (2,200 ft) above. Our route, a new line, lay straight up a steep ridge, presenting no problems except those expected when carrying heavy sacks, with skis on top, up endless slopes of steep sharp scree. Just below the camp the massive skull and horns of a Marco Polo sheep, *Ovis poli*, lay among the rocks, a bold creature indeed.

It was a relief to don skis and climb easily on skins for 300 m (1,000 ft) out of a hanging cwm and over a succession of tilted snowfields leading to a ramp beneath a large zone of tumbled seracs. Half-way up we passed the site of the Colorado Camp 2 and 'liberated' a useful amount of abandoned food and fuel.

Now the ice forced us to the left, and round each corner we found we could advance another few hundred feet into the maze. Although we actually crossed few cravasses, we skirted some real whoppers. Eventually we established Camp 2 in a safe snowbowl above the worst of the ice fall. Unloaded, the descent made superb skiing, but not without some anxious moments. At one place the only line skirted the top of one of the enormous precipices. A fluffed turn would have resulted in a world-record ski-jump.

After the planned three carries, we occupied Camp 2. Then we pressed on upwards in misty whiteouts, through a sequence of snowy cwms, safeguarding our route with bamboo wands, carefully recording the compass bearing to the previous one on each scrap of flag, while it, or the ski tracks leading from it, were still visible. It was a worthwhile exercise because, despite continuous poor conditions, we maintained steady progress and advanced on schedule.

Eventually we entered a zone of huge seracs to discover, well hidden at 6,370 m (20,900 ft), a lone tent. It was the abandoned Colorado Camp 4 – their top camp: we added another tent to establish our own Camp 3. At dusk we looked out through the icicles to watch the shadows lengthening over the desert hills far beneath and a red glow lingering behind the Russian Pamirs.

Then the storm hit us. Squeezed three into each two-man tent, we huddled in our sleeping bags for two unpleasant days, killing time by overhauling the black-smoking, fuel-guzzling pressure stoves on which life depended. We would have been hungry without the abandoned Colorado food – tuna salad, cottage cheese, shrimp cocktail and freeze-dried ice cream! This is when personalities fray, tempers crack and one learns the true measure of one's companions. But we were all still friends when the weather cleared and we could advance once more.

Navigation now was easy: it was straight upwards to the top. But even so it took over five hours to ski the next 600 m (2,000 ft).

We had to cut platforms into the steep slope to pitch Camp 4 at 7,000 m (23,000 ft) – two tiny tents lonely on a vast windswept snow slope. Having lost two valuable days, I decided to occupy Camp 4 after only the second carry. By now my plans had crystallized and I arranged two summit bids on succeeding days. I would lead the first, the larger stronger party, proving and marking the route, which next day Steve's smaller team would repeat while we remained up high in support.

Another storm hit us. This time we had little food and less fuel. It was far colder. We dozed and worried for a day and a night as the blizzard played weird music through the skis and poles stuck upright in the driving snow outside.

It was hardly dawn when I awoke. The wind had died. We were enveloped in thick cloud – visibility nil. I brewed tea and dozed again. Suddenly it was 9.30, the mist was streaming away and the sky above was blue. Now for the top! It took nearly two hours to get away, scraping the ice from our bindings and skins and digging out the tents, but all five of us were going strongly and I was confident there could be few difficulties ahead.

Although our summit bid went smoothly, the descent back to Camp 4 demanded strongly defensive skiing. Steve's party of three reached the top the next day in good style. From Camp 3 our descent to Base was swift but not easy. It was high summer, snowfields had become ice-slopes and many new crevasses had opened. We dismantled each camp as we passed through it, and our sacks grew larger and larger. On our arrival at Base Camp, Steve and I weighed our sacks at 44 kg (97 lb), the sort of load that makes skiing difficult, but walking on this sort of terrain impossible. However, our time had run right out and we had to clear the mountain in one go.

An epic night camel-journey brought us to the road ahead on the appointed day and our Chinese friends kept smiling all the way to the mandatory victory banquets in Kashgar and Beijing. We had got eight men to the top . . . it had certainly been a rather different ski holiday!

Fig. 126 overleaf   Muztagh Ata : Camp III at 8,840 m (20,900 ft).

Historical dates

These dates are taken almost entirely from Sir Arnold Lunn's "History of Skiing", published 1927 by the Oxford University Press.

2500 BC   Hoting ski found at Honne, Sweden, in 1921.

2500 BC   Rock carving at Rödöy, Norway, depicts a skier.

2000 BC   Kalvträsk skis and stick found in Sweden in 1924

2000–500 BC   Twenty-four rock carvings around Lake Onega and the White Sea, Russia.

AD 552   Dubious reference to skiing by Procopius.

629   Detailed raference to Turkic nomads using primitive skis.

618–907   Reference to the use of skis in the official history of the Tang dynasty.

1050   Memorial stone at Boksta, Sweden, shows a hunter on skis.

1150   Earl Rognvald of Orkney lists skiing as one of his 9 accomplishments.

1206   Infant King Häkon rescued by two men on skis.

1230   Publication of *Konungas Skuggsja.*

1521–2   Gustav Vasa flees from the Danes. The Vasa race commemorates this event.

1555   Detailed descriptions and drawings of skis by Olaus Magnus.

1574   Prof. Simler in *De Alpibus Commentarius* refers to the use of snow shoes by travellers for crossing Alpine Passes.

1628   Skis used in Devonshire, England, in the great frost of that year – ref: *Lorna Doone.*

1689   Valvasor, in *Die Ehre des Herzogtumes Krain* says that the peasants of Krain, Austria, were expert skiers.

1856   Snowshoe Thompson starts twenty years of carrying mail across the Sierra Nevada.

1860   The miners of Weardale, Cumberland, England, used 'skees'.

1870   First visit by people from Telemark to Christiania.

1879   Pioneer of French skiing, M. Duhamel, makes first attempt at Grenoble.

1880   Cecil Slingsby crosses the Keiser Pass 1,550 m (5,085 ft) in Norway on skis.

1883   Wilhelm Paulke given skis as a present as a schoolboy and tries them at Davos. Local carpenter copies them.

1883   Abortive attempts at skiing at Arosa in Switzerland and by the monks of Gr. St. Bernard.

1884   First ski ascent of a mountain, the Brocken in Germany, by two Norwegians, followed by two Englishmen.

1889   Norwegian O. Kjelsberg introduces skis to Winterthur in Switzerland and ascends the Bactel (1,119 m/3,671 ft).

1890   Englishman, Mr Knocker, introduces skis to Meiringen in Switzerland.

1890   Nansen treverses Greenland on skis.

1890–91   Munich Ski Club formed.

1892   Black Forest School developed using Norwegian technique and with Wilhelm Paulke as the leading light. Ascent of Feldberg highest mountain in the Black Forest.

1893   28 and 29 January: first genuine Alpine ski expedition by Christopher Iselin – the crossing of the Pragel Pass 1,554 m (5,098 ft).

1893   8 February Iselin and Jenny climb the Schild (2,302 m7552 ft) on skis in five hours and ski down in two hours. The real Alpine summit on skis.

1893   Crossing of the Mayenfelder Furka (Davos to Arosa) on skis by the Branger brothers.

1893   Swiss Ski Club formed.

1893   Paulke ascends the Oberalstock on skis.

1893–4   Col Bilgeri introduces skis to the Austrian Army.

1894   Sir Arthur Conan Doyle goes to the Mayenfelder Furka on skis. Enthusiastic group of Englishmen at Davos.

1894   Black Forest Ski Club (Paulke) formed.

1896   Zdarsky publishes *Lilienfelder Skilauf Technik.* Black Forest Ski Club hold first competitions.

1897   Dr Payot uses skis in Chamonix for visiting patients.

1897   January: Paulke traverses the Bernese Oberland without guides (route: from Grimsel, Oberaarjoch Hut, Grünhornlücke, Konkordia Hut, down the Gr. Aletsch Glacier to the Belalp Hotel. First major ski traverse. Ski mountaineering stems from this date.

1898   First ascent on skis of Piz Buin by F. Danzler and guide Guler.

1898   January: attempt by Paulke with Dr Helbling (after two days' skiing) on the Monte Rosa.
March: D. Schüster and H. Moser (guide) climb Monte Rosa on skis.

1898–9   Sir Arnold Lunn skis in Chamonix.

1899   First ski ascent of the Breithorn by Dr. Helbling, E. Wagner and H. Biehley.

1899   First fatal avalanche accident to ski-mountaineers: Dr. Ehlert and Mönnichs (members of Paulke's 1897 traverse of the Bernese Oberland) killed on the Susten Pass.

1900   Dr. Hoek (German) with guides traverses the Bernese Oberland; climbs the Finsteraarhorn and the Mönch.

1901   First ski ascent of the Finsteraarhorn by Dr. Hoek and guides Moor and Tannler.

1902   First ski ascent of Mt. Velan by Dr. Helbling.

1902   First ski ascent of Gr. Fiescherhorn by Dr. J. David and P. Koenig.

1903   January: Attempt on Haute Route on skis by Dr. Payot, Joseph Couttet, Alfred Simond and Joseph Ravenel 'Le Rouge', avoiding the Gr. Combin.
February: Dr. Helbling and Dr. Reichert cross on skis from Val de Bagnes to Arolla via the north side of the Gr. Combin and on to Zermatt via the Col D'Herens.

1904   First ski ascent of Mt. Blanc by Mylins and guides.

1907   First ski ascent of Allalinhorn by A. Hurter, Max Stahel, and guides Othmer and Oscar Supersaxo.

1907   First ski ascent of Gr. Combin by Marcel Kurz, F. Roget and M. Crettox.

1908   Traverse of the Dolomites (Waidbruck to Innichen) by H. Hoek and O. Schüster.

1908   Alpine Ski Club founded (President: Sir Martin Conway).

1909   First ski ascent of Gr. Glockner by Max Winkler and Strobler.

1909   Shackleton fails to reach the South Pole because the party did not use skis.

1910   Traverse of the Diablerets by F. Roget and M. Kurz and guides.

1910   2 April, Zermatt to Saas Fee via Adler Pass by Oscar Superaxo, Herman Kronig and party.

1911   F. Roget and M. Kurz ski from Bourg St. Pierre, over the Plateau du Couloir, Col du Sonadon, Chanrion to Zermatt, with first winter ascent of Dent Blanche. This is the first pure 'Classic' Haute Route, crossing the South side of the Gr. Combin.

1911   December: Amundsen reaches the South Pole on skis.

1912   January: Scott reaches the South Pole on skis.

1912   F. Roget publishes *Ski Runs in the High Alps.*

1917   First ski ascent of the Dom by Sir Arnold Lunn and J. Knubel.

1924   First traverse of Mt. Blanc on skis by von Tscharner (President of the Akademischer Alpen Club, Zurich).

1926   First ski ascents of the Meije and the Ecrins.

1933   12 February – 7 April. First ski traverse of Alps (Nice to Tyrol) by Leon Zwingelstein from Grenoble.

1956   Traverse of the Alps (Julian Alps to Nice) by Bonatti and three other guides.

1965   Traverse of the Alps (Innsbruck to Grenoble) by Denis Bertholet and four other international guides. 1,000 km (600 ml) in twenty-two days.
10 June, First ski descent of the Whymper Couloir, Aiguille Verte, by Sylvain Saudan.

1968   16 October, first ski descent of the Gervasutti Couloir, Mt. Blanc du Tacul, by Sylvain Saudan.

1970   Traverse of the Alps (Vienna to Nice) by Robert Kittl and three other Austrian Army guides. A heavily supported, low level crossing, completing 2,000 km (1,242 ml) in forty days.

1972   British Alpine Ski Traverse (Kaprun to Gap) by Alan Blackshaw and seven other amateurs, in forty-nine days with ascents of major peaks.

1973   2 August, first ski descent of Couturier couloir by Serge Cachat-Rosset.

1977   17 May, first descent of North Face of Aiguille du Midi by Anselme Baud, Daniel Chauchefoin and Yves Dietry.
29 May, first ski descent of North Face of Aiguille Blanche de Peuterey by Anselme Baud and Patrick Vallençant.
31 May, first ski descent of Arête de Peuterey by Baud and Vallençant.

Equipment check list

Exactly what equipment and clothing you carry obviously depends on the type of tour you are doing; but in any case it is essential to take only what is absolutely necessary, so that your rucksack is kept as light as possible. A heavy load will slow you down when going uphill, and when skiing downhill will contribute to throwing you headfirst into the snow with consequent delays to the whole party – and you will soon become very tired.

On an easy day-tour away from glaciers, many of the items listed below can be left behind; whereas a multi-day glacier tour in terrain where there are no huts will require in addition : tents or additional bivouac material, cookers, utensils, food etc.

The following is suggested for a high Alpine glacier tour lasting a few days, buying food at huts. Those not carrying ropes and cameras will be able to keep the weight down to about 8 kg (17 lb), while even the heaviest load in the party should be below 14 kg (30 lb).

Personal list:

Normal skiing or mountaineering clothing (e.g. ski salopettes or breeches, light gaiters, warm sweaters, cagoule, overtrousers etc.)
One spare set of socks and underwear.
Duvet jacket or equivalent warmth in sweaters.
Gloves and spare.
Warm wool hat and sun hat.
Sun glasses and goggles.

Sun cream and glacier cream for lips.
Water bottle.
Lightweight headtorch.
Rucksack with attachments for skis and ice axe, with waist belt.
Avalanche transceiver.
Glacier harness.
1 long prusik loop (a 3.3 m (11 ft) length of 6 mm tied with a double fisherman's).
1 short prusik loop (a 2.1 m (7 ft) length of 6 mm similarly tied).
2 lightweight screwgate karabiners (2,500 Kg/5,500 lb minimum).
1 lightweight snaplink karabiner (1,800 kg/4,000 lb minimum).
Ice axe and crampons.
Skins and harscheisen.
Ski mountaineering boots.
Skis with touring bindings, and sticks.
Camera and film.
Toothbrush and toothpaste.
Lunch snacks (e.g. 6 sweets and 1 chocolate bar per day).
Emergency food (e.g. 2 chocolate bars).

Group equipment

Ropes (50 m/164 ft of 9 mm for 3 people).
2 lightweight mechanical prusikers.
2 ice screws, and 1 lightweight pulley.
First aid kit and repair kit (needle, thread, glue, rivets, screws, tape).
Bivouac tents.
Lightweight snow shovels (ideally 1 per person).
2 sets of maps, 2 altimeters, 2 compasses and 1 guidebook.

Glossary of terms

Abseil	method of controlling one's descent by sliding down the rope. Also called 'rappel'.
Alp	summer mountain pasture.
Altimeter	instrument used for indicating height or weather changes by measuring barometic pressure.
Arête	snow or rock ridge.
Aspect of slope	the orientation of a slope, i.e. the direction it faces. A useful aid in navigation.
Avalanche	slide of rock, snow or ice.
Belay	the feature or device used for securing a rope, and the method by which one does this.
Bergschrund	the crevasse, usually very large, between the glacier and permanent snowfield (névé) above. Also called 'rimaye'.
Bivouac	to spend a night out on the mountain with a minimum of equipment. Can be planned or involuntary.

Bothy	rough rudimentary shelter, typically found in Scottish hills.
Brèche	steep-sided mountain pass.
Cagoule	long shell jacket which is waterproof and windproof.
Christiania	abbr. 'christie'. A turn across the fall-line keeping the skis parallel throughout.
Col	mountain pass.
Contour line	lines on maps joining points of equal height.
Cornice	overhanging lip of snow formed by wind on the lee side of ridges. Can be very big and can break, sometimes causing the slope below to avalanche.
Couloir	gully.
Crampons	frame of metal spikes attached to the sole of the boot, for climbing hard snow and ice.
Crevasse	cleavage in a glacier, occurring at right angles to tension.
Crust	a thin crust on the snow surface which may support a skier or may not (breakable), formed by sun or wind.
Cup crystals	large fragile crystals formed in the snow pack by temperature gradient metamorphosis. Also called 'depth hoar'.
Depth hoar	see 'cup crystals'.
Descendeur	device used in abseiling.
Duvet clothing	clothing made traditionally of down, providing excellent insulation. Ski mountaineers often carry a duvet jacket, modern ones being made of either down or man-made fibres.
Edges	the metal edges of skis.
Edging	forcing the edges into the snow to prevent side-slipping; done by rolling the knees uphill and simultaneously pressing them forward.
Exposure	either the sense of height, or the cooling of the body due to cold, windy conditions.
Fall-line	the direct line down a slope, i.e. the line a ball or loose ski would take.
Firn	strictly speaking, last year's snow; but the word is generally used to mean any well-consolidated snow.
Firnification	change of shape of snow crystals. Also called 'metamorphosis'.
Fluh	crag or precipice.
Föhn	warm south wind in the Alps, typically giving in the ski mountaineering season heavy falls of rain in the valleys and of snow on the mountains.
Glacier	moving masses of snow and ice, being continually fed by the permanent snowfields (névé) at the top and continually melting at the bottom (snout).
Graupel (n)	ice crystal formed by heavy riming. They are round in shape which means that they form a good lubricating layer for an avalanche, and it also means that they lose heat slowly so remaining unaltered for a long time.
Hail	a frozen water droplet which has not made contact with an ice crystal.
Hanging glacier	a glacier on a very steep face, frequently falling over a rock face. Ice avalanches from them can pose a very severe threat as they fall onto the main glacier below.
Harscheisen	crampons for the skis, used in conjunction with skins, enabling a traverse line to be maintained on hard snow.
Hoar	see 'depth hoar' and 'surface hoar'.
Icefall	a section of glacier with many crevasses and seracs, caused a sudden steepening in the gradient of the glacier.
Icescrews	tubes or pitons which are screwed or driven into ice for use as belays.
Joch	pass or col between two summits.
Jump turn	a slow turn in which the skis are jumped round the sticks, both skis being lifted clear of the snow. Used particularly in breakable crust.

Karabiner	snaplink used for securing harnesses, for attaching ropes to belays etc.
Kick turn	a stationary turn made either uphill or downhill.
Magnetic North	the direction in which the compass needle points, being pulled over to one side by the magnetism of the Earth.
Magnetic Variation	the amount the compass needle is affected by the Earth's magnetism.
Moguls	bumps on ski runs, either loved or detested.
Moraine	long pile of stones and debris pushed out from the glacier as part of its continuous erosion process on the underlying ground.
Mulde	deep hollow between the lateral moraine on one side and the valley on the other. Any avalanche coming down from the hillside above will go into this hollow; and so in avalanche conditions it should be avoided.
Névé	strictly speaking the high permanent snowfields above the glaciers, but loosely used to describe any well consolidated snow.
Pegs	see pitons.
Pitons	made of high-tensile alloy-steel and hammered into cracks in rock for belays.
Piste	track or trail made by skiers all following the same line, often rolled ('pisted') by snowtrack machines.
Powder	light fresh snow in which the skis sink, but easy to ski in.
Prusik	to climb up the main rope using loops of thinner rope and special hitches, which slide one way but which jam when loaded. Mechanical devices ('prusikers') make this much easier.
Randkluft	the large crevasse between the glacier and the containing rock wall.
Rimaye	see 'bergschrund'.
Riming	water freezing directly to an object due to wind, relative humidity and temperature.

Sastrugi	wind scoured snow, often forming hard ridges which are difficult to negotiate on skis.
Schuss	to ski straight down the fall-line without turns, resulting sometimes in involuntary high speeds and spectacular falls.
Serac	big unstable tower of ice found in ice-falls.
Skin	originally sealskins but now synthetic which are fixed to the sole of the ski to enable uphill climbing.
Slab	snow layer formed by the wind on lee slopes and susceptible to avalanche
Snow bridge	bridge of snow over a crevasse, sometimes strong enough to support a person, sometimes not.
Snow flakes	linked crystals.
Snow plough	the skis are placed in the 'V' position for gliding, braking or turning.
Stem	to push out the heel of one or both skis allowing the stemmed ski(s) to slide over the snow at an angle to the direction of travel. If both skis are stemmed, the position is similar to the snow plough.
Stem christie	a turn started as a stem and finished as a christiania (christie).
Sublimation	the process whereby solid turns to vapour without going through the intermediate liquid stage; and vice-versa.
Surface hoar	crystals which form directly on the snow surface by sublimation.
Verglas	film of supercooled water which has frozen on to objects to give a clear and smooth coating of ice. It is denser, harder and more transparent than rime or surface hoar.
Vibram	composition rubber soles specially moulded for climbing, as found on ski mountaineering boots.
White-out	snow condition of appalling visibility where it is impossible to distinguish between the gound and the horizon.
Windslab	see 'slab'.

Bibliography

Historical
A History of Skiing, Sir Arnold Lunn. Pub: Oxford University Press 1927.
The Guiness Book of Skiing, Peter Lunn. Pub: Guinness Superlatives Ltd 1983.
Ski Runs in the High Alps, Prof. F. Roget. Pub: Fisher Unwin 1912.
The Book of European Skiing, Malcolm Milne and Mark Heller. Pub: A. Baker 1986.

Guidebooks
(Other guide books are listed in the relevant chapters of Recommended Tours.)
Les Alpes du Nord à Skis, Anselme Baud. Pub: Denoel, Paris 1983.
High Level Route, Eric Roberts. Pub: West Col 1973.
Haute Route, Hartranft and Koniger. Pub: Rother, Munich 1978.
Haute Route, Seibert and Matuschka. Pub: Berg, Munich 1980.
Ski Mountaineering in Scotland, Bennet and Wallace. Pub: Scottish Mountaineering Trust 1987.
Alpine Ski Touren. Pub: Swiss Alpine Club 1977.

Instructional
Avalanche and Snow Safety, Colin Fraser. Pub: John Murray 1978.
Avalanche Handbook. Pub: US Forest Service 1976.
Mountain Weather for Climbers, David Unwin. Pub: Cordee 1978.
Mountain Navigation, Peter Cliff. Pub: Peter Cliff 1986.
Tourenskilauf, Erich Griessl. Pub: Rother, Munich 1978.
Handbook of Ski Mountaineering and Alpine Ski Touring. Pub: Ski Club of Great Britain 1973 (new edition due 1988).
A Chance in a Million, Bob Barton and Blythe Wright. Pub: Scottish Mountaineering Trust 1985.
Mountaineering, Alan Blackshaw. Pub: Penguin 1975.
Mountaincraft and Leadership, Eric Langmuir. Pub: Scottish Sports Council and MLTB 1984.
Modern Rope Techniques, Bill March. Pub: Cicerone Press 1976.
Ski Technique and Instruction Manual, Books 1 and 2. Pub: British Association of Ski Instructors 1983.
The Snowy Torrents: Avalanche Accidents in the United States 1910–1966, Dale Gallagher ed. Pub: United States Department of Agriculture 1967.
Cross Country Skiing, Ned Gillette and John Bostol. Pub: The Mountaineers, second edition 1983.

Back-Country Skiing, Lito Tejada-Flores. Pub: Sierra Club Books 1981.
Avalanche Safety for Skiers and Climbers, Tony Daffern. Pub: Rocky Mountain Books (Canada), Alpenbooks (USA) and Diadem (UK), 1983.

Index